The Noble Ca~

Michael Layton & Steph

To Mike

Very best wishes

Michael Layton

2024

First Published: November 2016, Bostin Books

First Paperback Edition April 2017, Bostin Books

Other books by Michael Layton and Stephen Burrows

Joint:Fiction:

Black Over Bill's Mother's

Keep Right On.

Non-Fiction:

Walsall's Front Line.

By Michael Layton

Non-Fiction:

Hunting the Hooligans

Tracking the Hooligans

Police Dog Heroes

Birmingham's Front Line

Violence in the Sun

The Hooligans Are Still Among Us (May 2017)

Author Biographies

Michael Layton QPM joined the British Transport Police as a Cadet in 1968 and then in 1972 transferred to Birmingham City Police, which amalgamated two years later to become the West Midlands Police, where he eventually reached the rank of Chief Superintendent.

On retirement from that Force in 2003 he went on to see service with the Sovereign Bases Police in Cyprus, and returned to the British Transport Police in 2004 where amongst other things he served as a Detective Superintendent (Director of Intelligence).

In the January 2003 New Year's Honours List he was awarded the Queens Police Medal for distinguished police service and finally retired in 2011, since which time he has acted as a consultant on crime and community safety issues, as well as taking up writing during the last three years.

Stephen Burrows joined West Midlands Police in 1983, working in Birmingham, Wolverhampton and Walsall. He performed a wide variety of roles, up to Detective Superintendent rank, including uniform command, complaints and discipline, (including internal and cross force enquiries) and CID command, (including Serious Crime Investigation, Child Protection and Head of Intelligence).

In 2002 he transferred to Warwickshire Police as Area Commander then became Detective Chief Superintendent, Head of Crime for the force, a post held for 5 years. He was trained as SIO, in Kidnap command, and all levels of Firearms Command amongst other skills. He retired in 2013 following thirty years' service, eleven

---

of which were spent at Chief Superintendent rank. He currently works part-time for The Home Office in the field of Communications Data.

DEDICATIONS

Michael Layton: To Andry for her continued support and to officers in the West Midlands Police, past and present.

Stephen Burrows: To Sue for putting up with the writing, and to my colleagues within the police service, wherever I have served, and especially remembering those no longer with us.

Table of contents

Foreword   Page 8

Introduction   Page 12

Chapter One. The Riot Police   Page 15

Chapter Two. The Special Ones   Page 43

Chapter Three. The Twilight World   Page 81

Chapter Four. An Ear To The Ground   Page 113

Chapter Five. The Grim Reaper   Page 164

Chapter Six. Early Mornings-Late Nights   Page 180

Chapter Seven. '999'   Page 240

Chapter Eight. The Sting   Page 282

Chapter Nine. Murder and Mystery   Page 340

Chapter Ten. The Rubber Heel Squad   Page 410

Epilogue   Page 427

Foreword

The striking gentleman on the book cover is Police Constable 118 'a' Thomas Wright. The imperious pose commemorates the awarding of a certificate from *'The Carnegie Hero Fund Trust'*, for bravery on the Thirteenth of February 1911.

Why this cover photograph? We reproduce the award citation in its original format, (Page 8). PC Wright risked his life to protect others. It was a runaway horse, not an armed terrorist, but nevertheless his heroism encapsulates the core principle of policing – that of protecting others; their lives, their property, their society.

We believe that the British police are the best in the world. We are not alone in this belief, as evidenced by the praise of commentators across the globe over many decades, even centuries, and the fact that foreign police forces still send their officers to Britain for training, and call in our professionals to assist on a regular basis. A continuing source of wonder abroad, especially in the United States, is the fact that we police 'by consent' and to date have not required every officer to carry lethal weapons, despite the ever increasing dangers presented by our evolving society.

The principles demonstrated by PC Wright stretch back to the formation of the police service by Sir Robert Peel, continued throughout the period we describe in this book, and remain at its heart to the present day.

The photograph of PC Wright, together with the other wonderful photographs of Birmingham City Centre, prior to modern development, were provided by Thomas Wright's grand-daughter,

Mrs. Frances Tebbutt, who is justly proud of Thomas and his service to the public. To Frances we give our grateful thanks for permission to use them. We hope that PC Wright would have been proud to be on the cover of this book and that its content demonstrates why policing is in truth *'The Noble Cause'*.

Michael Layton & Stephen Burrows (2016)

POLICE CONSTABLE (118 a.) THOMAS WRIGHT, Birmingham, 29 years of age, on the 13th February, 1911, at great risk to his own life, stopped a runaway horse in Fazeley Street, Birmingham. (Case 589).

This case was reported by Chief Constable C. H. Rafter, Birmingham, on the 20th May, 1911. The Chief Constable also furnished an account of the occurrence prepared by the Deputy Chief Constable and statements by witnesses.

Shortly after 11 o'clock in the forenoon of the 13th February, 1911, a powerful horse attached to a covered van laden with timber took fright and bolted in Paternoster Row. The horse shook off its bridle, and was galloping at great speed without a driver along Park Street towards Fazeley Street. Police Constable Wright was on duty in Park Street, and saw that there was imminent danger of a serious accident. He caught hold of the horse by the nose, the bridle having been shaken off, and ran alongside. The horse was going at high speed, and, owing to the absence of the bridle the constable found himself unable to check it. He succeeded, however, in turning it down Fazeley Street. Here it was on a down gradient with a heavy load. A short distance ahead a tramcar and a herd of pigs were coming towards the runaway. The street was otherwise in a crowded condition, and a serious accident seemed inevitable. Seizing the horse by the ear with the right hand, and holding one of the shafts by the left hand the constable endeavoured to prevent an accident by turning the horse against the corner of New Bartholomew Street and Fazeley Street. He succeeded in doing this. One shaft struck the wall of the building on one side of the corner, the other shaft struck a door on the other side of the corner. The shafts and the fore part of the van were smashed, the horse was thrown to the ground, and the constable was hurled through the door.

Witnesses speak in high terms of the courage shown by the constable, and state that he undoubtedly prevented an accident, which might have resulted in the loss of life and injury to others. The Deputy Chief Constable, in reporting the case to the Chief Constable on the 17th February, recommends the action of Constable Wright as worthy of special consideration, and describes it as the most courageous act that had come under his notice in the way of stopping runaway horses. Constable Wright was awarded a stripe of merit by the Watch Committee, and the Chief Constable commends his case to the Trustees as well worthy of recognition.

Police Constable Wright has been a member of the Birmingham Force for nearly 5 years. He is 29 years of age, is unmarried, and receives 28s. 6d. per week.

153. Police Constable (118 A) Thomas Wright, Birmingham, on the 13th February, 1911, at great risk stopped a runaway horse in Fazeley Street, Birmingham (Case 589). It was agreed to recommend that he receive an honorary certificate and the sum of £5.

Figure 1: Carnegie Award Citation, Thomas Wright

Figure 2 Carnegie Award Certificate, Thomas Wright

Introduction.

This is a book about policing, warts and all, written by former police officers, not journalists, TV producers, politicians, or so-called 'experts', but by two people who did 'the job' day in, day out, in uniform and out of it.

'The Noble Cause' is brutally honest, and deliberately so. The public tends to discern policing through the prism of television, encapsulated into half-hour episodes where every crime gets solved, or the two-hour special where the ace detective unravels the complex plot and emerges triumphant. Reality is often far different and happy endings are not guaranteed.

The job itself can be hugely satisfying, indeed the majority of officers and police staff love their work, finding it rewarding and meaningful, together with being a member of a 'club' that those outside the police service might never fully understand - a club with its own language, culture and humour.

On the other hand, it is dangerous, testing and sometimes frightening. Ordinary men and women with families put themselves on the line, both physically and mentally, and run the risk that the 20:20 hindsight of others after a split-second decision or incident will result in an enquiry, suspension, court, discipline proceedings, or castigation from every quarter.

Family and friends come second. Police officers see the worst of society, its inequalities, injustice, the effects of drugs, alcohol and mental illness. They witness the way that vulnerable people are often left to the 'thin blue line' to act as both guardians of society and social workers of last resort.

They have to confront and deal with pure evil and the lowest degradations of the human state. They have the horrors of murder, accidental death, suicide, domestic and child abuse, plus sickening violence imprinted on their minds, and have to find a way to cope, and remain the pillars of society that most are.

Most actually join in order to help people and to protect society. They learn from their experiences and undergo rigorous training. They want to make a difference, doing a worthwhile job. They ask for no thanks and often get very little.

The police service offers a myriad of roles, career paths and experiences with the ultimate in variety. No two days are the same. There is no certainty as to what will be faced during a tour of duty.

This book tracks the course of two very different career paths during the 1980s and 90s, one uniform, one CID, (Criminal Investigation Department), until they converge and somewhat ironically swop from uniform to CID, and vice- versa.

The recollections of other officers, working during that period, both embellish and expand the rich count of incidents. Also included, and rarely ever described to the public, are training courses and organisational structures that lie behind the officer on the streets, and his or her actions and reactions.

The book is structured with recollections from the co-authors, and grouped into chapters. They are deliberately written in two very different styles with a view to bringing the operational outcomes achieved through intensive police training together.

The book is designed to serve as a window into the reality of policing, its trials and humour, a window into this British institution that is rightly held up as being the best police service in the world. The incidents described occurred many years ago, but the basis of policing does not change, and the observations made are as valid today as they were then, and in the decades preceding them, through police history to the original oath that still pertains at the core of policing today.

(Michael Layton & Stephen Burrows 2016)

Chapter One

The Riot Police

(Stephen Burrows):

I was woken by the jarring sound of the telephone ringing. Not a mobile by the bed – there were no mobiles - this phone was downstairs and it was the wee small hours of Tuesday 10 September 1985. I was in demand.

"Handsworth's gone up," said the voice, "Your course is cancelled, get yourself into Acocks Green as soon as you can."

It was just four months since I had been involved in the riot at the Birmingham City versus Leeds match, and it seemed that disorder was stalking me.The previous day I had commenced my 'PACE' course. This was a week–long introduction to the recently enacted Police and Criminal Evidence Act which had changed every facet of prisoner handling, interviewing and evidence collection.

In fact it was the last 'PACE' course being held, and everyone bar a few older in service 'duckers and divers' had been trained. I was by far the youngest in service on the course, and just about to complete my two years 'Probation'.

I recount this fact because every able-bodied person on the course formed a public-order 'serial' for the Handsworth riot and thus I ended up in a rattling Transit van with an interesting collection of characters of some service length, wise in the ways of policing. I watched and learnt.

Once assembled, we were sent to Thornhill Road Police Station, Handsworth, where we were hurriedly fed and sat around the yard by the van awaiting orders. We must have arrived at dawn because I can remember looking through the van window as we drove past Lozells Road and seeing the smoking ruins that looked just like pictures of the Blitz.

There had been a temporary lull in the disorder and many weary colleagues, who had been on duty since the previous evening, were going off duty, to be replaced by us. Their faces and the devastation in the streets made me realise that this was the most serious and potentially dangerous incident I had ever been part of.

This sight did not dampen the spirits of my colleagues though. There was a line of vehicles, public-order vans, dog-vans and police cars, parked to one side of the yard at Thornhill Road, with their officer contents sat on the floor between the vehicles and the station wall. We were waiting for something to happen and inevitably boredom set in and the mischief making began.

This was the unfortunate moment for the local Superintendent to decide to hold a live press interview in the back yard on the other side of the vans.

The dog vans contained their complement of large German Shepherds, in the internal cages but with the rear van doors open to allow air to the dogs. Police dogs are not normally shy and retiring and these were no exception. They had produced the usual barrage of barking but had calmed down by the time the interview was to begin.

I imagine that the superintendent thought that the backdrop

of vans and officers ready to deploy would be very good on the television.

Some of us had a view of the interview but the superintendent could not see everyone sat behind the vans. As the first question was asked it was drowned out by a cacophony of barking from the dog vans. Silence fell and they tried again, but as soon as the superintendent began to speak the barking erupted once more. What bad luck!

This went on for some time until the superintendent ordered the dogs to be removed, adding some choice language that I doubt made the television.

This decision was effective, stopping the barking which had in fact been caused by officers sat behind the dog vans rocking them with their feet, upon a signal from those who had sight of the interview. Classic police humour, relieving the tension and getting a 'bite' from a gaffer too. A win–win!

It must have been about 10am when our wait ended. We were told that trouble had started again and into the van we climbed. I can remember the superintendent coming to the open back doors of the van and wishing us luck. I can still recall the feeling. I was going into battle.

I already knew that people had died the previous night, two brothers Kassamali Moledina, aged thirty-eight-years, and his forty-four-year-old brother Amirali, were burnt to death in the post office that they ran, after they decided to remain in the premises to protect it from the mob. Tensions were high and there were reports that many troublemakers from outside of Handsworth were travelling to 'have a go' at the police and maybe do a spot of incidental looting.

We were deployed to Heathfield Road, in public-order attire and had shields and what were termed 'NATO' helmets. There were people around, but mostly they seemed to be older locals, Asian and Black, upset and bemused by what had happened to their community - and all very clear and unanimous that it had not been done in their names.

The Asians in particular, who owned the vast majority of business in Handsworth, were incensed and vowing to mobilise as vigilantes to protect their livelihoods. Everyone blamed a small minority of black drugs-dealers and troublemakers who centred themselves around the Acapulco Café in Lozells where the trouble had started.

I was on the streets of Handsworth for a week after the riots and spoke to many locals, and not a single one blamed deprivation. In fact most of those arrested came from outside of Handsworth.

Relationships between the police and the local younger black community were not good and there were constant potential flashpoints, but ironically, the superintendent at Thornhill Road Police Station had been diligently pursuing a campaign to improve relationships with black youths, with some positive results, but it had now literally all 'gone up in flames'.

Many officers felt that we had become too soft, and let liberties with the law be taken in an effort to improve things, but that was an understandable reaction upon seeing Handsworth burning.

The community policing initiatives undertaken after the 1981 riots were seen as being very innovative and the riots caused huge disappointment. It has to be remembered that this was a period when rioting and confrontation involving black youths and the police was not uncommon across the UK, so anything with a prospect of improving relations was seen as worth pursuing.

Anyway, back to Heathfield Road. We drove around for a while but it seemed to be quiet so one of the more experienced officers announced that they were going to show me how to 'live off the land'.

The van driver found a row of shops containing a newsagent and general store that were open, and parked the van on the pavement outside. Officers disappeared inside the shops and then returned to the van. A short time later crisps and chocolates appeared in abundance.

My best memory of the Handsworth riot occurred shortly after the crisps arrived. I saw a black man, probably in his fifties; emerge from a house opposite the shops. He approached us and I awaited the expected harangue.

"Do you all want tea?" he enquired politely.

We nodded enthusiastically. About ten minutes later he emerged with a huge teapot and cups and saucers on a tray. We took tea by the side of the road in a quintessentially 'English' cameo that I expect was the sort of thing that made the British Empire great.

The morning passed and we were informed that the then

Home Secretary, Douglas Hurd, was attending to inspect the scene at lunchtime. We were deployed to the area. Crowds of youths began to gather on the street again and the mood changed for the worse. As a police officer you develop a sixth-sense for trouble, an ability to almost taste tension, and all my sensors were ringing.

Hurd was a tall man and I can remember seeing him approaching, surrounded by a cluster of senior officers. Suddenly bricks and colourful abuse started flying from the crowd towards Hurd, who beat a hasty retreat leaving us behind, thank you very much! Shields were swiftly gathered from the van and a shield wall formed.

A shield wall with officers behind it has an immediate effect on a disorderly crowd - they throw things at it, and this crowd did not disappoint, as bricks and bottles began to bounce off the shields.

We advanced, and I received my first and only experience of being petrol bombed in anger, as several were lobbed from the crowd.

The crowd broke and ran, leaving a milk crate containing half a dozen unused petrol-bombs which were seized as evidence.

We spent the rest of the day chasing groups of youths around the Birchfield Road and Heathfield Road areas. They rampaged through Birchfield Road Shopping Centre, and the Post-Office in Rookery Road was raided.

We eventually restored order later that night but the damage was done and burnt buildings, burnt-out and overturned cars, bottles, bricks and makeshift barricades littered the streets. Every time I see a war film I am reminded of that day.

The next day I returned and the plan was to flood the streets with police, but in conventional attire in a 'return to normality, if it's normal to have pairs of police officers every hundred yards doing a spot of 'evening all' and all that. I was with John Cudd, a seasoned campaigner, and we made a point of speaking to everyone we saw.

We made the national press - photographed with a young black boy who was wearing my helmet, a photograph that re-appeared in many subsequent articles usually with a byline about 'community police restoring relations'.

One moment I had been in the 'riot squad', then just twelve hours later, the 'community police'.

***

'Riot Police called in to quell disturbance' 'Riot Police bricked by mob' 'Riot Police accused of....

Who exactly *are* these riot police? Where do they come from, how are they trained, what do they do when there's no riot, and what's it really like on the other side of the shield?

We've all seen them on the news, in the papers. There they stand, behind a shield wall, helmets and visors, overalls and boots. Some have round shields and run about, sometimes with batons.

Well, there are some units that specialize in 'public-order,' a catch-all police term that covers a multitude of sins, from the brawling drunk on a Saturday night, through to the gang of louts causing trouble outside a pub at 'chucking out' time, to the full blown riot such as at Handsworth, Broadwater Farm, and Brixton.

In Birmingham, these units were called the Operational Support Group, (OSU). They trained together, deployed together and developed a high level of expertise and teamwork. Their 'day job' was public order in all its variations, although they were also used in other forms of policing, as they were a skilled, mobile and valuable resource. Thus, they could be found for example at:

• Political or other marches and demonstrations

• Football matches

• Pre-planned operations likely to result in public order issues, for example a drugs raid on a busy pub in the evening

• On patrol in city-centres or other locations where late night disorder could be anticipated, for example clusters of 'fast food' purveyors where inebriated youths gathered after a night out, such as John Bright Street in Birmingham. The queues for the late night buses in Birmingham City Centre were also a regular spot for trouble.

Returning to the question of 'who are the riot police?' the vast majority comprises officers drawn from regular duties. I was one of those officers, trained from police constable to superintendent, in 'public order'.

When I was first plucked from the streets at PC rank and informed that I was to attend a three-day 'Basic Public Order' course, the venue was Round Oak Steelworks, on which Merry Hill Shopping Centre now stands.

I can state with some confidence that any modern day Health and Safety representative viewing the site would probably faint on the spot. It was a disused factory, perfect for riot training, but far from safe. There were holes in the floor; metal projected in various places, and wires hung everywhere.

Visibility whilst wearing a helmet with visor down is not brilliant and in scenarios there was not time to think much about the surroundings whilst charging around under various types of fire.

The best part of the training was the lunch, the legendary 'cow pie' served up in a portakabin. The first exercise after eating always seemed to involve running and that pie could hang very heavy for hours in your stomach.

Before attending a basic course, the lucky officers received their very own set of equipment. In the early days of training, this consisted of a 'flame retardant' boiler suit, a cricket box, a sturdy set of boots with steel toecaps and a NATO helmet with visor. To this extravaganza of protection one added one's own standard issue gloves, belt and truncheon, and there you were, ready to face anything.

Later on, the equipment was enhanced with arm, elbow, shin and knee armour, better batons, and in-helmet radio systems that occasionally worked, but never replaced a loud voice bellowing commands.

The training venue was later moved to a corner of RAF Cosford, a vast improvement, with good facilities in the hangar buildings and plenty of space outside, clear of dangerous holes and obstructions.

I regularly trained in a number of techniques and scenarios, experienced at both these venues over the years in three ranks, namely constable, sergeant and inspector.

'What did the Romans do for us?' asked John Cleese in Monty Python's *'Life of Brian'*. The crowd in the film has many suggestions, but they didn't come up with shield tactics, which can be traced directly from the Romans to the Police.

The Roman armies didn't conquer the known world in hand-to-hand combat; instead they perfected the use of full-length shields to protect their troops from spears, arrows and horsemen. Enemy attacks broke against their shield-wall time after time.

Police tactics unashamedly stole from the Romans - we were facing bricks and petrol bombs rather than spears and flaming arrows, but the effectiveness of the shields held true two thousand years later. They were never intended to protect from firearms although they did possess some capability against low velocity weapons. The first time a firearm was used against public-order officers in modern times was at Broadwater Farm in October 1985, and marked a watershed moment on the streets of England.

Standard public order response does not include armed officers, but after Broadwater Farm, tactics including response by firearms officers were developed, and armed officers would be deployed behind the shields if accredited intelligence or events on the day justified it. It is important to state that the British police never deploy armed officers against an unarmed crowd in the UK.

The police issue full-length shield comprises a clear sheet of flame and impact resistant plastic around five feet in length. That length was not so good for tall cops because it meant one had to 'half crouch' forward when the shield was at rest, playing havoc with the lower back. The length was necessary to give mobility when walking or running – the shield would not drag on the ground, although as the height restriction for police recruits was removed and female officers took their rightful place in the shield walls, they tended to have straight backs, and some inevitable dragging.

Those shields were not light, and even ten minutes of training, holding a shield out in front of the body whilst moving, in full gear with helmet on, was extremely tiring.

Basic shield tactics involved building a wall of long shields and being able to move it forwards and backwards.

A public-order 'serial' usually consisted of a van containing a driver, who remained with the van, a sergeant, and nine constables. It was known in police slang as a '1 and 10'. If long shields were drawn, the nine constables operated in three shield parties of three officers, with the sergeant directly behind them, and often in physical contact whilst commanding.

The three officers would link shields and move with them linked, or stand ground by placing them on the floor whilst linked, crouching behind them. The protection afforded by three shields enabled up to two other officers with short shields or those in specialized roles such as first aid, evidence gatherers or 'spotters' to shelter behind.

If a shield wall was required the three officers would link to the other three- man teams quickly forming a nine-shield wall.

In terms of structure and deployment, there were three serials to a 'PSU', (Police Support Unit). Serials were formed from officers from the same division but different stations, all of whom were trained in public-order and kept personal issue kit in their lockers.

These officers all came from normal policing roles such as 999 response, neighbourhood policing, traffic etc. The OSU, (Operational Support Unit), had their own serials, each with a 'home' division that they would default to for non- public order work, thus 'Uniform Echo' covered Acocks Green, Stechford and Bromford Lane; the 'E' Division.

The Divisions have changed in size, shape and name over the years but the basic principle of having trained officers from 'normal' policing roles, equipped and ready to respond to a 'public-order mobilisation' still holds true. This provides an efficient, flexible and cost-effective response to spontaneous public disorder whilst allowing the majority of officers to concentrate on their vital day-to-day roles.

An inspector commanded each PSU, and thus was in charge of three vans and drivers, twenty-seven officers and three sergeants - a formidable force. Serials could come together, linking shields to provide ever-expanding walls.

A trained chief inspector and/or superintendent would be in overall command of a number of PSUs. This was a tactical role for which training was given.

The Command structure was broadly:

- 'Bronze' – PSU or multiple PSU Commanders, or in charge of a particular geographical area, or at an event for instance.

- 'Silver' - chief inspector or superintending ranks in overall tactical command.

- 'Gold' - usually ACPO, (Association of Chief Police Officers), ranks such as assistant chief constable, but also chief superintendents who had been trained as 'Gold'. This was supposed to be a purely strategic, logistical and organisational role, handling supplies of equipment, mobilization of serials/PSUs, and engagement with other agencies such as fire and ambulance, and media liaison. There was often a blurring of lines causing discord, due to the ranks, and sometimes egos, of some of those involved, and the ingrained rank structure of the police. The Gold commander was often tempted to meddle in Silver's tactics leading to tense moments.

Once basic shield tactics had been mastered, including putting a 'roof' on the shield wall by locking long shields above the shield wall, similar to that seen in the film *'Gladiator'*, we moved onto the next stage of training. A section of the trainees would be designated as 'the crowd' and supplied with ammunition in the form of wooden blocks cut from 4" x 2" timber.

You would think that care would be taken by the crowd not to injure their colleagues, especially given that roles were to be reversed during the day.

Nothing could be further from the truth, and much energy was spent trying to gain a body hit. The instructors exhorted the crowd to aim at the shields but to little avail. In the early days at Round Oak the odd piece of brick used to appear, but thankfully this practice was quickly stamped upon by the instructors.

The main sport for the crowd was to hunt for the sergeants, and especially the inspectors, and above, present at training, who were armed only with short shields and were trying to manage tactics and issue commands whilst keeping an eye open for flying blocks! Sometimes you could gauge the popularity or otherwise of 'gaffers' by the concentration of fire and I have been present when 50% or more of the missiles rained down upon a single hapless senior officer. I suspect that even the instructors enjoyed this but could not permit a smile!

The next challenge was learning how to break the shield wall to allow a variety of other tactics to advance through and into the crowd. It required exact timing due to the risk of the crowd being able to surge through the gap created. It also provided my biggest moment of fear of all public-order training.

Imagine yourself in line, shields locked across the road, filling it completely building line to building line. Behind you would be officers with short round shields, and big sticks, who could run with the lighter weight.

You needed to know who the 'link-men' were, and to listen intently for the order.

"Short shields coming through, break!" would be heard, at which point the link men, who would be in the centre of the wall, unlocked shields and pivoted forwards to left and right, dragging their half of the wall forwards and outwards towards the building line. The nearest officer to the building line acted as the hinge and, in effect the shield wall opened outwards towards the crowd like two gates.

At this point the short shields would charge through to take the ground. The long shields then broke, moved forward past them, and re-formed the wall.

The next stage of training was what to do if a barricade obstacle faced the shield wall. It was the same tactic, except that this time the wall would break to allow an armoured bulldozer or something similar through. These don't move too quickly so there was plenty of time to get out of the way.

Clearly there is a significant difference in the personal experience of this tactic between the link-man and that of the hinge-man. The link-man has a very difficult task. They have to describe a lengthy arc from the centre of the road to the building line whilst dragging the rest of their half of the wall behind them and heading for the crowd. This can be quite a long way in full riot gear whilst carrying a long shield and needs to be executed at the double to get out of the way of charging officers or the bulldozer.

In contrast, the hinge-man just has to execute a turn on the spot whilst admiring the speed - or panic, in the centre of the wall. I was a link-man quite often, and learnt to dread the news that the horses were to train with us.

As a link-man, stood in the middle of the road, knowing that if I didn't 'leg it' forward and outwards as fast as possible, two tons of horse might be colliding with me from behind, certainly concentrated the mind.

To increase the tension, the horses would come through at three speeds. I can still recall my first session as link-man. You were not allowed to turn around, so you could hear them clopping about and snorting, the bridles jangling, but you didn't know how close they were when the order came to 'break'. You just knew they were coming...

'Horses coming through, at the walk - break.'

So far so good - made the edge of the road easily.

'Horses coming through, at the trot - break.'

Not so much clearance that time.

Horses coming through, at the gallop - break.'

Bloody hell - sprint time! In my mind the instructors seemed to always wait until you could feel the horse's breath on your neck before ordering the break. I know I was not alone in my lack of enjoyment of this sensation and it was truly the most fearful I ever was in a riot situation, and that was just training!

Another segment of training was classed as 'building entry'. The training venues boasted a variety of structures built of plywood and steel to recreate doorways, stairways and the like.

Getting three long shields abreast through a standard doorway is not possible. Therefore there is a method of shields dropping out of the locked line and slightly staggered to negotiate doorways, stairways and the like, whilst maintaining an impenetrable wall ahead to protect the shield bearers. The key issue is knowing in advance who will maintain the lead and who will drop back and this is practiced at length, at various speeds and through numerous obstacles.

If there are people above dropping objects as the shield party is trying to enter, then the shield roof is employed. Shields are held above the heads and arms are used as a bracing and spring mechanism to take impacts. The instructors assured us that a good roof, properly braced, could withstand a considerable weight dropped upon it. We practiced whilst a variety of objects were dropped from a gantry built to simulate a first floor. The final run involved a fridge being levered onto us from about fifteen feet above. The shield roof took the impact easily.

The final significant training experience was fire, and in particular petrol- bombs. Understandably, officers were nervous about being doused in burning petrol and the first time one trains with real petrol bombs is somewhat of a 'test' to ones 'inner strength'.

Equipment-wise, the shields, boiler suits and boots resist fire although they aren't going to protect you if you stand in it for long.

Like walking across hot coals in bare feet, movement is the key to happiness!

Both long-shields and short-shields tactics are used against petrol-bombs. With a long shield wall, the impact sprays burning petrol onto the shield but a couple of steps backwards whilst kicking the shield removes the burning liquid which quickly burns out and the ground can be regained.

The best tactic however, is running through petrol-bombs with a short shield. The technique is simple, you run through the flames with a short shield in front, looking downwards to seal the helmet visor onto the chest. The boots, boiler suit and shield will not catch alight and the seal of the visor onto the chest prevents the up-draught of fire and heated air burning the face. Within a second or two you are through the flames and can continue charging the crowd. The only issue really is failing to create that seal onto the chest with the visor, and some eyebrows have been lost that way.

Once you have run through petrol bombs a few times, confidence in the equipment and technique is high, and Molotov's rarely posed a threat, they just looked horrific to the onlooker. As a final contingency, serials are equipped with a number of portable fire extinguishers in harnesses that can be employed if anything goes badly wrong.

***

I was a sergeant at Steelhouse Lane the next time I had occasion to put on the riot- gear for real, and it was back to Handsworth again.

The third Handsworth riot, (the others were 1981 and 1985), occurred on 2nd September 1991 when a power-cut plunged the area into darkness and sparked a looting spree in local shops. Two hundred police officers in riot-gear were called in to bring the unrest under control. Hundreds of shops and houses were looted and cars stolen.

I was on duty this time, at Steelhouse Lane, and covering Birmingham City Centre, which adjoins Handsworth. An electricity sub-station was damaged resulting in the Soho Road and nearby areas being plunged into darkness.

Groups of looters, both black and white, very quickly appeared on the streets and began forcing entry to shops, often by smashing the windows or doors. The majority of shops in the area were owned by Asians, and soon there were groups of shop owners and their families, many armed with hockey-sticks, standing guard outside their shop fronts.

Handsworth was always portrayed in the media as a flashpoint between blacks and the police, but relationships between Asian and black members of the community were if anything, even worse in the eighties and nineties, with numerous and often unreported clashes.

The situation that evening was therefore highly dangerous.

A force-wide public-order mobilization plan was initiated and I was nominated as a sergeant in charge of a serial of ten officers. We deployed in full riot- gear straight away due to the situation and linked up with other serials near to the centre of the disorder. We were formed into a PSU, under the command of a chief inspector, who luckily for us that night was highly competent at his job.

He outlined the situation facing us. A barricade of stolen cars had been built across the Soho Road, blocking it completely. Up to two hundred looters and rioters were in the area of the barricade, shops were being entered and some shopkeepers were defending their premises.

Luckily, the mob did not have any organised leadership or tacticians to hand. What they hadn't thought of was that they were easily outflanked by the use of the many surrounding streets and in fact, our serial was behind them, with another serial facing the barricade and drawing their focus and attention.

In one of the best executed pieces of public order command I have ever witnessed, a 'pincer' movement was put into action, timed so precisely that both serials hit the crowd at the barricade from front and rear at almost the same moment. The element of surprise was devastating for them.

We deployed from the van carrying short shields. By this time we were also equipped with knee, shin, elbow and arm protective pads, as well as metal asps, a telescopic metal truncheon that had much more impact than the old wooden one.

I have to confess that I took great satisfaction from being one of those thirty- odd officers with instructions to break the crowd up and get them dispersed. It has to be remembered that these people had looted, assaulted people, stolen and burnt cars, and thrown missiles. There was potential for even worse to come if not nipped in the bud. There was no quarter given and within seconds they were fleeing through the streets, never to return that evening.

We returned to our vans and spent a couple of hours roaming the area, encouraging straggling groups to go home. Few prisoners were taken, we needed to preserve numbers of officers on the streets, but it was a comprehensive rout all the same. Other officers secured the centre of Handsworth and peace was restored.

I was there and I saw what happened, who was involved, heard what they said. Handsworth 1991 was not a demonstration against deprivation, injustice, or police actions, it was pure criminality, and it was dealt with, but the cost to the law-abiding shopkeepers and residents of Handsworth was high.

My final tale of public order dates from 1994, and was back in Handsworth again. By now I was an inspector in charge of a response shift based at Thornhill Road.

Every incident in Handsworth at the time had potential to become a flashpoint for wider disorder. I had great admiration for the officers there, who had learnt how to diffuse or resolve many serious incidents, often at great risk to themselves, without precipitating a full-scale riot. Drugs dealing and firearms incidents were commonplace during a shift and were routinely handled with a minimum of fuss by a small number of hugely competent officers out on the streets, day and night.

Another feature of Handsworth at the time was the presence of a disproportionately large number of individuals, with mental health issues. This was during the period when 'care in the community' had started, which often seemed to be care by the police when the 'wheel came off'. If the unfortunate mentally-ill individual happened to be black there was the real potential for police actions to be misinterpreted and for community tension to rise quickly.

This was one such occasion, with an innocuous beginning. A routine call was received at Thornhill Road from a social worker. She had to visit an address just off the Lozells Road, the epicentre of the 1985 riots, to check if a mentally-ill individual, released from care, had been taking his medication as they had received reports that he was acting strangely.

Ironically, such information often emanated from friends, family and neighbours, but onlookers would only see the confrontation resulting and tended to react to the scene before their eyes, oblivious of the background.

Handsworth was a very difficult area to police because every police action came under scrutiny for racism or oppressiveness and could act as a spark that set off another riot.

An officer was duly sent with the social worker.

They had knocked the door at this persons address, and eventually, when it was opened, the occupant, a black male, had thrown a milk bottle full of petrol over them and produced a box of matches and a hand-axe. They took appropriate action and retreated – fast, and after a short chase the occupant returned to the house and shut the door.

As the inspector I was soon presented with this little problem to resolve. Clearly the occupant had not been taking his medication and was a danger to himself, neighbours and any member of the public unfortunate enough to come into contact with him. He could not just be left in the premises.

I have had many dealings with mentally-ill people over the years and the process in a case such as this was that the police were responsible for arresting the person under the mental health legislation and conveying them to a 'place of safety', inevitably a police cell. The reality is that cells are totally unsuitable for this purpose but this is what we had to work with at that time.

Once the dangers presented by the individual were removed, a long and laborious process ensued where medical practitioners were required to 'Section' the person in order that they could be conveyed to secure mental health accommodation. Places in such accommodation were however at a premium and jealously protected by the relevant representatives of medical and social services professions.

Everyone knew that the police were unsuited to, and unqualified for, caring for these unfortunate individuals but, such was the lack of medical and professional resource available, that the 'thin blue line' tended to become the resolution mechanism for all the problems that occurred where the public were involved.

My problem was simple, the situation required officers to be in protective gear, to the onlooker that would be 'riot-police' on the streets of Handsworth. It was unlikely that it could be resolved by negotiation, and the use of force against a black male by fully equipped officers could result in a confrontation that was likely to spread.

The bottom line however was that he had to be removed from the house, for assessment and treatment, or an unacceptable risk to the public would remain.

It was an afternoon shift and the weather was fine and dry so I couldn't rely on the good offices of 'PC Rain' to keep the curious from the streets. A low-key approach was out of the question as my experience indicated two likely issues would arise, a forced entry by officers with long shields, and a gathering crowd.

Luckily the local OSU serial was on duty so I had a team of well-trained officers at my disposal, together with my own, local, shift officers. I decided to divide my resources into two groups, the OSU officers in riot-gear and the local officers in normal uniform.

Off we all went to the house in question. The location could not have been much worse, only a few hundred yards from where the post office was burnt in 1985. It was a terraced house with a single front door. I sent an equipped team to the rear in case the occupant made a run for it. I used the normally attired local officers to form a cordon, with instructions to talk to any crowd that formed and to explain what was going on, this was not a time for secrecy.

Luckily I had a secret weapon on my shift. Anyone who policed Handsworth in the 80s and 90s would recall Pam Burrell, now Pamela Burrell-Clayton. I'm sure she won't mind me saying this, but in those days Pam was a substantial and imposing figure who had a party piece of 'flopping' onto struggling miscreants on the ground and sitting on them until they cried for mercy - it worked every time.

Pam is black, a rare sight in the police in those days, and was one of the best coppers in Handsworth. She was beautiful, could sing like Whitney Houston, and had the sort of personality that everyone wanted to be part of – a wonderful lady who brought joy to everyone who knew her.

I put Pam on the cordon and in hindsight I am sure that is why we got away with what followed. She talked, and talked, and the crowd of around two hundred listened and just watched. Handsworth was a very special place, with unique policing challenges; for example, within minutes I was aware of a group of people on a nearby rooftop filming us. We dared not put a foot wrong and the unfortunate occupant of the house was an unexploded grenade waiting to set off trouble.

To approach the door I chose a three man shield party with long shields to lead, two officers with short shields and myself behind them. This was very much a gamble, given the location and crowd, but I had a duty of care to my officers as well as the public and the occupant, so full protective gear had to be worn. It was a good job we did.

After the usual few minutes of banging on the door, a very agitated man opened it and began abusing us in the most colourful terms. This didn't bother me, but the axe he was waving about did!

We tried asking him a few times to put it down but this just resulted in louder shouting. I was very conscious of the gathering crowd and decision time as to how to resolve the situation was fast approaching. In the event my mind was made up for me when the man started hacking at the long shields with the axe.

This was an eventuality for which we had trained and I had total confidence in the OSU officers. I gave the order and we pushed forward swiftly as a group. Luckily, the layout of the house was very conducive to the tactic. It had a long, straight, hallway that led directly into a kitchen, and straight onto a solid brick wall.

I don't think the occupant was expecting the move. We ran him backwards down the hallway as he hacked again and again at the shields, but without much force as he was off balance, retreating.

It was a perfect move, and within seconds the man was pinned by the long shields against the kitchen wall, unable to move. More fortuitously, his axe was raised above his head at the moment of impact and thus his arm and the axe were pinned aloft by the shields. It took just moments to reach up and prise the weapon from his grasp and throw it behind us.

Moments later he was restrained and handcuffed, all without injury to anyone. I breathed a silent prayer of thanks and we were able to walk him outside and into the van without further problems. The crowd dispersed and I don't think the film from the rooftop opposite has ever come to light.

The final twist in this tale came later. Here was a man, clearly mentally disturbed, who had attempted to set fire to a social worker and a police officer, and hacked repeatedly at us with an axe. Criminal proceedings were not however appropriate due to his condition.

He could not stay in a cell forever; he was a medical case. I assumed that as social services had instigated the incident, they would be relieved that we had resolved it and assist us by returning the man to a secure hospital. I had reckoned without social services logic!

About two hours after returning to my office the telephone rang. It was the custody officer who informed me that social services were refusing to do anything because they had no secure accommodation. They were insisting that the man just needed to take his medication at which point he would be fine to go home!

They would not budge, even when I pointed out the facts, the dangers and that it was one of their own who had been attacked.

In the end I had to call out a doctor to 'Section' the man for assessment under the Mental Health Act, after which we were able to take him to a secure unit.

The whole incident probably tied up thirty officers for a whole afternoon and the result was - nothing. No crimes solved or recorded. This is somewhat typical of the sort of thing that the 'thin blue line' deal with every day, and which gets in the way of the police's proper role. The police are truly the social service of last resort.

Figure 3 Public Order Training - Petrol Bombs

Chapter Two

The Special Ones

(Stephen Burrows):

Police leadership training has passed through many incarnations in an effort to produce the right kind of leaders. Changes tend to reflect the environment, although in the case of the police, this can sometimes lag considerably behind external cultural, technological and societal change.

Since its inception, well over one hundred and seventy years ago, the British police service has been closely aligned to the principles of citizenship and community. A product of this alignment with the people it polices, is the concept that its leaders should be drawn from within its own ranks. This view has prevailed until very recently and has only been breached in the last few years by the introduction of direct entry at superintendent rank.

Further experiments are to be made in this vein but the 'jury is out,' as to whether the skills of direct entrants, drawn from outside the service, will be of more use than the years of policing experience gained from rising through the ranks.

Despite generally moaning about 'the gaffers,' it had once been a source of some comfort to junior officers that every single chief officer had started as a probationary constable and 'learnt the ropes' so to speak, from the bottom (most important) rank of the organisation, the constable.

Post World War II, police leaders tended to be drawn from a

military background with commensurate training and attitudes. As the 60s dawned, and the world changed, they appeared increasingly out of date and unsuited to a profession that was supposed to reflect the public and to act with its consent.

It was therefore no coincidence that the *'Special Course'* was introduced in 1962; at a time when there was an urgent need to attract applicants with the skills and character suitable for an accelerated promotion route.

The name itself was ill-chosen and a continuing problem. It eventually came to be called the 'APC' - Accelerated Promotion Course. To be a member of the Special Course was like having an albatross permanently affixed around one's neck.

Often viewed with suspicion, resentment, and sometimes open hostility, the Special Course officers had to constantly prove themselves and were often bullied or distanced from their colleagues with questions as to why they were deemed to be so much better than others.

The stated objectives of the 1962 Special Course at its inception were:

- To improve the career prospects in the police service, so as to attract good recruits, and,

- To provide training for young officers with potential to reach high rank in accordance with the principle that senior officers should be drawn from the service.

The Special Courses, and later accelerated promotion schemes, were always held at Bramshill Police College in Hook, Hampshire, an estate sold to the Home Office by Lord Brocket in 1953. This imposing Jacobean Mansion, set in extensive sculptured grounds, did little to expel the beliefs of other ranks that the whole enterprise amounted to an elitist 'club'.

The tale of my attendance upon the course will give some credence to that view. I hope though, that it will also demonstrate how the new course attempted to grapple with that legacy, although, in my opinion, ultimately gloriously, and even somewhat humorously on occasions, failed to overturn the establishment principles firmly mortared into it.

The College seemed to draw much of its inspiration from nearby Aldershot, and military officer training, and would not easily relinquish this approach.

It is worth setting out the ranks within the police service with a brief description of each:

Constable - The bedrock of the service - all officers are constables and swear an oath to the Crown when they join. Constables are not 'employees', they are servants of the Crown and as such many employment rights are barred from them, including the right to strike and unfair dismissal. They are technically always on duty and can be recalled to duty at any time and deployed in any role, anywhere a chief officer requires. They are subject to Police Discipline and Conduct Regulations including obeying any **lawful** order given by a senior rank. The majority of officers remain as constable, performing a wide variety of roles and they are the most important people in the police service.

Sergeant - The first managerial rank, usually first-line supervisor of a small group of officers on specialized teams such as in CID. On a uniform 999 response shift in larger forces, dependent upon structure, there would have been several sergeants rotating through roles such as custody officer, patrol sergeant and 'controller' - sending officers to jobs from a Control Room.

Inspector – Broadly, in charge of a team, or section, such as a response unit or specialist units, a geographical area, or a CID office. Numerically, normally supervising anything between twenty and forty officers and staff.

Chief Inspector - A much broader managerial role, and the first step into senior management. Spheres of responsibility differ greatly, they can command a geographical area, or be the deputy on a larger area, or cross-force team.

Superintendent - A key command role, responsible for whole areas, departments, cross-force functions and several hundred officers and staff.

Chief Superintendent - Can be in command of a single large function or group of functions, such as 'Head of Crime', or can command a single function across a force such as all uniform policing. In the eighties for example, West Midlands Police was grouped into geographical divisions headed by a chief superintendent, each division comprising two or three sub-divisions commanded by a superintendent.

Assistant Chief Constable - The first 'ACPO', (Association of Chief Police Officer), rank. There may only be one ACC in a force, or several in larger forces, each having responsibility for groups of functions such as 'ACC Crime' or 'ACC Operations'. ACPO officers are also usually required to take on national lead roles and are expected to develop policy and practice and perform spokes-person roles for the service nationally, for instance in liaising with the media. In general, ACPO roles set the force strategy.

Deputy Chief Constable - One deputy per force, they do as the title suggests, deputise for the Chief Constable. They usually act as Head of Discipline, (called Professional Standards now), and have national roles.

Chief Constable - The lead and figurehead for the force - accountable to the Police and Crime Commissioner now, but in the eighties, the Police Authority.

***

Let us begin with a brief, and personal, pen-picture of the Special Course, the Police College, and police leadership training in 1985, when I first encountered them - with everything centred around Bramshill.

The mansion was preserved in all its fading glory, and housed the commandant and administrative staff. Several rooms were left for meetings, whilst two housed bars, one where formal dress was required, and the other casual.

The grounds contained a large lake, (in which fishing was

permitted, and which boasted a small boat), walled gardens, an imposing mile-long driveway and the inevitable deer herd beloved of English country houses.

The Home Office had clearly inspected this beautiful building and its estate and decided to improve it by erecting as many cheap and monstrous buildings as could be crammed in directly next to the mansion. Thus there was a large dining hall, classrooms, and a quadrangle of 'accommodation' that resembled nothing so much as a prison camp.

Such was the standard of these domiciles that it had clearly been felt that senior officers needed something more suited to their status. Thus a series of new accommodation blocks were constructed at the bottom of a hill where, the more 'important' visitors were housed. The scars upon the landscape were completed by a mini housing-estate for residential staff, and a large gymnasium, housing squash courts, badminton courts and weights.

By the 80s, Bramshill was 'the place' for those with ambition to go further in the service to attend and network. For this wasn't just somewhere one went to sit in a classroom, a whole cultural experience had evolved around the course structure.

I attended the second year of the new Special Course. This was a brave attempt at modernizing a course structure that had evolved during the previous twenty-three-years. The main courses held at Bramshill at this time were:

The 'Overseas Command Course.' This was a residential course for senior officers from other countries, particularly from the African

Continent although attendees came from all over the world. They were resident at Bramshill for six months.

I think the idea was that they would learn how to police 'the British way', i.e. with consent and without breaches of human rights. I'm not sure how successful this inculcation was, but they always seemed to be enjoying the experience hugely. We had very little day-to-day contact with them other than seeing their colourful procession of uniforms, with much gold braid adornment, around the campus and at mealtimes. The Overseas Command Course continued right up until the College closed at the end of 2014.

The 'Senior Command Course.' By the eighties this had become the premier course in policing. Candidates could only get onto it via a rigorous selection process. The gateway to ACPO, (Association of Chief Police Officer), ranks, it was a lengthy residential course where every attendee received a crucial final grading that tended to determine their pecking order in succeeding in being selected for assistant chief constable posts when advertised by forces around the country.

Somewhat like the draft pick in American football, each year forces would hold back on advertising their vacancies until the latest batch of embryonic chief officers emerged from this course clutching their hard-won grades. An 'A+' pretty much guaranteed a swift elevation to ACPO, anything below 'A' carried the danger of repeated applications throughout the years to come, an experience that drained many an ACPO hopeful of the will to live as they underwent endless selection panels, exercises, and 'rubber chicken' dinners with the Police Authority members of whichever was the latest force with the coveted vacancy.

The 'Intermediate or Junior Command Course.' This was a course for chief inspectors in the main, in preparation for higher ranks. This course fitted somewhere in between the Special Course and Senior Command Course but linked to neither, standing alone as a management and leadership course for both the 'special' ones and their colleagues who had been promoted at a normal pace.

The 'Special Course'. As stated previously, the aim of this course was to prepare future leaders of exceptional calibre. Successful attendees were promised an accelerated promotion path. Upon selection they were promoted to sergeant and within a short period of completion, were to be promoted to inspector by their forces.

There was an expectation that, having reached inspector whilst young in service, they would be able to progress to senior ranks by competing with their conventionally promoted colleagues in force. This had led to mixed success with many attaining senior rank, but problems were appearing with the numbers applying, the time it was taking to pass through the ranks, and the wastage rate, as prospective ACPO members suffered the pressure of continual competition and assessment.

There was also a view that the system was in some sense 'cloning' future leaders with a narrow range of views and illiberal attitudes that did not meet the challenges of modern, 80s, society. It was also very formal, with a significant militaristic influence.

The sergeants attending Bramshill for the year's duration of the course experienced a fall in status from supervisors in force to 'junior' ACPO 'wannabe's', treated as such by those on the Senior Command Course and staff, many of whom of course had passed through the same suffering and expected others to do the same.

There was a distinct shortage of female applicants, many of whom struggled to combine family commitments with residing for a year in Hampshire, and nearly everyone was a white male.

Special Course members were paraded and inspected and were expected to learn the conventions of etiquette in the dining hall. It was like recruit's initial training with quasi-aristocratic or military officer knobs added on.

***

The culture of Bramshill itself is also worth a light touch walk-through. I always felt that the mansion house and grounds had engendered delusions of grandeur on the part of the directing staff and ACPO. There was a tangible sense of it being the 'Chief Officer's club', and this was the perception of the majority of rank and file police officers that I worked with.

Activities in the dining hall provided a focal point for this attitude. There was a dress-code for meals. The commandant, senior directing staff and visiting guests sat on a raised dais at the front of the hall. Imposing portraits of previous commandants and Her Majesty looked down upon the diners.

When I first attended, meals were very formal and it was rumoured that table etiquette was monitored as part of the assessment of the original Special Course. Learning the direction of 'passing the port,' and how to eat peas correctly on the back of the fork were essential skills to be cultivated.

However, it was on the legendary 'Dining In Nights' that the College excelled itself. These events took place every six weeks or so and were well attended by senior ranks who would stay the night to enable full enjoyment of the proceedings.

This was a black tie, silver-service event. Guests were allowed and were often, (but not always), wives and husbands. Drink flowed, the port was passed in the correct direction, there were speeches, entertainment, and a jolly good time was had by all.

On my first Dining In Night I will never forget leaving the hall to find a very senior officer vomiting into the bushes. Drunken forays on the boat on the lake were also a regular occurrence. I was never comfortable with the excesses of Dining In Night and could not reconcile them with the conservative formality of a police service that prided itself upon being drawn from and representing the public.

It smacked of elitism and I felt that it had little place in the police service. During later years these attitudes of excess faded away and thankfully Bramshill became a normal training establishment.

The other side of the coin was the overt and visible snobbery I encountered, and the often negative or bemused attitudes displayed towards the new Special Course.

***

This was the environment into which the new Special Course was launched.

It was divided into four stages:

Stage 1 - Those selected for the course were to be promoted to sergeant on the 1 September, if not already holding that rank, of the year preceding the course. They would thus carry out the full duties of sergeant in force for a period of six months prior to attendance.

Stage 2 - (Part One) - A three months residential course in April, May and June. The aim of this part was to identify the strengths and weaknesses of an individual and to provide them with the knowledge and skills to become a more effective manager. Each officer was to have a personal development plan based upon individual needs. Instruction was to be given in the following areas:

- Writing effectively.

- Public speaking.

- Research skills.

- Effective reading.

- Leadership development.

- Team building.

- Problem solving.

- Stress.

- Assertiveness training.

In addition, the 'Lincolnshire Exercise' would take place in which the student was expected to exercise management skills by role playing. At the close of this stage the student was expected to be aware of his, or her, own personality and behaviour.

Stage 3 - 'Sandwich Section'. This was spent in Force for a period of one, or two years during which the officer was required to:

• Study for, and pass, the Inspectors Promotion Examination.

• Undertake projects assigned by College Directing Staff.

• Attend seminars at Bramshill. Suitability to progress was then evaluated by the chief officer of the force, which in reality was the relevant assistant chief constable, the director of the Special Course, and the director of the extended interview process.

Stage 4 – (Part Two of the course) - A six months course at Bramshill. All students attending were promoted to temporary inspector, and this part focused upon preparation for being an inspector with one eye on the longer-term. I quote from a pamphlet which provided guidance: *'It is also thought necessary to make provision on this course for a consideration of problems pertaining to more senior police management as well as making provision for a study of relevant political, economic and social phenomena.'*

I should say at this point that this chapter deals purely with Special Course Part One for two reasons. Firstly, I did not attend Part Two, which is another story. More importantly, Part One of the course was the challenging and experimental section, certainly in a police context, and probably at that time at the forefront of public service training regimes anywhere.

**

Those eligible to apply for the new course in 1985 were:

'All Constables who have passed the promotion examination for sergeant, and all sergeants who in both cases, on 1st April of the year of applicationare not over 30 years of age andhave not more than 10 years' service.'

In special cases the age limit could be extended to thirty-five – for ex armed forces applicants for example. There was also a provision for: *'Constables who pass in all three papers in the most recent qualifying examination for promotion to Sergeant and are within the top 200, (in England and Wales in respect of marks gained), are entitled automatically to be interviewed by their Force Boards if they are eligible as above.'*

This was how the hand of fate, in the form of my local superintendent, propelled me into the selection process, as I had indeed come in the top two hundred in the 1985 examination.

I was sat writing a report in Acocks Green Police Station one day when the 'Super's' hand laid upon my shoulder and I was informed that I was being put forward for a Force Selection Board. This represented a change of plan as I had wanted to become a detective and join the drugs squad, but I figured it cost nothing other than a spot of effort to apply. I duly completed and submitted my application form on 17 February 1986.

Before moving on, I should mention the Graduate Entry

Scheme that in reality produced the majority of Special Course members.

Graduates underwent the selection process before joining the police and thus were not required to undergo the normal selection process of Force, Central, and Extended Interview Boards. Of course this did nothing to assist those labeled Special Course and the epithet 'graduate wankers' was often heard from others on the shift.

On 22 April 1986, I attended the first stage of selection, the Force Interview Board, comprising the Assistant Chief Constable, (Personnel and Training), Superintendent (Training), and a Police Federation representative. Much to my surprise I passed, and was sent forward to the next stage, the Central Selection Board.

This one-day event took place at the Lancashire Police Training School near Preston on 18 June 1986. Central Selection Board comprised two interview panels, each of around forty minutes. One panel comprised an ACPO officer, a Superintendents Association member, a Police Federation representative, and a Non-Service Member, (NSM). The second interview was with just the NSM.

This was the first occasion upon which I encountered the concept of the Non-Service Member, a role that featured in all of the selection procedures for the Special Course, the Senior Command Course, and their replacements.

The NSM was a non-police person nominated by the Head of the Home Office Unit, Civil Service Selection Board. If this was an attempt to introduce the outside world into police leadership selection it was rather limited in breadth. As I once observed whilst being interviewed by an NSM, there weren't any NSM factory workers or similar.

They were described as being, 'someone of great experience in some other branch of public service, in education or industry. To generalize, they tended to be establishment figures palatable to the Home Office. As evidence for this assertion, I note that all four NSM's on my Extended Assessment were Knights or Ladies of the Realm.

The questions asked in interviews tended towards what has best been described by some as 'blue sky'. This allowed candidates to demonstrate the ability to think and express themselves widely and creatively whilst under pressure, and to demonstrate their knowledge of current affairs. Much reading of broadsheet newspapers was thus encouraged in the run-up to these assessments, and debate raged as to the relative merits of The Times, Telegraph, or Guardian. The Sun and Daily Mail tended not to feature.

Thus, in interview I encountered such questions as:

'How do you think the inflation rate in Israel would affect you if you lived there?' and,

'What are your views on the conduct of the Rhodesian elections?'

The latter question came from an NSM who later revealed he had been one of the organisers!

This sort of thing provoked incredulity when related to colleagues back at the nick who would shake their heads in wonderment.

To my surprise, I passed, and headed off to the next and final stage, Extended Interview.

Numbers were limited to a maximum of one hundred and thirty two in 1985; of which thirty-three came from the Metropolitan Police's own Selection Board, not Central Selection. Candidates attended for three days, and were seen in groups of five or six, by teams of three assessors, each team consisting of two senior police officers and a Non-Service Member.

The procedure was daunting, and there were many pale faces present at breakfast the first morning, not much eaten, and more than one trip to the toilets on the part of some. One memory I have was the number of people who confided that they didn't really know what they were doing there - none of whom I saw again so presumably they must have failed.

I think self-belief was an important factor in getting through, a piece of advice I often passed on in later years – if you don't really believe inside that you are ready, why should the assessors, promotion board, or job interview panel think differently? There was no pass quota, candidates either reached the standard required or not. I believe that this was true, and the assessors applied themselves admirably to the task in hand.

Candidates were required to arrive before dinner, 5pm on Saturday 2 August 1986 in my case. Following the meal they received a briefing and completed a form detailing interests, some *'views on life'* and *'two or three controversial topics of a non-professional nature you would be prepared to discuss'* in interview. I note that I wrote *'sanctions'* and *'nuclear energy'* on the top of my joining instructions so they must have been my chosen two. Funnily enough, they are both still controversial issues.

The procedure then went as follows:

Day One: The first morning was occupied by a 'Written Appreciation' exercise. Candidates were given a file of papers to peruse that required a decision on a 'fairly complex' non-police problem. There were several possible solutions, none right or wrong. The requirement was to produce a written report giving a decision and justifying it by detailing the rationale used to arrive at it. This was more difficult than it seems due to the time constraints.

The trick was to read quickly, making notes as one went, decide on the solution, the structure of the report, and get on with writing it. Not finishing the report in the time allowed, or not making out a justified decision were the key reasons for failure. Spending too much time reading was the main tactical issue.

A numerical 'Intelligence Test' followed before lunch.

Lunch was pre-occupied with anticipation of the afternoon's 'Group Discussion.' I always hated these. The group of five or six candidates was sat around a table with the assessors watching. A topic or topics were thrown into the middle of the table and discussion ensued, or battle raged, dependent upon one's philosophy of life. The make-up of the group was key to success or failure.

The best advice was always to say a few things and try to be inclusive, bringing in those who had said nothing or seemed to be struggling. This always gained extra marks. Unfortunately there always seemed to be at least one person, usually male, in each discussion who ignored this advice and sought to talk over everyone, challenge everything said and impose their view on others. They always failed the exercise but could destroy the chances of others. Some groups got together in advance and made pacts to allow everyone to speak but were sometimes betrayed when the time came for combat.

Once this bout of gladiatorial effort was complete, it was time for evening meal then the 'General Information Test', a language-based reasoning exercise.

Day Two: This began with the first round of interviews, and during the day candidates were rotated through the full panel and NSM interviews.In between interviews two more tasks were undertaken.

A second written exercise, the 'Drafting Exercise', comprised drafting a reply to a difficult letter from a member of the public in 'suitable and tactful' terms. Telling them to *'f... off and get a life'* was tempting but not recommended.

The final task was the 'Committee Exercise'. Another opportunity for combat, or teamwork, my comments as regards the group discussion apply equally here. The group were given a number of practical problems with each group member taking turns to chair and run a discussion of the problem.

The task of the Chairperson was to, *'make a clear proposal and then co-ordinate the ideas of others'*. The Committee Members were equally under scrutiny to join in and produce ideas, although I confess that I felt more like punching the egotistical one(s) who loved to hog the limelight, but I clearly successfully disguised that emotion from the assessors.

The final act was to vote individually on the one or two people in your group that you saw as most likely to succeed as senior officers and, quite bizarrely, the one or two that you would most like to have as holiday companion. I guess this was recognition that for most people, senior officers were best left alone, and definitely not to be taken on holiday. My subsequent experiences in the police tend to support this view!

My group comprised six hopefuls, only two of whom succeeded. To my amazement I was one of them, receiving the coveted letter on 13 August 1986. My police career was about to change beyond my imagination.

I was promoted to sergeant on 1 September 1986 and posted to Steelhouse Lane with that label of 'Special Course' firmly applied. Everyone assumed that I was a graduate entrant but in fact I believe that I was the first non-graduate to successfully apply in West Midlands Police.

***

The new 'Special Course Part One' awaited me. The previous year, the first 'new style' course had run, and the description in the official booklet had changed subtly from that given above. It may have hinted at what was to come, but I can still feel the disbelief of us attendees on the first day, first input, which I describe later. The description now stated:

'This part of the course will embrace both assessment and development in communication, problem solving, interpersonal skills, stress assessment and team building modes. Exercises in Brecon, Snowdonia, and Lincolnshire provide the opportunity to combine all the skills in leadership and team building modes where the student is faced with unfamiliar surroundings in which to test himself.'

The course began with a week long familiarization in the autumn of 1986. I journeyed down to Bramshill on a Sunday afternoon and was immediately confronted with the mile-long, arrow straight, driveway leading to the mansion house in the distance. It made an impressive statement that was slightly ameliorated by the more workmanlike structures of the training and residential buildings.

There were over thirty of us on the course, and I was one of only two non- graduates. Many of my course colleagues were from 'Oxbridge' with a large contingent from the Metropolitan Police. Our first encounter with the new style course came when we met as a group in one of the rooms in the mansion.

This was no ordinary classroom, it had oak paneling, tapestries hanging on the walls, and faded furniture of the sort I had only seen in National Trust properties. The whole experience to that point had already made me feel out of place and wondering whether a mistake had been made - was I 'out of my 'class'?

We sat in anticipation, and then the door opened and in walked an individual portraying what I can only describe as 'effeminate affectations'. This was not a problem, but to this day I'm not sure if his style was an act designed to 'confront our thinking' or a genuine behaviour pattern.

In due course I grew to admire him greatly, and his attempts to confront the established thinking and norms of the police. He had created the concept of the new course, together with the Course Director, and they both deserve plaudits for this brave attempt to change and modernise police leadership training.

Our three police chief inspector Directing Staff were introduced, and also the Course Director, whose moustache and demeanor made me instantly think of a Spitfire pilot in the Battle of Britain.

Our friend from earlier then delivered a quite extraordinary input for police officers to receive, describing what Part 1 was really about in his view; namely self- development.

We were to learn to know ourselves - our strengths and weaknesses, expand our minds, and seek 'self-actualization,' a concept from 'Maslow's Hierarchy of Needs Theory'.

The process for achieving this state would not however involve Mescaline, LSD or any other mind-blowing drugs. Instead we would be divided into small groups remaining together throughout Part 1 for 'Group Encounter' sessions, where every minute detail of our reactions and performances as individuals, and groups, during the exercises to come could be debriefed and discussed. We were informed that this submersion in self-analysis could lead to vivid dreams - unfortunately not so in my case.

We were recommended to read some literature of a mind-expanding nature; in particular I remember *'Wind, Sand and Stars'* by Antoine de Saint Exupery, and *'Siddhartha'* by Herman Hesse. I am ashamed to state that it took me a while to realise he was talking about a Buddha figure and not someone called *'Sid Arthur'*, but I eventually caught on. (I would recommend both books if you are exploring the meaning of life). Clearly I had some personal journeying into the depths of my soul ahead of me. Introspection would be the keyword during the weeks to come.

That evening I decided to go to the gym, my mind filled with excitement at the unexpectedly innovative, and liberal nature of the course. I have always been a rebel, and chafed at many of the stuffy and restrictive 'norms' of the police culture, and structure, with its rigid hierarchy and discipline. *'At last'* I reflected, *'A breath of fresh air.'*

My reverie, as I walked, was interrupted by a question from a much older man, clearly a member of the Senior Command Course, "What part of the armed forces did you serve in?" he said, nodding towards the tattoos on my arms, a relic of a misspent, but glorious youth, the tattoos now visible for the first time at Bramshill below my T-shirt sleeves.

"None of them, I was a biker," I responded in my best 'Brummie' accent together with an engaging smile.

He turned on his heel and marched off without another word,

my first encounter with the police establishment had occurred.

***

Following the week of familiarisation, I returned to my sergeant duties at Steelhouse Lane Police Station in Birmingham City Centre for six months. The full course commenced on Monday 30 March 1987 and once more I traversed the long driveway towards the mansion.

By the time I had driven the mile to the mansion I had gone from a role with responsibility and status in Birmingham, to the bottom of the pecking order at Bramshill. We were accommodated in the quadrangle I mentioned earlier.

The blocks were akin to basic army barracks, no en-suite bathrooms in those days, just a sink in the room that could double up as a urinal in a late-night emergency. Furniture consisted of a single bed, bedside table, wardrobe and mirror, 'Spartan' I think it is called. Upon occasion, brown water would flow from the taps and legend had it they were fed from the lake.

I should mention the other members of my course. They were, on the whole, clever, witty, innovative, brilliant company, and good friends. I have not seen most of them for nigh on thirty years. A number have reached, and some still hold, very senior positions in policing, whilst others left to pursue pastures new. One played rugby for England and became a journalist, one a diplomat. One of the nicest and most liberal took a decision to open fire when commanding armed officers and faced the most searching enquiry into a firearms incident ever held in this country, with courage, dignity and professional brilliance.

They were in fact special people, and nothing I say about activities upon the course is in any way derogatory to any of them. It is fair to say that they embraced the philosophy of the course in varying degrees, ranging from the 'I'll just get through it' school of thought, to the 'I'm totally into this, it's changed my life' response, but such is life, and people and the world would be less rich if it were otherwise.

And what of me? Well I was enthusiastic, and attempted to give self- development a good go, which is why I ended up disappointed I suppose.

I am not about to recount every detail of three months of intense and constant self-development work. As is often said, 'you had to be there,' immersed in it, to understand the potential for altering the way one thought and reacted. It was in fact quite disturbing at times to have one's innermost thoughts and habits dissected and challenged by others. Therefore, I will pick some choice nuggets to give you a flavour of the experience.

***

Let us begin with 'assertiveness' and the giving of 'feedback'. These were techniques that were inculcated into us very early in the course, the tools of challenge, dissection and encounter sessions. I'm not sure if they were supposed to be separate issues but in my mind, and others on the course, they became as one.

The key to assertiveness, we were informed, was to

disassociate emotion from the statement of assertion. The idea was, if you said your piece in a matter-of-fact manner, the recipient would not get angry and punch you on the nose. We were taught this framework. I have to confess I was never any good at it, and still can't dissociate emotion from my opinions.

To this technique was added the giving of non-judgmental feedback. This fitted nicely with assertiveness because it was about making observations about behaviour, statements made, and views of others in a way that was supportive and non-threatening. This often took place within the group-encounter sessions and some people cried as a result, or sulked for days - perhaps we needed more practice.

Anyway, the giving of non-judgmental feedback and the assertiveness statement became conflated, and permeated our days to an extent that outsiders would have found puzzling. Being police officers, a healthy dose of cynicism and humour was added, and it was not unusual to hear strange conversation such as, "Can I give you some non-judgmental feedback. Stop hogging the fucking cheeseboard at dinner, it pisses me off because there's none left for me."

We definitely became a bit weird, and one doesn't share deep emotions and inner-feelings with others without forming a close bond. I think for most of the group very close friendships formed quite quickly, some were more than friends; at least one couple got married and are still together.

I gradually became aware that the other courses, especially the Senior Command Course, were unsure what to make of us and were questioning a course that promoted such 'hippy-dippy shit'.

Another feature of the course was the lack of any sort of discipline, incredibly rare in a police environment. We were told that *our* learning was *our* responsibility, and thus up to us how we dealt with the course. For instance, there was a timetable, with exercises, visiting speakers, classroom inputs, but apart from being polite to visitors it did not seem to matter greatly if one was on time, or indeed engaged. It was a regular occurrence for students to be 'missing in action' following a heavy night before, or if bored, for the newspaper to be produced and read in class.

One spectacular example of this laissez-faire was the day we were asked to divide ourselves into two groups for a later exercise. This was at around 9am one morning. By lunchtime we had failed to divide and a number, myself included, had got so bored with the debate that we left the others to it. We never did create two groups. I'm not sure if that was actually the exercise, and whether we passed or failed, that was just how it sometimes was on this mind-bending course.

Another day, and another affront to the senior officers, from the members of the 'hippy' sergeants course - the 'beautiful boat' episode.

Upon arrival in the classroom our eyes feasted upon craft items - card, scissors, glue, tape, and all the components of a good afternoon in infant school. This time the instructors divided us into groups, lesson learnt I think, and after all we only had three months.

"We want you to build a boat that is beautiful and will sail on the lake for ten minutes," was the instruction. It might have been five minutes but I distinctly remember the boat had to be beautiful.

The reader seeking assurance as to police innovation and resourcefulness can rest safe in the knowledge that several wonderful and beautiful boats were constructed. We then set off in procession to the lake, instructors in the lead, carrying our craft proudly aloft. Our path led us past the ground floor classrooms of the Senior Command Course, and I recall with some enjoyment the sight of jaws hitting ground as we paraded past with our boats.

There were two major off-site exercises, 'Lincolnshire' and 'Snowdonia,' both a week in duration. I think the idea was to provide experience(s), build team and individual leadership skills, and generate plenty of material for debrief in those group sessions by way of a spot of non-judgmental feedback.

Snowdonia was actually a week long 'Outward Bound' course at Aberdovey. The bad news was that alcohol was banned; but the good news was that no-one was searched!

This week was all about team-building. In hindsight it was a wonderful time, and I had the opportunity to try a number of new experiences. These were designed to tease out fears and enable one to overcome them with the help of colleagues, remember – 'self-development' was the mantra.

It is a sensible approach to look at the week in terms of fears confronted. Everyone has a pet fear - mine was, and still is, heights. I can do depths, water, blood, faeces, decaying and dismembered bodies, cold, hot and spiders but I wobble on top of stepladders.

The first test was abseiling off some cliffs at Barmouth. It wasn't too high, perhaps fifty feet, but over eight feet was a good as a mountain to me. They didn't tell us until we got there that we had to climb up first! All the safety gear was provided and we were roped from the instructors at the top and I managed to conquer going up okay.

At the top I assumed we would just come down the same way, but the abseiling gear was set up a little further along, fiendishly above a large cave mouth. This meant that we could abseil for about ten feet and then had to push off and hang in space in the cave mouth with just the ropes to support us. Two moments of gritting teeth then, once going over the edge, once kicking off the cliff face and letting go bar the ropes.

Actually I went over the edge easily, I had seen others do it and it didn't look too bad. I even kept my eyes open. I descended by pushing off the cliff and letting rope through the winch mechanism until I reached the apex of the cave mouth.

I can remember stopping and breathing deeply. One of those 'shit or bust' moments that policing occasionally throws at one. I definitely shut my eyes and pushed off and....I hung happily in mid-air. A few operations of the rope mechanism and I was back on terra-firma. That fear conquered - or so I thought.

The next heights moment was cunningly disguised in another fear for many, and became my worst moment of the week. We were informed that we were going pot-holing in a disused slate mine. Several course members suffered from claustrophobia and that was the focus of worries as we journeyed in the minibus to our appointment with a hole in the ground. I assumed that this would be more crawling and squeezing, than hanging and dropping, and I was happy that I could do that, so spent the time helping to encourage others, including one of my group members who was extremely upset at the prospect but courageously committed to attempting it.

Upon arrival we disembarked, dressed in caving gear, and made our way into the mine and along a tunnel. I was waiting for it to narrow and for the squeezing to start, but we halted and gathered around a small hole in the floor covered by metal plate.

"This is where we get in," announced the instructor, removing the plate to reveal a hole around thirty Inches Square. I looked at it dubiously and noted that a metal ladder twelve inches wide was affixed to the side of the hole, hanging into the Stygian depths below. It suddenly dawned upon me that this pot-holing would involve heights, but this time underground and in darkness.

The revelation of the hole was the final straw for my claustrophobic group member who had been growing increasingly distressed in the tunnel. All the exercises were voluntary of course, we could not be ordered to do these things, and anyway that was not the course style or philosophy as we were responsible for our own learning and development. The person decided against proceeding and was taken out of the tunnel to await us.

I hated that ladder even before I stepped on it. Understand, that this was not a solid affair, it was segmented and hung in mid-air through the hole and down into a cavern below. In effect I would be descending from the cavern roof on a swinging ladder with no rope for about forty feet. It was as bad as I feared, the ladder swung about wildly, my headlamp beam careering around the walls as I descended. At least I had gravity on my side going down but I knew that the only way out was to climb back up it and that thought was to be on my mind during the next hour or so in the mine.

I had no problems in the mine, including another short abseil and some narrow passageways. In fact I quite enjoyed it, I have always loved 'The Lord Of The Rings' and imagined myself in Moria, didn't spot any Orcs though!

Eventually we returned to the ladder. I can remember standing at the bottom and looking up, thinking, 'I can't climb that'. Unfortunately it was the only way out. I stepped onto the bottom rung and began the climb. Having watched the instructor and others who had climbed before and were used to it, it was clear to me that there was a technique to rope ladders and they sped up without a problem. Sadly, I didn't have the technique, which involves using the much larger thigh muscles to push up, rather than pulling up with the arms/biceps.

I reached the halfway point and realised that the fear had turned to panic and I had been using my arms, which were now protesting that another pull up of my body weight would be the last. I experienced that moment of 'freeze' one often sees in films, so it does happen in real life.

After around a minute that seemed like an hour I forced my mind back into gear and concentrated on using my legs. I reached the top safely and lay on the tunnel floor gasping. This was a major learning experience for me. I had forced my mind to rationalise its way around a primal fear and overcome it. There is a saying in the police, 'What doesn't kill you makes you stronger', and I realised the truth of that on that day. I still don't like heights but I have stood on many a tall building since and overcome the stomach churning.

Water is another fear for many people, but this one wasn't for me. I am a strong swimmer, used to snorkelling and have tried scuba diving. Others were not so happy. At the end of this section I describe a team competition, and one exercise was for the whole team to stand in a swimming pool and submerge for sixty seconds. This proved really difficult for some and I admire them for achieving the task.

Anyway, we were taught to sail in training dinghies, which was a wonderful experience. Then we were taken to a sandbar revealed by low tide, that stood in the centre of the River Dovey estuary. Upon the sandbar were a collection of pallets, ropes and barrels. We had to build a raft before the tide came in and row it to shore about half a mile away. It was time for a quick survey of group skills. Luckily, one of us was an experienced sailor and knew knots – a key skill in this scenario. We promptly fashioned a raft and proudly paddled across using pieces of wood as oars. It held together perfectly and we only got our legs wet.

Other challenges included orienteering, spending the night in a log cabin in the middle of nowhere and the usual *'get the team from A to B without touching the ground'* sort of thing.

The grand-finale was a team competition. Older readers may recall a television programme called *'The Great Egg Race'*. Teams had to overcome a series of puzzles and physical challenges and score points to receive clues to locations and progress to where a final winning prize was hidden. This was a similar format.

We were split into three teams and the tasks began, orienteering up the nearby mountain, solving puzzles, submerging, and so on. We were given twenty-four hours to finish the competition and it was up to us how we allocated time and resources, including sleep time. We split ourselves according to skills and got on with it. All three teams finished neck and neck on the beach near to Aberdovey pier where an alcoholic prize awaited, buried in the sand. We shared it on the beach in the sun.

The other out of Bramshill 'experience' was the 'Lincolnshire Exercise'. This actually featured in a Sunday Times article on one occasion and had been running as part of the old style Special Course for years.

We were shipped out to a hotel near Grantham for a week. The exercise took place in a small village in the wilds of Lincolnshire. The villagers routinely volunteered to 'act' in the scenarios and had done so for years. The village hall was turned into a 'police station' and we took it in turns to be PCs, sergeants and inspectors.

Various tasks were fed to us during the week. The test was to sort them out whilst taking turns role-playing the various ranks. I'm not sure how previous year's visits went, but there were a large number of officers from big cities such as London, Manchester and Birmingham on my course and the green fields of sleepy Lincolnshire seemed to us like heaven on earth to police.

I can recall lying on a panda car bonnet in the sun in 'PC' mode, in a country lane, surrounded by fields as far as the eye could find see, waiting for a job. And waiting, and waiting. To put this into perspective, as a response PC at Acocks Green the shift could easily, and routinely, clock up a hundred jobs on an afternoon shift. In Lincolnshire it seemed that one would be the norm. Eventually the radio crackled and I was deployed – to a theft of pedal cycle. I just about coped with that one.

We waited for the 'big job'. We knew there would be one. Finally it arrived, and I was in a PC role again. An 'animal rights demonstration' was reported at a nearby poultry farm. Off we went in a transit van, about ten of us as a public order unit. In light of my public order experiences a bit of a demonstration at a poultry farm acted out by people from a sleepy village was not going to be too daunting.

As the van travelled we looked at each other, West Midlands, Metropolitan Police, Merseyside, Greater Manchester. Between us we had experienced Brixton, Handsworth, Toxteth and other riots - we decided on our strategy.

I think the idea was that we should police the demonstration, allow it to proceed, negotiate, that sort of thing. There were about twenty villagers with placards pretending to be agitated. We alighted, 'arrested' and handcuffed half of them, put them in vans, took all the placards for evidence and sent the rest home. It took about five minutes. I can recall a very bedraggled looking line of 'protesters' sat in the 'police station', and a certain sense of 'coolness' from the instructors.

Frankly, 'Lincolnshire' was a bit of a joke - I don't know if it carried on for long afterwards.

The end of the course approached. It is fair to say that I had embraced the philosophy wholeheartedly in the first few weeks, but as time went on my belief began to sour for several reasons.

I realised that the instructors were out on a limb and that the self-development approach was too radical to be accepted by the establishment. I couldn't help but sense that a very large question mark, imbued with a 'traditional', conservative and reactionary attitude, was displayed towards us by a number of, if not all, of the people at Bramshill.

I also began to feel quite strongly that, out of the classroom, the company of the 'Oxbridge' graduates seemed more desirable to some Directing Staff than my own, a non-degree holder with a Brummie accent and tattoos. In fact I cannot recall one specific senior instructor ever talking to me for the whole three months of the course. I discussed this with the other non-graduate and he felt the same. This may have been just a perception, but for me it splintered the revolutionary and radical philosophy put forward on that first day.

I had also realised by this time that my return to force would simply put me back into the rigid and conventional police environment with no power to change anything, until, and unless, I advanced to senior rank, and even then it would be a continual battle.

It was also apparent that a number of my course colleagues were simply playing the game until the three months ended.

Finally, I felt that we were 'guinea pigs,' and that the whole enterprise had the potential to seriously affect candidates psychologically, and I felt that the people in charge were not professionally qualified to deal with that. I know for a fact that a number of people were deeply affected by the course, in particular the group- encounter sessions.

In the final analysis, I felt that I had been sold a concept that later did not live up to expectations, but as I stated at the start of this chapter, it was a brave attempt at changing a rigid, hierarchical and traditional organisation.

Looking around, there are a few holders of senior office, products of the 'new' Special Course, who do display liberal and change-orientated attitudes and behaviours.

Alas, my personal view is that they are few in number, and that 'the establishment', and tradition, which is not necessarily a bad thing, still holds sway. That 'summer of love' philosophy has never taken hold.

Figure 4: Mansion house, Bramshill Police College - circa 1986

Figure 5: Caving - the hole and the ladder

Figure 6: Abseiling over the cave mouth

Figure 7: Rafting across the estuary

Figure 8: Sailing

Chapter Three

The Twilight World

(Stephen Burrows):

In 1989 I accepted a new, and very different, challenge. Thus far I had worked in uniform, but now I was to lead the 'Plain Clothes' team at Steelhouse Lane Police Station as its sergeant. It was already a successful team of about eight officers.

There was a force-level 'Central Plain Clothes Unit' that predominantly dealt with obscene publications, prostitution, and the like. My unit had been modelled upon that, but our activity was focused on Birmingham City Centre as we were staffed by 'F Division' officers from Steelhouse Lane and Digbeth.

During my tenure in post the remit of the unit changed, as did its name, to 'F Division Support Unit', as cuts in resources began to bite, and some of the traditional activities of the unit began to be questioned in terms of value for money, impact upon crime, and indeed whether it was ethically the correct thing to be doing as society changed. In this chapter I chart some of those changes in the team's focus as society and the objectives and styles of policing evolved and altered.

***

The ethical question related more to the policing of 'cottaging' than anything else.

'Cottaging' is a UK gay slang term referring to anonymous sex between men in a public lavatory, primarily but not exclusively, or cruising for gay sex. The term probably emerged in Victorian times as many of the public lavatories, especially in London, had the appearance of being small cottages.

Prior to the Sexual Offences Act 1967, most of which was repealed by the 2003 Act of the same name, homosexual activity of any kind between men was illegal and often subject to harsh punishment historically.

The 1967 legislation legalized homosexual acts *in private,* between *two* consenting males aged twenty-one, or over. This was the legislation in force during the period to which I refer. It specifically did not include a public toilet as being in private, thus such activity remained illegal even after the 1967 Act.

Looking back over the decades from our modern, liberal and enlightened attitudes, it now seems barely believable that the police spent valuable time and resources policing public toilets, but we did, and this was one of the activities that the plain-clothes unit specialised in when I took over.

To be fair, I was told by the senior management that complaints had been received about the activities taking place in a number of male toilets in Birmingham City Centre. My subsequent experiences did evidence the fact that behaviour that could have both frightened and intimidated members of the public using the toilets for their correct purpose was rife.

The main offence we policed was outlined in the Sexual Offences Act 1956, (not repealed by the 1967 Act):

'It is an offence for a man persistently to solicit or importune

in a public place for immoral purposes.'

There was a further, more serious, offence of 'Gross Indecency', relating to inter-male sexual conduct that dated from Victorian times and had been used to convict Oscar Wilde. This was one step down from buggery, which was a separate offence, and retained an element of Victorian punishment.

Gross Indecency was defined thus:

'Any male person who, in public or private, commits, or is a party to the commission of, or procures, or attempts to procure the commission by any male person of, any act of gross indecency with another male person, shall be guilty of a misdemeanor, and being convicted thereof, shall be liable at the discretion of the Court to be imprisoned for any term not exceeding two years, with or without hard labour.'

Thus, the 'dark art' of policing the lavatories had importuning, and gross indecency, as the key pieces of legislation with which to apply sanctions.

Putting it into more simplistic language, nodding, winking and masturbating, whilst displaying an erect penis, was importuning, whilst being caught in a urinal fellating another man was classed as gross indecency.

An arrest for either offence spelt out ruin for many a career and marriage, and the actual legal penalty was often far less severe than the ruination of a man's reputation that could, and sometimes did, result in suicide. With this fact in mind we did try and caution all our offenders, unless there were aggravating features, and we also tried to keep details from the press.

Policing appeals to the hunting instinct within man, but it is offenders not animals we track. We developed a sophisticated technique of arresting offenders in the toilets. It became almost a sport. It sounds like madness now, but there were a set of rules and techniques evolved from experience, custom and practice, that we followed.

We worked in teams of three. We did not have radios as they could not be concealed, thus we developed a set of hand-signals. We would not act as 'agent provocateur', it was not lawful. Thus, we would enter the toilet, stand at the urinal and pretend to urinate, with our penis out of sight, in fact often not even out of our trousers. In our view, the potential offender had to make some move or effort to actively importune.

The offence includes the word 'persistently'. Police custom and practice, interpreted that as:

First visit was to use the toilet

Second visit was coincidence or realizing that there was more toilet use required.

Third visit was 'persistent'.This may sound somewhat unreal but there were many occasions when offenders would return five or six times in a short period before arrest.

Only one of us would be in the toilet at any one time and we would try to achieve at least two of us being importuned separately as that was much better evidentially.

Our main area of activity was the Manzoni Gardens toilet close to the Bull Ring Open Market in Birmingham City Centre. I had never done this kind of work before and I was amazed at the level of activity. We could have arrested at least ten, or more, a day, but we thankfully had other things to do. Surprisingly, the majority of those arrested were married and I do not think were actually gay, they just obtained a thrill from the experience and had become addicted to it in some way.

We also arrested those from professions that historically seemed to have attracted a proportion of gay men such as actors, ballet dancers, vicars, male nurses and scoutmasters. The problem for professionals such as nurses, and for instance teachers, was that we had little discretion and had to notify their employers of the arrest.

All in all, I had some interesting moments in the toilets, including:

Being cornered by a very large black man with his erect penis out who would not take 'no' for an answer but became somewhat deflated when I produced my warrant card. To this day I suspect my comrades on the day of deliberately leaving me in there with him for a joke as we had monitored him, acquired the evidence, and arranged for two of us to be present at the time of arrest. There were a few rather tense minutes as they were late in arriving and seemed very amused when I recounted the tale.

Being chased by the local legend, *'tripod,'* so-called because his member was the size of a third leg. I can verify this; it was at least a foot long, as it was waved at me. He could have made a better living in pornography than his supposed profession of waiting tables in a local Indian restaurant. He followed me from the toilet, and I am glad I wasn't a member of the public as he was quite menacing. He must have twigged something was wrong because he suddenly ran for it up the subway and we lost him. I never encountered him again.

Having a man ejaculate on my shoe. He was walking towards me, masturbating and I don't know if it was the shock of the warrant card and the word, 'police', but he ejaculated at that exact moment. I was not impressed! Luckily the shoes suffered no lasting damage.

Being chased by a student from Lancaster Circus toilets. He actually ran up behind me as I left the toilets, and tapped me on the shoulder enquiring whether I was a 'giver' or a 'taker'? I replied, "Neither. I'm a police officer and you're nicked." Whilst it could be extremely amusing at times, I think we all felt increasingly uncomfortable about using police time in a way that was clearly becoming out of step with the values of a changing society. I for one was not sad to see that particular policing deployment fade away, to be replaced by more worthwhile activity.

**

One of our other functions was to attempt to befriend the city-centre 'rent boys' in an effort to protect them, and to gain intelligence. There were a small number of these boys, usually aged around thirteen to seventeen, who regularly provided male prostitute services to an older male clientele.

Most of the boys were very vulnerable and had a sad story to tell, of broken homes, being sexually abused, drug and substance use, and many were 'in care' but with limited engagement with Social Services in those days. Some of them just slept rough on the streets.

Looking back, it is scarcely credible that they were left on the streets, but there was no support mechanism in existence and the police were neither equipped nor trusted by them sufficiently to provide the help that they needed.

We heard many stories of them being hired for 'parties' by groups of older men, or going to a man's accommodation, both highly dangerous activities.

Today, I have no doubt that a team would be set up jointly with Social Services and medical expertise, but there was no prospect of that happening back then. The boys, the victims and only witnesses, were anti-establishment, often criminalized, under the influence of drink or drugs, and making what to them seemed a reasonable amount of money. In other words they were hostile witnesses and not once did we obtain information that we could act upon.

Senior officers knew all of this and thus it was not a policing priority. The onset of performance measures earlier in the decade was beginning to have an effect, sparse resources were being channeled towards detections and arrests; the rent-boys were a potentially resource-intensive stone that lay unturned.

Our role was deemed purely one of gathering intelligence and maintaining a set of sources we could talk to should the worst happen and one of them was murdered. As the era of measuring the police and a 'business' approach gained hold, the policing of the rent boys, and the toilets, faded into history until the more modern child abuse scandals that have raised the profile of child-abuse to its current height.

***

Another role undertaken by the team was that of supporting the Licensing Inspector for Birmingham City Centre. This comprised of interviewing prospective licensees, visiting and issuing warnings to licensees if they were keeping a disorderly premises, and best of all, visiting licensed premises undercover to gain evidence of offences. Being paid to go into pubs and clubs!

We also made a special point of visiting gay bars and clubs – linked to the rent-boy intelligence issue, a particular favourite being 'The Jug', under the arches near Livery Street.

I really liked this establishment, the atmosphere was non–threatening, the clientele knew we were police officers and treated us well. The owner was a real character, reminding me of the 'Dick Emery' spoof character whose stock phrase was 'You are awful, but I like you'. I can still remember him saying, *"The only trouble in here is the Lessies dear boy, the poofs are fine!"* They did however run a very risqué floor-show, and we usually diplomatically excused ourselves before it started.

Policing is full of these 'grey area' decisions, where one aim, for instance forging relationships and trust, can be in conflict with enforcing a law. The bedrock of British policing is the trust invested in individual officers to use their power of discretion in an appropriate and uncorrupt way to resolve this sort of difficulty, and I believe that we did our best to achieve this balance in an ethical manner.

This is however also one of the most dangerous areas for police officers, who have to be scrupulous in their decision-making and be able to justify why a minor offence might be subsumed beneath a greater good, lest the murky waters of corruption allegations and professional standards enquiries beckon.

Licensed premises are a minefield for police officers, and a tightrope has to be walked between law enforcement, supporting licensees who are trying to 'clean up' troublesome establishments, maintaining a professional relationship and weighing the ethics of the various temptations on offer.

These are not just the obvious free drink, or free food, but the breaching of confidentiality by careless chat and the offer of other so-called 'soft bribes', such as event tickets, gambling, or sexual relations, that could place one in a position where favours could be called in later by a licensee in trouble.

So many officers got themselves into trouble or have been compromised over the years that it is understandable why the frequenting of pubs and clubs dwindled to virtually nothing, apart from large 'raids' or 'chucking out time' visits. Many officers would not dream of setting foot in a pub alone, yet there is a rich vein of information and support to be gleaned there, and most customers are pro-police and glad of the chance to chat and see that the officers are human beings like themselves.

***

When I took over the unit, the other line of work occupying our time was 'obscene publications'. This all seems rather tame now that the world has an avalanche of every kind of depravity at its fingertips via the internet, but in those days the availability of pornography was strictly controlled, for fear of its corrupting effects. Who can say now that this thinking was incorrect, given the horror stories about some murderers and sex-offender's consumption of violent or obscene pornography?

The Force Central Plain Clothes Unit tended to pursue the actual pornographers themselves, but with the city-centre as our stamping ground we had many establishments retailing magazines and videos. These establishments were supposed to comply with the rules of 'The Obscene Publications Act 1959', a piece of legislation still in force today - a case of 'Canute and the sea' if ever I saw one. Of course, where there are rules, someone breaks them and that was where we came in.

The legislation, as usual, required some interpretation and experience, and case-law had provided some guidance over the years, although the area of pornography was, like policing homosexual behaviour, or 'rent boys', another moveable feast for policing as societal values and standards changed.

Obscene publications law is a classic example of a law that passed parliament and then required substantial case law to actually decide what it meant.

The definition of 'obscene' in the Act is that an article is taken to be obscene if the entire article,

'Is, if taken as a whole, such as to tend to deprave and corrupt persons who are likely, having regard to all relevant circumstances, to read, see or hear the matter contained or embodied in it.'

The test is based on 'persons', it is not sufficient for an individual to be depraved or corrupted, and you have to show that a significant number of people likely to read it would become corrupted.

'Article' is defined as, *'anything containing material that is read or looked at, any sound recordings and any film or other picture record.'*

'Publisher', is taken to mean anyone who *'distributes, circulates, sells, lets on hire, gives, or lends it, or who offers it for sale or for letting on hire, or 'in the case of an article containing or embodying matter to be looked at or a record, shows, plays or projects it'*

Later legislation amended this section to include the transmission of the article electronically, possessing obscene articles for publication or sale, and also extended 'obscene materials' to cover photograph negatives.

Despite these attempts to update the obscenity laws, they have dwindled in use, especially following the advent of the Internet, and alternative legislation such as offences relating to child protection are employed. The point at which the public 'at large' deem anything obscene has moved and is still moving, and prosecution for anything bar child pornography or publications depicting crimes and violent abuse is now rare.

Back in the late 80's though, the offenders tended to fall into two groups.

The first were newsagents and the like who failed to display soft pornography correctly, drawing complaints from mothers and other concerned citizens.

These related to the type of magazine, the contents, the front cover and the position on the shelf.

The second group traded in the 'under-the-counter' stuff.In terms of content, the rough guide was that sexual intercourse, erect penises and open vagina lips were obscene and should not be on general sale. Having read the vagueness of the definition one can understand how difficult the law was to apply, as police officers had to physically read, or watch material, and try to decide if it would 'deprave or corrupt' the general public.

This may sound like an interesting way of earning a living but I can assure you that boredom quickly sets in and the majority of films were of poor quality, and devoid of plot or characters; in other words extremely tedious and repetitive!

Those who have ever read magazines such as 'Playboy', 'Men Only', or 'Fiesta', will recall that models were always tastefully posed with legs closed and male genitals were obscured or flaccid. This is one of the reasons why nudist magazines such as

'Health and Efficiency' enjoyed a purple-patch of sales, as the pictures of happy nudists could sometimes include angles not present in the carefully posed 'upmarket' magazines.

The front-covers were supposed to be carefully composed, or offending areas covered in some way, such as with a cellophane outer with opaque areas, or brown paper. They were also supposed to be displayed on the 'top shelf'. These measures were supposed to prevent male innocents being corrupted by eye contact with the female anatomy in all its glory.

There were other magazines that were more 'hardcore' and sold by sex-shops alongside videos. These sometimes appeared for sale on newsagent's shelves and we would check the retail outlets for transgressions in regard to sale and placement and advise accordingly. We rarely had to prosecute these sorts of establishment but we did on occasions receive genuine complaints from the public that required action.

The porn shops presented us with another challenge. In terms of the legislation, the level of 'depravity' necessary to corrupt someone over eighteen-years- of-age, who chose to enter a sex shop, was considerably higher than schoolchildren in a newsagent shop buying sweets. Thus we tended to look for really extreme material, usually not on display. To gain evidence we would have to conduct 'test purchases' and then assess the material - another interesting use of public money.

By 'extreme', I mean videos depicting criminal acts, as these tended to have a victim and offender. To illustrate changing times, bear in mind that in those days the depiction of illegal homosexual behaviour, more than two persons, could be obscene, as could sado-masochism a la *'Fifty Shades of Grey'*. The holy grail of the hunt was however the 'snuff movie.'

We were regularly informed that these videos existed. They were supposed to depict a real death, clearly a very serious criminal issue, even if consent or suicide were allegedly involved. We seized a number that purported to be the real thing but they were obvious fakes. We never did find the real thing and I am open-minded as to their existence back then. Today it would not surprise me at all!

***

In due course our focus moved to new problems.

The first of these was the prevalence of overt, 'street-level', drug dealing. Complaints from residents in areas surrounding the city-centre began to come in, and senior officers started to ask questions as to why their plain-clothes officers were spending time on policing the toilets and 'soft-porn', when greater damage with attendant public disquiet was being produced by drugs.

As with pornography, there was a force-level Drugs Squad that focused on higher-level dealers. The 'F' Division problem was mainly cannabis dealing on the street because that was what disturbed the residents.

Many volumes have been written about cannabis and whether, and how, its sale and use should be controlled. Actually, the drug in those days was in a much milder form than that available now and the evidence then suggested it was relatively harmless

94

unless taken in large quantities when it could cause psychosis. I met a number of individuals, in Handsworth particularly, who suffered from this condition because of significant cannabis usage over many years, and some were dangerous to the public because of it. However, in general, in my personal opinion, it was a drug probably less harmful than tobacco.

The problem with cannabis dealing was not the actual drug; it was what happened when dealers began purveying their wares in a particular location.

On the 'F' Division this situation tended to be focused upon public houses in the Highgate area. The pubs in this ward were situated amongst houses and tower blocks, with many families and elderly people resident.

We would speak to the licensees, and some were compliant, but others were either intimidated into turning a blind eye or were complicit in the dealing. Many licensees seemed to resign themselves to the activity but insisted that it took place outside, which suited us.

I think this was because a number of police raids of licensed premises had resulted in licensees losing their licence, livelihood, and home. Most were tenanted premises, owned by large chains such as Mitchells and Butlers who were fully supportive of us, and ruthless in removing tenants who transgressed. They did not want adverse publicity and drug-dealing impacted hugely on the premises and its profits if it took hold.

It was like watching a disease take hold. A dealer would set up. They would bring with them a cohort of lookouts and bodyguards, and as they became more sophisticated, couriers – often youths as young as ten on bicycles would be employed.

The stash of drugs would often be hidden nearby and the dealer would take an order, generally using a public phone box, as there were no mobile phones in those days, or from a walking or vehicle-borne customer. The youth on the bicycle would go and fetch the goods and the deal would take place. This technique prevented the dealer having to personally hold the drugs in case police arrived and searched him. In those days all of the dealers were men.

As the 'infection' progressed, the customers would arrive from a wide-range of society; the clearly criminal, the down-and-outs, the addicts, students, buyers who then supplied friends. For them, the dealer was potentially a doorway to hell, because cannabis is what is also known as a 'gateway' drug.

The dealer had to get his supply from a dealer higher up the chain. That dealer, or those further up, would, and still do, seek to expand their market by selling different and more addictive drugs, especially cocaine, crack cocaine and heroin. They are not averse to providing 'free samples', to get buyers hooked.

Word would get around that drugs were available and as custom increased prostitution would sometimes surface. Many of the prostitutes used drugs and a number of their 'pimps' supplied them with drugs as a form of control. Incidents of violence blossomed and areas were blighted, as dealers fought for territory. In some streets residents became frightened and intimidated and the more vulnerable stayed indoors.

This was exactly the situation in Highgate around a small number of pubs, presenting a challenging enforcement problem.

The result was *'Operation Pacifist'* which ran throughout the period I was on plain clothes and after I left. The nature of the beast was that as you took one dealer out another was waiting to step into the vacuum created and supply the customers.

Our first task was to gather intelligence regarding the locations being used. This came from sources such as residents, councillors and informants. Sometimes we even received names and these could be researched to provide photographs from previous arrests.

Once we had sufficient information, the licensee would receive a visit from the licensing inspector, or myself, be put on notice that drug-dealing would not be tolerated, and support was offered. If this worked, fine, it was the most efficient way of solving the problem. If not, they had received fair warning, and it would go much worse for them if they allowed their premises to be used for supply, which was a criminal offence in itself.

If dealing continued in the premises we could gain evidence by using undercover officers if possible, arresting purchasers as they left, or raiding the premises at an appropriate moment. Even if everyone threw their drugs on the floor as we entered, it was still 'curtains' for the licensee and they would be removed.

Happily for us though, the fashion in Highgate was street dealing.

Having gathered intelligence and approached the licensee, the next step would be to discreetly obtain suitable observation points. Providing a window for the police to look through could be a risky enterprise for locals who allowed us to use their own premises, so we mainly used vacant council flats. The local council was very supportive – acting in the interests of their residents, and we were always able to obtain suitable observation points, usually in local tower blocks.

There is case law regarding observation points and identification, stemming from the stated cases of R v Johnson and R v Turnbull. These cases set out the factors that make a location suitable evidentially, and the procedure should an address be required to be kept secret at trial in order to protect the occupier.

R v Johnson, (1988) states:

'The person does not have to fear violence in order to be protected. If, however, the location can be revealed without identifying the occupier, then it should be revealed.'

R v Johnson also set out the correct procedure when using observation posts:

The police officer in charge of the observation, who should be of no lesser rank than sergeant, should testify that he had visited the observation posts & ascertained the attitude of the occupiers to the use of the premises & to disclosure which might lead to their identification. An inspector should then testify that immediately before the trial he visited those places & ascertained whether the occupiers were the same persons as those at the time of the observations and confirm that the attitude of the occupiers remains the same. It is not necessary to go through the same procedure where the building is unoccupied. There is no occupier whose interests need to be protected.

Moving to R v Turnbull, this case law ostensibly applies to witness identification evidence, but it is also directly applicable to the evidence an officer in an observation point gives, and must be borne in mind when assessing the site, compiling logs of observations and when writing statements for court. It is a key piece of case law relating to identification, and is worth reproducing. It demonstrates the legal parameters and pitfalls we had to operate within in order to successfully arrest and prosecute dealers.

These are the guidelines given:

'If the situation arises where the case against an accused depends wholly or substantially on the correctness of one or more identifications of the accused which the defence alleges to be mistaken, it is imperative the judge should warn the jury of the special need for caution before convicting the accused in reliance on the correctness of the identification(s).

Additionally the judge should instruct them, (the jury), *as to the reason for the need for such a warning and should make some reference to the possibility that a mistaken witness can be a convincing one and that a number of such witnesses can all be mistaken.*

Secondly, the judge should direct the jury to examine closely the circumstances in which the identification by each witness can be made. Some of these circumstances may include: For how long was the accused under observation by the witness? At what distance was the witness from the accused? What length of time elapsed between the original observation and the subsequent identification to the police?'

This meant that prospective observation points had to be visited by myself and assessed in respect of both Johnson and Turnbull.

Operation Pacifist was constructed to follow this legal framework in order to maximize the prospect of guilty plea and conviction.

Within an observation point, officers were equipped with official 'log books' within which all relevant notes were entered. These log books were tendered in evidence and were the officer's 'original notes' for reference in the witness-box when giving evidence at court, often months later. A usual defence tactic was to attempt to throw doubt on when the notes were written in order to fatally undermine a case.

Great care had to be taken to preserve the probity of the 'log books' in terms of originality, authorship, and timing.

We also acquired good cameras with zoom-lenses to photograph the deals. Such photographs were of course useless without supporting evidence, as they would just show two people apparently stood talking, which is where the arrest teams came in.

We would operate with two or three pairs of officers in unmarked cars, supported by officers in uniform in marked cars. In those days, we often had to use our own cars, which were far from ideal, but later we acquired a revolving stream of used cars for the purpose.

The process itself was simple. Observations were kept on the dealer and photographs taken of suspected deals. A description of the buyer and vehicle, if used, was circulated to the arrest teams. As the buyer drove, or walked away, they were followed until well away from the dealer, when the marked car would stop and search them and arrest them if drugs were found, which was obviously pretty much every time!

The buyers would be caught in possession of small quantities of drugs that were seized as evidence. They were interviewed in order to obtain evidence regarding the supplier. They usually had no links to, or friendship with, the dealer and had little hesitation in being helpful and 'grassing them up.' Thus we would have a strong case, the intelligence, the observations, the photographs, the buyer arrest and the drugs.

The drugs could be forensically examined if necessary to prove they were from the same batch and if the dealer were to be found in possession, could be matched to his drugs too. This negated any defence that the dealer was in possession for 'personal use' only, a substantially lesser offence than dealing.

The observations and buyer arrests would continue until we had three or four and then we would move in and arrest the dealer, who usually had nothing on them and came in quietly protesting their innocence. Sometimes we were lucky and found the 'stash'.

In interview, the offender was confronted with the evidence and in the majority of cases would admit the offence but try and minimize it. As far as I can recall, we had very few 'not guilty' pleas at court once the defence had seen the evidence. The buyers were dealt with in accordance with charging rules at the time. They were in 'possession', not suppliers, and if they had no previous convictions were often cautioned, but a number ended up before the courts.

Operation Pacifist was hugely successful and we made many arrests over the months and years. We got to the stage where we would send someone out to see who was dealing and could be up and running within an hour.

***

The impact of changes in society and demands upon policing continued, and the focus on arrests and detections and the impact of new types of criminality, squeezed the old tasks out. Instead of toilets, rents boys and Playboy magazines, we spent our time on the streets. The unit was renamed the 'F Division Support Unit' and we began to assist in uniform on occasions, and formed part of public-order mobilization plans, and patrols for the division.

We were equipped with new covert radios comprising a box held under the arm in a hidden shoulder-harness, with a transmit button on a wire passed down the sleeve into the palm and a wireless earpiece that sat out of sight in the ear. No more talking into a pocket concealing the bulky old radio with a wire into the earpiece.

Ironically these days we could have walked around all day

with a phone in our hands and headphones visible and no one would blink an eyelid, but back then you may just as well have had 'police' in neon lights on your forehead if you had a wired earpiece and all the bad guys knew it.

We transferred the learning from Operation Pacifist into other endeavours. Vehicle crime was rife in the city-centre, focused on the car parks. Vehicle security was really poor and most cars could be entered with a screwdriver to punch the door skin and pop open the lock. Alternatively a piece of wire with a loop on the end; coat hanger wire was favourite, was fed through the window rubber to lift the door lock button. CD players were the target then and fetched a fiver a time from the receivers.

Some car parks began to implement 'secured by design' principles and employ patrols and cameras and these did have an effect on crime, pushing it towards the unprotected car parks, of which Masshouse Car Park was the prime example, and a honeypot for vehicle thieves.

Using our proven practices, we obtained observation points for Masshouse Car Park, set up arrest teams in plain clothes at key locations outside the car park, and the fun began. It was like shooting fish in a barrel. There was something about the criminals that drew one's attention and it got to the stage where we could recognize them for what they were before they even thought about screwing a car.

We often saw them acting suspiciously but not entering a vehicle and would then stop and search them, usually discovering gloves, screwdrivers and loops, which together with the observation evidence was good enough for a charge of 'going equipped'.

What continually astonished me was the skill of some of these youths who could enter and 'hotwire' a vehicle, or remove the CD player in seconds.

Christmas was another opportunity to work the streets. We used to always put on an operation with a seasonal title such as *'Operation Jack Frost'*.

We deployed singly, or in pairs, throughout the city-centre, with a couple of observation points in support, usually having an 'eyeball' on New Street, especially the ramp area, and the corner of New Street and High Street. We would usually work at this for around a month in the run up to Christmas, targeting shoplifters, pickpockets, street-robbers and 'nipping in the bud' any potential for disorder.

By the time we had finished each year, we would have walked a couple of hundred miles, knew every part of the city-centre like the back of our hands, most of the regular criminals, and made lots of arrests.

***

Another new area of work surfaced for the team and we scored what I think was one of the earliest prosecutions in the country. This topic is rife in the modern world, in fact completely out of control due to globalization and the Internet, and it is fascinating to look back nearly thirty years to the time it first began to become a serious problem.

In late 1988, the 'Copyright, Design and Patents Act' became law. It is in fact still the law covering copyright to this day. In brief it protects the following types of work:

- Literary - Song lyrics, manuscripts, manuals, computer programs, commercial documents, leaflets, newsletters and articles etc.

- Dramatic - Plays, dance, etc.

- Musical - Recordings and score.

- Artistic - Photography, painting, architecture, technical drawings/diagrams, maps, logos, etc.

- Typographical arrangement of published editions - Magazines, periodicals, etc.

- Sound Recordings - May be recordings of works, e.g. musical and literary.

- Films - Broadcasts and cable programmes.

The Plain Clothes Unit had always had links to trading standards, a council- run department that was under-resourced and tended to concentrate on pub measures, dodgy market stalls, poor restaurants and the like. Unbeknown to us however, the explosion in counterfeiting had become a serious problem for commercial companies and the new legislation brought in some real 'teeth' in terms of powers to search, seize and arrest, and substantial punishments for offenders.

Commerce had become increasingly frustrated with what they perceived to be a lack of action as regards counterfeiting, both from trading standards and the police. To be fair to both, trading standards were fully committed, and the police tended to regard this area as a civil rather than criminal matter, and of course had other priorities in respect of protecting people rather than intellectual property.

The passing of the Act changed that, leaving no doubt that this was a criminal matter costing manufacturers, retailers and the exchequer a vast amount of money that should have been added to the UK economy.

The legislation was given Royal Assent and became law without being noticed by the police, but eventually one of my officers received a call from trading standards on behalf of *'Athena'*. We soon were placed into direct contact with this firm.

Athena was best known for producing, and selling, artistic photographs and designs on posters that adorned many a student bedroom wall. In those days they were a multi-million pound enterprise with their own shops. They owned the copyright to many well-known photographs, including the female tennis player scratching her bottom, and their posters were being counterfeited everywhere. They were keen to use the new Act to score a victory, by a prosecuting a retailer of counterfeit goods, and had spent considerable time and money identifying such miscreants.

As it happened, near the top of their list was a stall in the Oasis Market in Birmingham.

Locals will nostalgically recall the Oasis. It was a collection of independent stalls in a maze of corridors purveying everything from 'joss-ticks' to 'kung fu' equipment. It had a definite 'hippy' and edgy feel to it, and indeed, as a teenager I frequented it for fashionable clothes such as flared trousers, cowboy boots and elephant ear shirts - it was after all the seventies! My abiding memory of the place is the smell of patchouli incense.

Athena had located a stall on the lower-level selling counterfeit copies of their posters and supplied us with the necessary evidence to take action. I discussed it with my senior officers at the time and we decided to have a go. What could be simpler? It would be a first, and it was only a market stall.

We set the date, and a couple of the lads had a walk through and confirmed the stall was open and trading. We swooped and arrested the vendor, conducting a search of the stall and the storage area prior the offender being whisked off to Steelhouse Lane for interview and charge.

After he had gone I can remember looking across the piles of stock and the boxes in storage and realizing that there was a lot of stuff! Upon investigation there were indeed many hundreds of posters, but also piles of 'T' shirts bearing music group logos that were clearly bogus too, in fact just about everything on the stall looked bogus. I couldn't only seize part of the stock and leave other suspected counterfeit goods to be sold, so the whole lot had to be seized for later enquiries. The only vehicles we had were plain police vehicles so these were stuffed to the roof with posters and 'T' shirts providing a somewhat hilarious sight. We managed to acquire a small van and filled that up too.

The next question was where to store it all? The detained

property store was at Digbeth Police Station. Such stores tended to be run by grizzled old staff that had seen everything, and this one was no exception. He looked at me with incredulity as I explained the extent of my haul. Firstly he explained, there was no room for 'that lot', and secondly, he wasn't about to book it all in individually, we would have to do it and he would provide us with the property register to do so.

I scratched my head until someone remembered the basement. I hadn't even known there was a basement at Digbeth Police Station but it was a Victorian building with many nooks and crannies. Down into its dusty bowels we descended and discovered an area large enough that could be secured.

It took all day to book the seized goods in, but it seemed a good job and Athena was over the moon. They were very helpful in identifying their counterfeits but shrugged their shoulders when it came to the T-shirts, which glorified groups of the moment such as 'The Cult' and 'Inspiral Carpets'.

It was clearly a moment for delegation, so I appointed an officer to take charge of the case and life moved on. I was aware that a prosecution in respect of the posters took place and that the court had ordered their destruction. Attempts were made to trace the copyright owners for the T- shirts without result. The stall owner knew they were bogus so was not about to claim them back and an impasse was reached.

Time passed, I left the Unit and the memory of the Athena job faded. One day I received a phone call from a colleague at Digbeth, demanding to know what the score was with all the T-shirts that were filling the basement that they now wanted to use.

Those, by now rotting, T-shirts were in limbo. The stall-holder had disowned them, the copyright owners had not been traced, no prosecution in respect of them had taken place and thus a court had not ordered their destruction. They were of poor quality and deteriorating badly. A pragmatic decision had to be taken and they were destroyed.

I like to imagine that late at night, an officer wandering the basement of Digbeth might hear strange footsteps and encounter an apparition -a ghostly '*Inspiral Carpets*' fan, rotting T-shirt hanging from his skeletal frame.....

Figure 9: New Street at Corporation Street, Birmingham - circa 1970's

Figure 10: Bull Ring Market, Birmingham - circa 1970's

Figure 11: Manzoni Gardens, Birmingham - circa 1970's

Figure 12: High Street looking towards Oasis, Birmingham - circa 1970's

Figure 13: Bull Ring, Birmingham - circa 1970s

Figure 14: The Rotunda, Birmingham - circa 1970's

Chapter Four

An Ear To The Ground

(Michael Layton):

I did not like the idea of working in Force Headquarters but I wanted to get back into the CID and this was where the job was so there was nothing to debate. I had been out of mainstream policing for more than a year and would need to adjust quickly. As I entered the detective inspector's office in the Force Intelligence Bureau (FIB) on my first actual working day, on the 9 May 1990, it was clear that things were going to get interesting very quickly.

The establishment for the department, for inspectors, was two, and two people were sat at their desks looking rather bemused at the new arrival. We could all count and I was the third.

I went out into the main office to introduce myself to the staff and was met by rows of desks all facing the same way. It was like being at school. I was met with courtesy and curiosity. Whilst there wasn't that many staff in total, there was literally hundreds of year's police experience in the room and I did not match that profile.

Each officer had set responsibilities and jealously guarded them. They had become 'experts' in their subject matters and that was their focus.

The head of Force Intelligence at that time was Detective Chief Inspector Phil Ellis, who had also just arrived, and had already set about introducing a number of new initiatives. During the course of our later police service, as fellow chief superintendents, we developed a close personal friendship which was to continue into retirement.

One of the sergeants was an extremely experienced intelligence operative who was well-respected in the force and within the prison service. He had been in the department for twelve years and remained passionate about the subject. He was the department's lead on providing training to officers from different police forces and organisations. He ran several courses a year at Tally Ho Police Training Centre, in conjunction with the No 4 Regional Criminal Intelligence Office.

I duly attended one of the courses myself, (Course 2/90), as a student, together with sixteen other police officers and police staff, and added yet another course photograph to my collection as we posed; a motley crew of all shapes and sizes, for the camera, in the grounds of Tally-Ho Police Training Centre.

Another officer was the 'guru' of all things technical within the department, and in particular the Force Intelligence database. He had been in situ for nearly eight years. The reality was that no-one else had a clue what to do if anything went wrong with the system and when he was on leave it was extremely difficult to resolve problems. He was a very knowledgeable, but strong-minded individual, who knew he had the 'power of knowledge' and I worked hard to make sure that his knowledge was slowly spread to others.

Other officers came under similar scrutiny and most lived up to the challenge of moving forward, whilst others moved on with good grace. One of the existing detective inspectors considered his own future and retired.

It is traditional for police officers to have a formal leaving party and most do. It is a chance for officers to bring their partners in from the shadows and to at least acknowledge their sacrifice to the job with some kind words from a senior officer. Humour is generally the order of the day for part-one of the speech and stories solicited from former colleagues and friends can sometimes be akin to being 'savaged' whilst part-two is generally designed to leave the recipient with feelings of warmth and sadness at the impending departure.

Slowly, but surely, the department started to change shape and we became much more high-profile.

***

One of my staff, Richard Shakespeare, had worked on Operation GROWTH (Get Rid of Wolverhampton's Troublesome Hooligans) and had consulted with me whilst I was working on Operation Red Card dealing with Birmingham City's organised hooligan element.

He was one of the younger generation, having been there for less than a year, and a hard worker with a broad 'Black Country' accent. In his role in Football Intelligence he developed good links with the National Football Intelligence Unit and we started to contribute to the national picture on a subject that was close to my heart.

Richard retired from the police service in 2007 and recalls, *"Before being posted to the Force Intelligence Bureau I worked as an undercover officer on Operation GROWTH and travelled all over the country. The operation proved to be very successful and we ultimately made eighty-seven arrests. You had to think on your feet very quickly and soon learnt the little tricks that hooligans would adopt to identify the opposition. For instance when you were asked for the time by some stranger it was really about trying to identify where you came from by virtue of your accent.*

In my role in FIB I was responsible for gathering football intelligence on hooligans affiliated with Birmingham City, Aston Villa, Wolverhampton, West Bromwich Albion, Coventry and Walsall, plus some non-league clubs where there was a potential for violence.

As part of my duties I attended high-risk matches for all these clubs, in plain- clothes, and where possible videoed potential trouble spots. Detective Inspector Bob Vercesi was my line-manager and often came out with me to give me some support.

All of the clubs had a hooligan element but numbers varied. Walsall was the least troublesome of all with the 'main boys' numbering no more than ten at that time but they could still draw support and needed to be monitored."

In the 70s the club's hooligan element formed a group known as *'Junction 9'* which came from the fact that the ground's location was close to that junction of the M6 motorway. They developed a reputation for 'punching above their weight' particularly when it came to their Black Country rivals, Wolverhampton's *'Subway Army'.*

Richard continued, *"Walsall FC was 'in my veins' because*

although I grew up in Wednesbury it was just on the other side of Bescot Sidings and I used to go to Fellows Park ground as a kid. It was a quaint old place. At the Railway End there was a chain link fence that you could climb under and avoid paying if you were lucky.

One of their famous players at that time was a guy called 'Bernie Wright' the number nine centre-forward, also known as 'Bernie the Bolt' who was a high goal scorer. In the closed season he used to repair brick walls at the ground.

I was also a Police Cadet at Walsall and used to attend Walsall Technical College so knew the area well."

Richard continued, *"As I have said Walsall was relatively quiet compared to the other clubs but I do recall that in 1988 they played at home to Bristol City in a 'play-off' game. There was a pitch invasion, with major disorder, and two police vans overturned. I was actually pictured in a local newspaper with two other officers arresting someone on the pitch.*

After ninety four years of being home to Walsall FC, Fellows Park was replaced by the new Bescot Stadium in 1990 and it was much easier to police. At the old ground the local police and British Transport Police used to have to escort fans, using dogs and horses, to the railway station but the new stadium was right next to it.

PC Dave Hughes worked as the Football Intelligence/Football Liaison officer at Walsall and he always worked tirelessly behind the scenes to make sure that policing arrangements were pitched at the right level.

I do remember one occasion when there was trouble at Bescot, I think it was in the 1990/1991 season. I had some information from Hereford's football intelligence officer that a group of risk fans were going to turn up at Walsall and I covered the match. Sure enough a group aged from their teens to mid-thirties turned up.

There was a lot of disorder in the away end and uniform officers moved in and swiftly made a number of arrests. They basically started fighting with the police and were drunk, aggressive, and vicious. Eventually the police cell-block underneath the stadium was full of Hereford fans. At that time 'Football Watch' was in place which meant that any supporters breaching ground rules were ejected, and anyone breaking the law was to be arrested.

The key to dealing with football hooligans was to show no fear but occasionally I used to have to pull Bob out of the way when it looked like things were going to 'crack off'. On one occasion we were outside the social club next to the ground when some opposition fans found themselves being confronted by Walsall fans with police officers somewhere at the back. People were surging backwards and forwards and there was a real danger of a stampede.

As much as I respected him I literally grabbed Bob by the scruff of the neck and pulled him into the doorway of the club. Some officers used to call him 'Mr. Grumpy' because Bob was always straight-faced but I got on really well with him and he thanked me afterwards for looking after him."

***

Steve Barnbrook retired as a sergeant, after thirty years' service with the British Transport Police, much of it as a Scenes of Crime Officer, and has his own memories of another football related incident in the Walsall area:

"*Prior to starting as a SOCO in 1991 I was working in uniform with the Mobile Support Unit doing football duty at Witton Railway Station on a Saturday for an Aston Villa game.*

I was instructed to escort some Villa fans on a train from Witton to Walsall with PC Roy Higgs. When we got on the train it was already packed full of shoppers from Birmingham. Within minutes of departing, for what was about a twenty minute journey, we became aware of a fierce fight taking place in one of the middle coaches of the train. Some of the fans were fighting with up to twenty black youths and it was proper fighting with punches and kicks being exchanged. Some of the shoppers were screaming with fear and we struggled, totally outnumbered, to get control.

It turned out that the black youths had started the fight and a number of them were from a well-known family that lived just up the road from Green Lane Police Station in Walsall.

I called up on the radio asking for police attendance at Walsall Railway Station but resisted shouting for assistance as I didn't want those fighting to realise that there was only two of us on the train.

I arrested one of the black youths and managed to handcuff him, whilst Roy arrested another, but because he was struggling so much he couldn't get the cuffs on.

We arrived at Walsall and found no-one there waiting for us. I managed to hold onto my prisoner but with some encouragement from the others Roy's broke free and ran off into the town centre and got away.

Cutting a long story short we got the prisoner to Green Lane Police Station and the custody sergeant told us that he knew the prisoner well and that he was only fifteen years old we would need to fetch his mother. He also told us that we wouldn't be going anywhere without a van load of police officers to support us. I was a bit surprised but sure enough when we got to the address, which was in a cul-de-sac, the mother was waiting for us on the doorstep, and about twenty youths hovered in the background not best pleased to see us. The local officers told us that if we had gone on our own the police vehicle would have been turned over – I believed them!"

***

The Force Intelligence Bureau started to become well-known with other intelligence agencies and we increased our links with Regional Criminal Intelligence Units, and Regional Crime Squads, to get a better understanding of cross-border crime.

As time went on I also attracted secondments into the office from my old force, the British Transport Police, and another from the Ministry of Defence Police. The first seconded officer from the BTP, Paul Majster, had previously worked with me as a police cadet and we were in fact close friends. There was however a clear understanding that 'work was work' and when he came in late one morning after a 'heavy night out' he got hit with 'both barrels' in front of the rest of the office.

Later that year eleven field intelligence police officer posts were returned to divisions and we were left with a core group of individuals who focused on such things as drugs, vice and pornography, football, traffic, Crimestoppers, the Animal Liberation Front, and bogus officials engaged in burglaries where the victims were often elderly or vulnerable.

We were in the middle of a 'sea-change' and some, like the traffic officer who got himself fully trained as an analyst, survived, whilst others struggled and a couple of police officers whose job purely entailed data inputting went back somewhat reluctantly into operational policing in uniform.

On Tuesday 17 July 1990 I went to Stafford Prison to see an old informant from my time as a detective sergeant at Steelhouse Lane Police Station. He had been convicted and sentenced and was looking to pass some information on. He had been good in his time but he led a complicated personal life and was in truth very vulnerable. He gave me the information and I promised to contact his mother who in turn had been helpful to me some years before. Neither of them ever knew about the common bond that we had between the three of us.

I saw him again on the 24 August 1990 in Stafford Prison to verify some of the information, which I had already passed on to an operational team, and then re- registered him officially as an informant which required giving him a 'pseudonym' and number. Further meetings followed and whilst it was not easy managing an informant in my current role it worked well in terms of personal credibility.

On Fridays of each week we began to adopt a higher profile as the FIB became a key player in the weekly 'Tension Meetings', which were usually chaired by the Assistant Chief Constable (Operations), and were designed to give the force an early indication of the potential for major public order to occur. We were in the spotlight and expected to deliver meaningful intelligence but it brought me into routine contact with the senior command team in the force.

We were also involved in 'Key-Task Commanders' meetings involving the use of *'Alpha Control'* which was a dedicated facility at Force Headquarters and was opened when major incidents occurred. People were actually starting to ask for our involvement, and I found myself routinely engaged with covert policing units, including the force surveillance team, where I had previously displayed limited skills.

Following an establishment review we also subsequently embarked on a big programme of civilianization, and recruited civilian intelligence researchers, a briefing officer, and a number of criminal intelligence analysts, who were trained in analytical processes using a technique called ANACAPA, (a private company name).

We had literally hundreds of applicants for jobs and I spent hours paper-sifting and interviewing candidates. We found some first-class people who really contributed to the department and made it an attractive place to work. Gone were the days of it being classed as a pre-retirement home. Gone also were the days of the department being something of a 'male preserve' as the gender balance of our new staff tipped very much to being female. It would have been fashionable to be able to say that as a result there was less swearing in the office, but sadly this did not prove to be the case, and occasionally the women were the worst offenders!

One of our success stories was the appointment of nineteen year-old Darren Ratcliffe to a position within the department in November 1990. Darren was profoundly deaf, had no speech, and also suffered from Ushers Syndrome which affected his vision. I interviewed him for one position, together with the Force Equal Opportunities Officer, and although he was unsuccessful we felt that he had potential and employed him under a Supernumerary Scheme.

He loved computers and fitted in quickly with staff, some of whom started to learn sign language, in order to communicate. One of our new Detective Sergeants, Eric Hughes, who was an excellent officer, was one of those who learnt sign language and in a subsequent force newspaper article said about Darren,

'He taught me all the swear words first of course, and he's always telling me off for not trimming my moustache. He jokes about me having to lift it up for him to lip read'. We all had a copy of 'Work Survival Signs' which I kept in my pocket but apart from mastering 'Thank You' and 'Very Good Work' I failed miserably.

Darren always found a way with a bit of a 'cheeky grin' to get his message across. He subsequently received the regional West Midlands Young Deaf Achiever Award and went to London to be part of the forces bid for being an outstanding employer in relation to its approach to working with people with hearing disabilities. Darren got to stay in the Strand Palace Hotel with his mother Val, who was a licensee in Darlaston, and to visit the Café Royal in Regent Street.

The Force subsequently achieved a third place award.

As we progressed we developed the concept of establishing dedicated intelligence cells for certain types of major incidents, with operational field intelligence officers to assist in developing the intelligence picture, and analytical staff to develop target profiles and such things as sequence of events charts. We were providing a service to the force which was designed to add value to investigations and operational staff gradually started to see the benefits.

***

In January 1991 Steve Barnbrook became a Scenes of Crime Officer covering the whole of the Midlands but again recalls working in the Walsall area,

"Bescot Sidings bordered on the Friar Park Estate, in Wednesbury, which was well-known for having a high crime rate. The estate was used to re-house families from slum clearance areas in the early 1930s and faced some real challenges. I often attended to burglaries of the railway offices within the sidings and on one occasion a safe was stolen. Several of the fingerprint identifications I made led back to Friars Park.

I dealt with another safe job just outside Bescot at Tame Bridge Railway Station. On this occasion the burglars broke into the office, and tipped the safe, which must have weighed a ton, onto its side. They then removed the metal plate on the back and drilled through the reinforced concrete inner-casing with a jack hammer. It would have taken hours of hard graft to get into it and when they finally managed there was less than £20 inside in change!

On the Bescot Curve, just outside the Sidings, freight trains used to stop at a particular signal, waiting for permission to enter, and when the locals got to realise this they used to raid the wagons looking for whatever they could steal.

The saddest case I recall was a young lad who was found burnt in one of the empty goods vans by a rail-man who was in tears when we got there The overheads had tripped earlier and the lad had touched the live cables after climbing on top of an oil tanker.

He was still conscious and more worried about the state of his clothing, which was all black from head-to-toe, and about getting into trouble when he got home. He was taken to the Burns Unit in Bath Row Birmingham but later died. He was with some of his mates at the time who panicked and left him. When people found out they were hounded out of the Friars Park Estate for not helping him."

***

At the beginning of 1991 Phil Ellis's services were required elsewhere, on a temporary basis, and I became the acting head of the Force Intelligence Department. That arrangement lasted for nine months, during which I directly managed the departments twenty-eight police, and civilian support staff, the vast majority of whom I had by now interviewed and selected.

On the 4 February 1991 the results of a chart which I had completed, were produced in a personnel report form by the West Midlands Police Employee Management System. The report described one of my performance characteristics as someone who *'enjoys risky ventures. Very independent and self-confident. Someone who prefers to tell rather than sell...'* As a self-confessed autocrat I wasn't too uncomfortable with the report's findings.

During this period I was closely involved in the preparation of a major contingency plan for the opening of the International Convention Centre in Broad Street, Birmingham. I was later afforded the opportunity of acting as an observer for a major exercise which was aimed at testing those procedures. It was multi-agency and involved the police and military, as well as a large number of umpires who logged and scrutinised every element of the proceedings.

Everyone had a very complicated set of rules, policies and procedures to comply with, during a developing 'hostage-taking terrorist scenario.' Chains of command were complex and needed careful handling. Whereas the military was very disciplined, and rank-orientated, the police service encouraged officers to be accountable for personal decision making based on roles and experience. Sometimes the two approaches were not compatible.

During the course of my police service I have witnessed, or been involved in several similar exercises, which are designed to be as realistic as possible. Decision making by senior officers is rigorously tested and stress levels are usually high leading to significant character changes in some individuals. This exercise was no different and everyone was trying hard not to be the focus of negative attention.

On this particular day I remember one senior CID officer

who was so focused on what he was doing, as he made notes, that he had the misfortune of inserting the nib of his fountain pen into his nose. It pierced the skin and he suffered a heavy nosebleed which refused to stop. At the same time he was summoned to the Chief Constables Command Group, to provide an update, and finished up presenting himself with a large twist of tissue paper inserted into one nostril. It was not his finest hour and I felt for him.

'Danny', a Special Branch officer for seventeen years, who I have worked with closely in the past, volunteered to be one of the 'hostages' for the exercise and recalls:

"I volunteered to be an Israeli member of the Olympic Committee, which was meeting to discuss where the next Olympics was being staged. We had to go to the BBC before the exercise started to get made up, and my hair was greyed to make me look as if I was in my fifties. We had photographs taken so that they could be used for intelligence purposes at a later stage. There was about seven of us, a mixed group of men and women.

The exercise started on a Friday and I found myself locked up in the 'stronghold' for three days, completely shut off from the outside world, and with the doors barricaded. There were four or five 'terrorists' some of whom were wearing Arabic headscarves, and carrying weapons that were capable of firing some very loud blank bullets. They were trying to make everything as realistic as possible and everyone got into the role-play, as we were body-searched. We were advised to speak when we were spoken to, and that if we started confronting the 'terrorists' they would most likely respond physically. I took the hint and remained compliant.

Any food that we got had to be obtained via police negotiators and we lived off 'hot cans' for three days, and slept on the floor at night in sleeping bags. At least one 'hostage' was taken out and 'shot' by the 'terrorists'.

On the Sunday morning I was tied to a chair and had a fake bomb tied around my neck. As lunchtime approached the SAS burst in and killed all of the 'terrorists.' Lots of noise, flashes and bangs and it was all over. All the other 'hostages' were dragged out unceremoniously from the room, but I had to wait until a bomb explosive expert was able to remove the device from my neck, as a man dressed completely in black looked on breathing heavily through a respirator. I was very glad that he was on our side.

We hadn't had a wash for three days and wore the same clothes throughout. It was good to have a shower and I decided that volunteering was perhaps not for me in future."

***

On the 30 July 1991 I had the opportunity of visiting the Royal Ulster Constabulary in Northern Ireland for a two-day visit with two other senior officers. Ostensibly we were tasked with looking at how we might be able to improve our approach to intelligence by learning from their good practice. We took off from Birmingham Airport and after one run of the drinks trolley, and one gin and tonic, landed some three quarters of an hour later.

We were met at Belfast Airport by a police driver who initially took us into a police office where we were introduced to a detective sergeant, who with a flourish of a small key opened a drinks cabinet on the wall and welcomed us to Northern Ireland in a traditionally warm manner.

We then made our way through the barren streets of Belfast to reach the RUC Headquarters and on the way the car we were in, which was an unmarked vehicle, suffered a flat tyre. I have never seen three grown men in suits, with English accents, change a tyre as quickly as we felt completely exposed, whilst the driver remained composed in the front seat, secreted under which was a firearm.

Throughout the day we were introduced to various senior officers, and various further drinks, culminating in a very late evening meal in good company at the 'Tedworth Hotel' in Bangor. Their marketing literature for a new weekend offer belied the darker side of life in the province and read as follows,

'Your Maxi Weekend starts on Friday evening with dinner in our restaurant which overlooks Bangor's new Marina, the County Down Coast, and Belfast Lough. On Saturday morning after a full breakfast you can explore the town of Bangor and the many attractions of North Down or unwind in one of the hotels residential lounges......'

All of this for the princely sum of £59.95 per person.

It was described as a fairly safe area although unusually there had been a terrorist bomb attack on British soldiers the week before. As we drove the sheer beauty of the green countryside served only to heighten the sense of tragedy about the place. You could not fail to admire the quiet courage of these officers, who lived with real threat of death and injury on a daily basis, yet remained totally focused on their duties.

I had come into contact with RUC officers previously and they were invariably great characters, who learnt how to live with constant danger, whilst retaining a quick-wit and a sharp sense of humour. Whilst the contents of my jacket would have revealed a pen, the contents of our driver's would have revealed yet another firearm which he carried with him at all times.

I do remember that the window catches on my first floor hotel bedroom were broken, and totally insecure, and fear of abduction, coupled with sleeping on a full stomach made for a restless night and a few nightmares. It was a totally irrational feeling but I was in a hostile environment where violence was an everyday reality and police officers were considered legitimate targets by the terrorists. I was happy when dawn broke.

The following morning, with some severe headaches being nursed, we were offered the opportunity of going out with one of the Force Surveillance units to see Belfast at street level. Two of us accepted the offer, rather foolishly in hindsight, and I spent the next few hours with a single-crewed surveillance operative who in fact was English.

The vehicle we travelled in was nothing short of a mobile armoury and it needed to be. We did a tour of the area where two off-duty British soldiers had previously been blocked in their car by other vehicles and subsequently abducted and murdered by a unit of the IRA. Three years later I saw a video, whilst on a course at the Police College in Bramshill, of the incident which was captured from a military helicopter camera hovering overhead, but which was powerless to respond.

One of the soldiers had a pistol which he fired into the air as they were surrounded but as he ran out of bullets it was 'game over' for them. It was a truly savage incident which I have never forgotten, and I vividly recall one of the killers leaning out of the vehicle containing the soldiers and punching the air in triumph - sheer mindless madness!

As we sat in the police vehicle surrounded by taxicabs, and stuck in traffic, in a community which was completely alien to me, I could only guess the terror of those two men as they faced death. One of the two corporals actually came close to escaping before finally being overwhelmed. It was a sobering experience and one which I should have politely said 'no' to if I had really thought about it. Removing my tie was the rather pathetic best I could do to blend in.

We subsequently visited the Holding Centre, where those arrested on terrorist charges were routinely interrogated, and viewed the brick walled rooms which many suspects chose to count as they declined to respond to police questioning.

Interviews create unreal situations as opponents play 'cat and mouse' with each other, with only a side of the table to distinguish one player from another. Most of the terrorists, of whichever political persuasion, had been trained to frustrate interviews. In any event they knew that if they were released they would be 'debriefed' by their own 'organisation', to assess whether they had given information, or in extreme cases been 'turned' into informants. The penalty for this was torture, and certain death, so for most silence was the safest option.

After meeting intelligence staff we made the journey home. In truth I probably didn't learn much in the way of new intelligence techniques but I learnt a lot about the strength of man and how people survive. I have always hated violence of any kind and the sheer futility of one man using violence towards another in the name of religion and politics just seemed totally futile to me.

On the day of the Birmingham Pub Bombings, as a young police constable, I had witnessed columns of uniformed officers marching from Digbeth up into the city centre after the bombs had gone off. It was an unreal sight which I witnessed from a Midland Red bus that was bringing us back from Birmingham Airport where we had been waiting for the body of a dead IRA bomber to be flown out. These are pictures that remain in your mind and stay with you.

CID investigations into serious crime, and Special Branch investigations into terrorism incidents, were conducted routinely in two 'parallel worlds' in the West Midlands area, and the wider UK, and 'Danny' recalls,

"It was like being within a Force, within a Force, for security reasons. Everything was on a 'need to know' basis and it didn't matter what rank you were, if you didn't need to know it, you weren't told it. We ran our own surveillance, and had our own sources. We felt privileged. We were not allowed to be elitist but one of the chief constables once remarked that if the CID messed up knuckles were rapped, but if the Special Branch messed up he would get the sack."

***

On the evening of Friday 4 October 1991, against my better judgement, I was persuaded to go to a charity boxing match at the Tally Ho Police Training Centre. Everyone was dressed up in dinner suits and I was advised not to sit anywhere near the ringside as my white shirt was likely to end the night covered in blood spots and other unmentionable stains.

I hated any form of violence and I hated this. As the evening went on and the levels of alcohol consumption rose it was like listening to the baying crowds of a Roman amphitheatre and it left me feeling cold. I left as early as I could and have never repeated the exercise.

At the end of October 1991 I visited Ilford in London to meet with officers from the Metropolitan Police, together with Detective Sergeant Steve Trenbirth, who had worked with me on Operation Red Card. I wanted to do something different again and we had started to research the viability of conducting an undercover 'sting' operation to buy stolen property from criminals.

In the first eight months of 1991 there had been an increase of 21% in burglary dwelling house offences, and a 32% increase in respect of robbery, and theft from the person offences, in the West Midlands Police Force area. These offences generated millions of pounds worth of stolen property circulating within communities and we wanted to tap into the 'market.'

On Tuesday 22 October 1991 I submitted a draft proposal suggesting that we set up a similar operation to that deployed successfully in the Metropolitan Police area where bogus premises were set up using undercover officers to buy stolen property. It got tacit support for further development but my impression was that people were cautious and wanted to look at it in 'slow time.' In reality it was to be nearly three years before we were actually able to bring an operation of this nature to fruition.

On Thursday 19 December 1991 we celebrated another Christmas with a function in the police bar at Steelhouse Lane, and I was about to see yet another year out. Out of the blue an opportunity arose however, at the end of December 1991, to apply for a Regional Chief Inspectors post in the newly created National Criminal Intelligence Service.

The advert read 'Post holders will be in at the birth of an exciting new national organisation and will be providing the vital link between the regional office, force intelligence bureau, dedicated law enforcement units and NCIS Headquarters. They will require to have experience in criminal intelligence matters and need to be dynamic and innovative'.

As soon as I became aware of it I decided to 'put my hat into the ring' and had absolutely nothing to lose given that the door 'in force' had been temporarily closed. In fairness to my Force though, the ACC Personnel said that if successful they would be willing to promote me on a temporary basis, to this particular post, and also said that in this specialist role 'it would be difficult to find a stronger candidate.' I could not have asked for more and the rest would be down to me. I knew that I would still need to get through a Force Promotion Board in due course, if successful, in order to be made substantive.

In the interim I tried to be supportive to the new incumbent Head of FIB who was a very well-known character in the Force, somewhat flamboyant, but with a lot of operational experience. He was very personable and energetic but we did not always see 'eye to eye' so I had to adjust quickly to get things done.

Soon after starting he suggested that we should operate like front-line news desks and group staff together in 'pods' with signs hanging from the ceiling for each area of expertise. It was actually an imaginative way of marketing the office and went down very well.

It was not long before our new structure was to be put to the absolute test in one of the most testing and demanding cases I have ever been involved in.

On the 21 January 1992 a letter was sent to me by Tony Mullet the new Director Designate of NCIS, and former Chief Constable of West Mercia Police, inviting me to attend an interview for the post I had applied for. There had been a large number of applications and at least two colleagues had been paper sifted, but I was through to the next stage, although the timing could not have turned out to be worse.

***

On the morning of Wednesday 22 January 1992, Stephanie Slater, aged twenty-five- years, was kidnapped by Michael Sams, a toolmaker with one leg. Not known to her at the time he had already murdered eighteen year-old Julie Dart, after abducting her in July 1991 from a street in Leeds.

Using a false name, and after some meticulous pre-planning, he arranged to meet Stephanie Slater, a sales negotiator with Shipways Estate Agents, ostensibly to view an empty, semi-detached, property at 153 Turnberry Road, in the Great Barr area of Birmingham.

At the property, the viewing of the house started as normal until they entered the upstairs bathroom whereupon he attacked her, and tied her up, before removing her from the house and taking her away in a vehicle. She was then kept prisoner at a workshop by the River Trent in Newark in Nottinghamshire.

For eight days she was blindfolded, bound and gagged whilst being kept in a home-made 'coffin' inside a wheelie bin, which had been laid horizontal, in conditions that were clearly meant to terrify her into submission.

Within hours, Sams made a ransom demand, and during one of the calls that were made he was described as having a Nottinghamshire accent. One call was subsequently traced to a public call box at a service station in Nottinghamshire.

The Force Intelligence Bureau was tasked with setting up a dedicated Intelligence Cell as part of the Major Incident Room at Nechells Police Station under the operational name *'Kaftan'*. It very quickly became a linked enquiry with West Yorkshire Police, and other national law enforcement agencies, and the gathering of intelligence was put at the very heart of the investigation. Suddenly we were put under a very large 'spotlight'.

The new head of FIB was part of the senior management team, as well as acting as the Intelligence Coordinator, and Regional Crime Squad liaison officer, whilst I was the Intelligence Cell Manager and ran the team from two portacabins in the back yard of the Police Station.

Two of the staff worked full time conducting intelligence analysis and the whole of one wall of one of the portacabins was covered in a continuous 'sequence of events' chart which was constantly pored over for clues. You could not afford to be distracted with this type of work and it was sometimes difficult for the two of them to get the 'peace and quiet' they needed to get on with their job, due to problems with space.

Other members of the Intelligence Cell, included Detective Sergeant Eric Hughes, who was a meticulously hard worker, a gentleman, and extremely loyal to me personally.

We were tasked with various intelligence functions and Eric's job was to maintain a complex file, with DC Kelly, which contained comprehensive details in relation to profiles of the 'Victim' and 'Kidnapper(s).' It was a hugely important job and senior investigators relied on the information to assist in some of their decision- making. There were lots of senior officers on the investigation, all occupying different roles, which made it difficult at times for us to deal with competing demands.

In the early days of the investigation some senior CID officers in the Force were openly skeptical about what the

Intelligence Cell could produce, and West Yorkshire Police did not put a similar structure in place for their enquiry.

By now Phil Ellis was on the Regional Crime Squad, and occupied an important role on the enquiry, so it was good to have someone around who I could have a decent conversation with.

One officer was imbedded within the Regional Crime Squad, whilst two others, including Richard Shakespeare, were responsible for Prison Intelligence. Another officer was employed full-time on researching financial lines of enquiry, and leads from recovered exhibits, which provided valuable information to police search teams at a later stage of the enquiry. All of them were initially posted to ten-hour shifts but they soon became the very minimum hours of working.

A further five officers worked directly to the head of FIB doing twelve-hour shifts around the clock to give us a 24/7 intelligence and communications capability with which to provide support to some of the staff deployed covertly.

Whilst there might be long periods waiting for the phone to ring, or a radio to transmit, they would have to act swiftly and in accordance with some very complex procedures if certain things started to happen on the ground. It was the biggest deployment of FIB staff in the new structure that we had ever undertaken, and a big challenge to our reputation as an effective department.

As part of the contingency plan for Operation Kaftan we attended all of the daily briefings for the operational teams, and provided an intelligence update, as well as conducting specific intelligence briefings. We always encouraged staff to be open in these sessions.

Experience told us that 'good ideas' were not necessarily within the gift of senior officers and we needed all the ideas we could get. Initially some of the briefings were held at the very end of long tours of duty, which meant that the room was full of extremely tired detectives, but the timings were later amended.

Other members of the police staff in FIB assisted within an Incident Information Centre set up by the Force Operations Department, at Force Headquarters, which took calls from members of the public in response to press appeals.

We left a 'skeleton staff' at Headquarters to try to keep the day job going. At one point this team was near to breaking point and I had to fend off requests to take even more staff away. This was a 'highly charged' enquiry where staff routinely worked at least twelve hours a day, day-in-day-out, and stress levels were high. These were the jobs that made careers, or broke them, and all the time there was a victim out there who needed help.

In the middle of all of this I attended my interview with the NCIS selection panel at 9.45am on Wednesday 29 January 1992 at the West Mercia Police Training School.

There had been no time for preparation but it was a fair interview and I knew that I would not have long to wait for the result. I was not feeling over-confident however due to the fact that the Head of the Region had already been identified as being a West Midlands Officer, and with six forces in the region I did not believe that they would want to fill the two top jobs from the same Force. After the interview I went back to the Intelligence Cell at Nechells, and prepared for another very long day.

Later that evening, the manager of Shipways followed some complex instructions from Sams as to how to deliver a cash ransom, which was ultimately left on the bridge parapet over a disused railway line in the Pennines near Barnsley.

Despite a huge effort involving covert policing techniques Sams managed to take the money and escape from the scene, using a moped to avoid being tracked by police. Throughout these events I was in the office, with members of my team watching events unfold. I had already been on duty for nearly twelve hours, but I had to be there, it would have been unthinkable not to be.

It was an extremely tense time and I felt for the senior officers who were tasked with making massive split second decisions in such a charged environment. The moment when the cash disappeared along with the attacker was a 'black moment' which was felt personally by everyone, whatever role they were performing. The next move would be in the hands of the kidnapper, and now that he had the money people feared the worst, and yet within hours he was to surprise many of us with a move that had not been predicted.

In the early hours of Thursday 30 January 1992 Stephanie was actually dumped by Sams at the end of the road where she lived with her adoptive parents, and he drove away undetected in the darkness.

Whilst this was a huge relief for the enquiry team it was clearly far from over, and if anything people became even more determined to find the kidnapper. Thus far he had been playing a very successful game of 'cat and mouse' with organisations which had vast resources at their disposal, as well as numerous experts. It was simply unthinkable that he would be allowed to win.

This was proving to be a massive investigation with so many lines of enquiry all over the country. The HOLMES staff were working flat out maintaining the computer inputting, indexing, statement reading, and allocating Actions to the outside enquiry teams, who knew that any one of those Actions might hold the key to the enquiry. There was no room for 'prima donnas' and forces and organisations that might normally be somewhat competitive with each other were forced to put such issues to one side. This was not about being seen as the best, it was about getting a result. The time for claiming any credit was not at that moment in time.

From a regional perspective West Midlands Police, as the second biggest force in the country, saw themselves as 'key players', whilst West Yorkshire Police, as the biggest force in the North East, regarded themselves as equals.

Later that day I was informed that I had been successful at interview for the NCIS job. There was no time for celebration, in the midst of all the intense activity, but I was very happy with the outcome, and had no hesitation in accepting the job. Instinctively I knew it was time to move on yet again.

During the month of January 1992 I worked fifty-eight hours overtime, which increased to ninety seven hours overtime in

February 1992, the equivalent of working six weeks in a normal four week period. Even in March 1992 when I left the investigation I worked another thirty five hours overtime and the reality was that home life in that three months consisted of sleeping, one hot meal a day, and possibly one day off a week, if we were lucky. Everyone was in the same boat – it was unrelenting as people pored over every minute detail of the case even down to the type of food the victim and offender had consumed.

In short there was no home life during this period and when officers subsequently completed an anonymous debrief form, which I later scrutinised, it was suggested that a letter of thanks be sent to the families of staff involved expressing appreciation for their support.

At work, in the early days, sausage sandwiches from nearby cafes were the order of the day, until the arrival of mobile kitchens. We ate at our desks.

Criminal intelligence analysis was still a relatively new concept in policing and we had to manage the expectations of the uninitiated, who often thought that the process could produce some sort of magical answer. Following Stephanie's release we also started looking more at identifying radius areas based on predictions of the minimum, and maximum, times she might have travelled from the place of kidnap to her home following her release.

Another FIB DC Joe McCallion, was responsible for traffic intelligence, and he was supported by PC Bob Nockalls, who focused on mapping and routing issues. We used traffic officers, mainly officers on motorbikes, to physically drive all of the possible routes, within speed limits, and came up with options for other officers to explore given that by now we were looking for other 'landmarks.'

One of those radius lines was in fact very close to the area in which Sams had his workshop in Newark, but at that point it was just one possibility in a 'haystack' of others, as the walls in our portacabins filled with yet more charts and maps. As enquiries continued however, we became more and more convinced that the place in which Stephanie Slater was detained was in an area to the east of Nottingham which became colloquially known as the 'Golden Triangle'.

Ultimately Sams was a man who transcended a number of force borders during the course of his criminal activities, which made the task of apprehending him even more difficult. Parts of the investigation related to the rail network and once more I found myself liaising with old colleagues from the British Transport Police, and an officer was seconded to us for a time.

At the same time Helen Skelton, the Senior Analyst who I had recruited in FIB, spent valuable time doing a detailed comparison of the Stephanie Slater and Julie Dart incidents to identify common features, of which there were many. This work provided a valuable insight into the skillset of the suspect – all we needed was a name.

In early February 1992 an artist's impression, in colour, of Stephanie's attacker, wearing glasses, was released to the media, and although not known at the time it proved to be a remarkable likeness.

Ultimately it was the power of the media that would be a 'tipping point' in the enquiry and Sams undoing. The Force Intelligence Bureau also circulated a Special Police Bulletin, to all Forces in the UK, which included a description of the suspect that now described him as having a soft Yorkshire accent. A 'voice analyst' who had listened to tape recordings of his voice had confirmed it as being from a specific area in the north of the UK.

Later that month a second bulletin was circulated, with a description of an Austin Metro which was believed to have been used by Sams, as yet another piece of the jigsaw puzzle was put in place.

On Thursday 20 February 1992 the TV show, Crimewatch UK, featured details of the case and the police made public a tape recording of the kidnapper's voice which was recognised by Sams first wife.

On Friday 21 February 1992 Michael Sams, who had an address in Nottinghamshire, was arrested, and his workshop was located at Newark on Trent. He was initially taken to a police station in Birmingham for questioning and on Sunday 23 February 1992 was charged with the abduction of Stephanie Slater, as well as blackmail and unlawful imprisonment. Following court appearances in Birmingham he was then taken to West Yorkshire where he was interviewed about the murder of Julie Dart and subsequently charged.

Sams gave detailed accounts of his involvement in the kidnapping of Stephanie Slater and the work of the Intelligence Cell continued unabated for a while, to support the enquiry team, which was now focused on preparing a detailed prosecution file. I remained as head of the Intelligence Cell, but managed to reduce the staffing levels after the 'dust had settled.' I was just over a month away from moving from FIB and it made sense for me to stay on the investigation whilst the department tried to return to some sense of normality.

* * *

Richard Shakespeare has his own memories of this enquiry, but for entirely different reasons and recalls,

"I was one of the first officers to be posted onto the job which very quickly went from being a missing person enquiry to a major enquiry. Initially I was involved in supporting some of the more technical aspects of the job but after Stephanie was returned home I started working with another officer doing prison intelligence. Basically we were tasked with visiting prisons all over the country to look at the backgrounds of convicted kidnappers, and serial killers, and to see if any of them had been 'celled up' with someone who had been recently released from prison.

On one particular day we were up in North Yorkshire to begin with and then got a phone call, I think it was from DS Steve Trenbirth, asking us if we could visit an address in Peterborough. Someone had made a phone call suggesting someone as a possible suspect and we were asked to go and get an 'elimination' statement to ascertain his movements on the day of the kidnap. It was very low-grade intelligence and we were just asked to get a feel as well for what type of individual he was. For the purposes of the rest of the story I will refer to him as 'Jack'.

145

We went to the address given and an older man answered the door who identified himself as being 'Jacks' father. He confirmed that Jack lived some forty metres away in some maisonettes and after phoning him to tell him two police officers wanted to speak to him he walked down with us to the address.

We knocked on the door and got no reply and after a while his dad got fed up and went home. We knew he was in so we carried on knocking every now and again and stood outside for what seemed to be about twenty minutes.

Finally Jack appeared at the door; a middle-aged man, tall, dark hair and balding, wearing a T-shirt and denim jeans but no shoes or socks. He looked slightly red and flustered but invited us in and led us up a narrow stairway to the first floor where we turned left into the living room, which overlooked the street.

The other officer with me sat on the sofa, and I sat on a chair whilst Jack went to occupy the seat next to me nearest the door, no more than two feet away. As he bent over to sit down he reached behind his back and pulled out a handgun that was black and shiny and a bit square shaped. He slapped the bottom of the gun and I heard a crack in the palm of his hand as if he had engaged the magazine. At this point he pointed it at the side of my temple!

The other officer sat there in absolute amazement unable to say anything and to a degree froze. Having not long come off undercover work I tried to stay calm and work out the options. Jack said, "The bells are under the clock", as if it were some sort of code. I didn't know what the code word might be but I had already decided that he was obviously completely unhinged. He demanded to see my

ID again and I gently placed my warrant card on the small table in front of us, at which point he lowered the gun to examine it.

I had already decided that to try and disarm him was too risky and there was literally no means of escape so I tried to talk our way out of the situation. It was strange but at that moment the image I had in my head was of the contents of my head being on the back wall behind me, but it made me calm and I almost accepted my fate, whatever it was going to be.

I started to trivialise our visit and said that he looked nothing like the kidnap suspect and that they had obviously sent us to see the wrong man. I explained that we would just need a short statement clarifying some details, at which point we would be on our way.

For his part 'Jack" - with the gun in his hand in his lap at all times, started to tell us about his 'girlfriend' and made reference to working for the SAS and the Security Services.

What I did not realise until later was that Jack was actually talking about himself and his 'women's side'. There was no girlfriend. He was a transvestite with a complete wardrobe full of women's clothes and I am guessing that it took him twenty minutes to answer the door because he was dressed as a woman at the time, and needed time to transform himself back into a man.

I wrote the statement as he sat there with the gun and finally the other officer tried to chat to him as well in an effort to keep him calm. Amazingly Jack then asked us if we wanted a cup of tea, an offer we gratefully accepted!

Whilst he was out of the room the other officer discussed

147

jumping out of the window but I persuaded him not to on the basis that we were bound to injure ourselves and in any event he could still shoot us from the window if he wanted to.

Finally I could hear him coming back and the sound of a tray with cups on rattling which reassured me as I realised that he wasn't coming back in with the gun pointing at us. He put the tray down, gave us our tea and then removed the gun again from the back of his trousers and sat with it on his lap.

We drank our tea and after assuring him that he would never hear from us ever again he took us back down the stairs and let us out. We had parked the car by Jack's father's house and walked very briskly to it in silence and drove off.

I drove a short distance away, pulled over and then took the deepest breath of my life.

We went straight round to the local police station and after some discussions between their senior officers and ours, Cambridgeshire Police came up with a plan.

I called Jack up and told him that we had missed a signature on the statement and asked him to call in at the local police station at 10am next morning to sign it, which he agreed to do.

On the way home to Birmingham that day we stopped off for just one whisky in a pub to calm ourselves. Because of the hours we had been putting in I hadn't been home properly for six weeks and should have been home that day. I rang my ex-wife to tell her that I would be late and that someone had pointed a gun at my head. I remember her saying "I've had a bad day as well. The kids have been really naughty today." I came to the conclusion that she had either misheard me or didn't care. Either way these are the things that keep your life real!

Next morning Jack turned up at the station and was arrested by a firearms team and at the same time another team executed a warrant at his address where they recovered about thirty guns, all of which were illegal. It also turned out that he had been debt collecting, armed with a gun and they cleared up loads of offences. Clearly he wasn't involved in the Stephanie Slater case."

***

Michael Sams was eventually sentenced to life imprisonment for the kidnap and murder of Julie Dart and the kidnap of Stephanie Slater. At his trial he admitted the kidnap of Stephanie Slater, but denied the murder of Julie Dart, however three days after being convicted he confessed.

At the beginning of October 1993 the media announced that Stephanie Slater had been awarded the sum of just £5,000 in compensation from the Criminal Injuries Compensation Board for 'suffering and distress.' At the time she was quoted as saying "Some people have said that I should have got more but I am quite happy. No amount could compensate for what Sams did to me."

Taking all the circumstances into account this case could only be described as a truly remarkable story of 'survival against all of the odds' and a unique enquiry which I have never forgotten.

In February 1995 Stephanie Slater released a book titled *'Beyond Fear'* about her ordeal in which she disclosed that within hours of being kidnapped she was raped by Sams, in his workshop, whilst handcuffed, naked, and blindfolded. She said that she had kept her secret for two years because she did not want to upset her family, or want people to know that she had had sexual contact with her kidnapper.

She was quoted in the press as saying, *"I went through hell at that man's hands but I didn't want people to know he had touched me because I felt dirty enough. I became obsessive about cleanliness. I used to have a bath twice a day, shower three times a day, scrub myself until I bled."*

In serious cases today victims are entitled to make 'Impact Statements' to the courts detailing the effects that crimes have had on them, and their families. Such words can in truth be really powerful in giving a voice to the innocent.

The response from Sams, serving his four life-sentences in Wakefield Prison, was to issue a statement via his solicitor denying rape and stating that he was going to commence libel proceedings.

***

On the 31 March 1992 I left the Force Intelligence Bureau and on the 1 April 1992 was promoted to Temporary Detective Chief Inspector, (Deputy Head of the Midlands Region), of the newly formed National Criminal Intelligence Service.

In accordance with Section 43 of the Police Act 1964 I was seconded to what was called Central Service by the Home Office, to an organisation which was to become the forerunner for today's National Crime Agency.

On the 1 April 1992 the National Criminal Intelligence Service officially began operating and we were initially based in quite basic office accommodation at Bournville Police Station in Birmingham. We covered six force areas, namely West Midlands, West Mercia, Staffordshire, Warwickshire, Leicestershire and Northamptonshire, and had officers from each of these Forces represented on the team, selected from the interviews carried out.

One of those interviewed for a post turned out to be one of the strangest interviews I have ever participated in. The officer adopted a totally inappropriate stance for his interview. He looked unkempt, and as if he hadn't combed his hair, and even had a pencil behind his ear. Albeit we were in a fairly relaxed atmosphere he removed his jacket and slouched in the chair.

He was unable to answer a number of the questions and in others adopted a flippant attitude and when asked why he wanted the job replied, "I have a wife, children and a large mortgage to support." When asked a question about his CV he appeared not to recall the content. During the interview he stopped and made comments such as "What am I doing here"? - I didn't know it was going to be like this." He concluded the interview by saying now it was over he intended to join the other candidates for a 'Balti' and referred to a Government document on the new organisation as a 'guide for insomniacs'.

Had it not been for the fact that we were involved in setting up a new body, the success of which we would all be personally judged on, it would have been hilarious and definitely the stuff of 'after dinner speeches'. Needless to say he didn't get a job despite the fact that his force had no hesitation in fully supporting his application.

The only other experience that came close to this was years later when I was interviewing someone for a CID post in the British Transport Police. The candidate walked in and dropped his mobile phone onto our desk as he went to sit down. In trying to grab it he knocked over a glass of water, which went over all of our papers, and the phone broke into pieces that scattered across the floor. Needless to say he didn't get a job either.

We had our first team photograph taken in the reception area of Tally Ho Police Training Centre in Edgbaston, Birmingham, with most, but not all of the twenty-three staff, smiling for the camera. Exciting days were ahead but I could not guarantee how long the smiles would last for as we faced the challenge of merging six different police cultures. Two of the staff were seconded from the BTP, and MDP, in line with similar attachments I had arranged in the FIB.

Four other regional offices had been created in the UK, in London, Bristol, Manchester and Wakefield, and we were all linked to the NCIS Headquarters, in Spring Gardens, near to the Albert Embankment, south of the Thames in London, where the bulk of staff in the organisation would eventually work.

The former National Drugs Intelligence Unit, the National Football Intelligence Unit, UK Interpol Office, and Organised Crime, and Counterfeit Currency Units all based in various Metropolitan Police buildings were pulled together – sometimes with a bit of 'kicking and screaming.' At its inception NCIS started with about four hundred police and civilian staff, plus about twenty-five Customs officers in total.

The Home Office had originally promised NCIS a new super computer system called NIX but eventually the whole project was scrapped through lack of funding and we finished up with an adapted version of a system called INFOS which the Metropolitan Police used, but which constantly strained to maintain effectiveness.

At the same time it was recognised that the organisation would struggle due to a lack of administrative support as, although the annual budget was £25,000,000, there was no 'new money' in the start-up costs.

Great emphasis was placed on the ability to conduct crime pattern analysis, and the linking of crimes, and initially offences of Murder/Attempt Murder, Kidnapping, Blackmail, Serious Sexual offences, Robbery involving the use of a Firearm, and issues of special interest, were identified for analysis work to be conducted in what were classed as 'serious crimes.'

Likewise 'major criminals' were identified and 'flagged' for attention. In order to gather intelligence on them we could do a number of things but were not allowed to do mobile surveillance, deploy our informants in a participating role, or conduct operational activity.

From the outset we worked closely with the No 4 Regional Crime Squad, which covered the same area, and fortunately I knew many of the officers seconded from the West Midlands and generally got on well with them. Every month I attended the No 4 RCS Branch Commander meetings and was well received.

John Carrington was the very first Head of the Midlands Regional Office and I was his designated Deputy. He quickly became involved in a number of 'national' issues relating to new policies and procedures, and for much of the time I was left to run the office. John also attended a number of training courses and I frequently performed the role of acting Head of the Regional Office.

Initially we were somewhat top heavy with managers and also had a detective inspector with responsibility for the field intelligence officers, who was classed as an Intelligence Coordinator, and a senior H.M Customs Officer who had been brought in to look specifically at intelligence relating to drugs, and specifically offences of drugs importation. Both of them had lots of service and experience but it made for a bit of a difficult mix from day one.

Bringing Customs officers into NCIS was about trying to develop a multi- agency approach to national and international organised crime. It was exactly the right thing to do but historically the police and Customs had not routinely shared intelligence, and indeed at times seemed to be in competition with each other - traditionally rivalry had been fierce.

Part of my duties also included being the 'Controller' for all NCIS registered informants handled by my regional field intelligence officers. This meant keeping detailed records of all proposed, and actual meetings, direction in terms of the dissemination of intelligence gleaned, and recommendations as to payments to be made. Some of the staff had brought existing informants with them over to the new organisation, and we were always looking for opportunities to cultivate new ones. We generally got that chance when someone was arrested, or when an individual simply was motivated by revenge.

Informants are rarely motivated by being public-spirited whilst at the same time few of them ever became very rich from the experience as they were mostly paid on results only. It was, and is, a very dangerous area of police work, both in terms of the personal safety of officers, and the informants, but also the real potential to find yourself facing a discipline enquiry should things go wrong. At such times records would be searched in minute detail for omissions or errors.

I also acted as an 'Authorising Officer' in relation to the use and deployment of covert technical operations, and to legally obtain records from other organisations, when required, for investigation purposes. On a more mundane front I was required to attend at least six regular meetings, some of which I chaired.

I always looked forward to our Operational Intelligence Meetings where I would practice the art of being a 'sensitive autocrat'. I was happy to listen to anyone, and there was never a shortage of people with an opinion, but after what I perceived to be a respectable period of dialogue I would signal an end to discussion and make a decision. I have always taken the view that any meeting lasting more than one hour was a wasted meeting and I tried to stick rigidly to this principle.

I was constantly providing inputs on NCIS to local CID Courses, visiting regional forces, and routinely on the train to

London to visit NCIS Headquarters regarding various operational, and policy issues. Some people love the 'feel' of being in London but I hated the Tube, the constant bustle of crowds of anonymous people, and wasted time staring out of the window of crowded trains. It felt like we were very much the 'poor cousins' in the regional offices, and I had little appetite for the 'bright lights.'

In August 1992 the West Midlands Police advertised again for chief inspector vacancies and yet again I put myself through the process which entailed both a paper- sift, and extended assessment, before a final interview.

This time I got through the paper sift stage and, on Sunday 1 November 1992, attended an extended assessment process at Tally Ho Police Training Centre where, with other candidates, I was tested on a group discussion, an operational exercise, problem solving, a presentation, letter drafting, and a mock TV interview.

It was an exhausting day, at the end of which I was mentally drained and I headed for the nearest bar for a pint. Overall though it went well and I received a solid final grade after three Assessors studied my every movement throughout the day. They sat in the corners of the room we were in, making copious notes on clip boards. We were the 'goldfish in the bowl', and they were the 'cats' looking to see if we made a fatal mistake!

At 11am on Tuesday 8 December 1992 I had my final board interview and then it was a matter of waiting. I was in 'Sam Wellers Bar' in Birmingham with some British Transport Police colleagues by 1pm and the first pint went down very quickly! I was subsequently notified that I had been successful.

In December 1992 John Carrington circulated a Christmas card to all the staff. He had a quirky sense of humour and had superimposed the heads of all of the team onto an old photograph of police officers in Victorian police uniform.

During the week commencing the 11 January 1993, I attended meetings in Leicester, Northampton and Worcestershire and then on the 15 January 1993 I attended a formal meeting with the other successful candidates, and the West Midlands Police chief constable, in an office at Lloyd House Police Headquarters. We sat in a line listening intently to his words of advice before, one-by-one, he announced where each officer was going.

It should have been a moment for quiet satisfaction however he completely forgot to mention me and I quickly realised that as a 'seconded officer', away from every day activity in force, he really didn't know who I was. It took the shine off the whole occasion and left me feeling very thoughtful and deflated.

On the 18 January 1993 I was promoted substantively to the rank of detective chief inspector still classed as an 'S' Division 'seconded' officer in the same role at NCIS. I was then constantly engaged in meetings with senior CID officers from the six Forces, and planning meetings for the move to new premises, as well as doing presentations on NCIS for Intelligence, and CID Courses, and the West Midlands Police accelerated promotion scheme, called SIPS for Constables.

I was a bit like being a car salesman selling a concept and a product that many people felt that they did not need. Due to John's commitments I found myself regularly continuing to run the regional office so time passed quickly. I made a lot of connections, some of which stood me in good stead later in service.

In March 1993, as we approached the end of the first year, I submitted a report outlining a number of potentially wide-ranging proposals which would enable the regional offices to grow. This involved such things as fraud, stolen vehicles, offender profiling firearms, and the use of undercover operatives, but my sense was that politics and money would not make it easy to make progress, in an organisation that in my opinion was very 'London – centric'.

On the 21 March 1993 we moved to new offices and I was tied up interviewing new staff. On Friday 2 April 1993, the Express and Star newspaper carried an article entitled *'Crime-fighting team moves to new office'* which announced the opening, the day before, of the new regional office for NCIS at commercial premises at the Waterfront, in Brierley Hill.

We were still growing in size, but at this point had about twenty police officers and civilian staff who were tasked with providing intelligence. We were equipped with INFOS, the NCIS Intelligence Computer system, which would be linked to the other areas. Everything we did had to accord with the Data Protection Act and was subject to a complex system of evaluation. Our office accommodation was brand new with a high level of security.

Whilst the idea was to be located away from police stations, and to adopt a low profile, it nevertheless would not take long for determined criminals to find us and any breach of security would be highly embarrassing. The staff loved the place not least of which because it was situated within walking distance of the large Merry Hill Shopping Centre.

John Carrington told the newspaper that the aim of the new centre was to provide a *'dynamic and creative'* intelligence service and went on, *'our targets are major criminals who commit serious crimes of regional, national, or international significance. We have prepared dossiers on more than one hundred major criminals over the last year, which have been forwarded to Regional Crime Squads, Police Forces and Customs. About sixty of those criminals have been arrested for offences varying from robbery to drugs.'*

A photograph of John and myself appeared in the article talking to one of the civilian staff. I was wearing a 'floral' tie that you wouldn't be seen dead in now and still had a full head of hair but it didn't take long for me to start losing it!

I was really pleased with the figures, as at the end of the first year the organisation as a whole had prepared some two hundred intelligence packages, which had led to one hundred and eighty arrests. I felt that the figures showed that we were definitely holding our own. Despite all the 'people' challenges I enjoyed the freedom of working on a national basis and whilst I didn't get the chance to do any of the exciting foreign trips I felt pleased to have laid some solid foundations.

At the beginning of July 1993, I attended a public-order command awareness course for three days to enable me to act as a 'Silver Commander' in public order situations. As something of a career detective I had never carried a riot shield in anger and I wanted to make sure there were no gaps in my skills.

It was time to start thinking about other options and on the 13 July 1993 during my career review with John Carrington I indicated that I was looking to leave. He gave me a 'glowing' report but did not try to change my mind. The West Midlands Police were about to start a major reorganisation and I wanted to be part of it.

In his feedback I was described as, '*a good team builder who certainly does not 'suffer fools gladly' and was never afraid to confront difficult situations whether or not I had faced them before'*. It seemed that I now had another label which was to remain with me for the remainder of my police service.

On the 19 July 1993 I submitted a request to return to the West Midlands Police. In many ways it might have been argued that I had achieved my aim, after all I had achieved promotion, but the reality was that many of my NCIS colleagues stayed on for the 'long haul' and finished up achieving several promotions without moving, indeed I recall one London based inspector eventually reaching the rank of superintendent and then becoming the civilian head of the same unit. He travelled all over the world in the process whilst the view from my office window was a canal, and a car park.

On the 27 August 1993 I had a phone call from the West Midlands Police personnel department identifying a vacant detective chief inspectors post and asking me if I could take the job at the earliest opportunity. I was on the move and asked to terminate my contract with NCIS with effect from the 26 September 1993, which was duly agreed.

On Friday 3 September 1993 I paid my first visit to

Willenhall Police Station, in Walsall Borough, to meet the uniform Chief Inspector Gerry Nicholson. I had never been to the station before and didn't know the area at all. He was an absolute gentleman who welcomed me warmly, and remained supportive in the following years.

On the 6 September 1993 I received a nice letter from the Deputy Director General of NCIS Simon Crawshaw, a former Deputy Assistant Commissioner in the Metropolitan Police, thanking me for my efforts and that was it.

I had a leaving do at the office on the 7 October 1993, where John Carrington did a humorous 'slide show' of pictures including some of me as a child, one of which was on a donkey at the seaside, one in a Marine Cadets uniform at the age of thirteen years, and several later in life where I was sporting a full beard.

The staff were highly amused, as he captioned each photograph with something related to my work in NCIS, but it was not malicious and I was happy to let him have his moment.

He also presented me with two cartoon pictures one of which showed my head on the body of a bulldog eating 'problems' from an NCIS food bowl.

The second showed me operating an NCIS 'ACME Target Package Generator' which showed a counter of 102 packages produced against zero for the Customs. Behind the machine was a 'counselling suite', which was a less than subtle reference to the amount of time I had spent trying to sort people and problems out.

Figure 15: Detective Inspector Michael Layton

Figure 16: Force Intelligence Bureau - 1990

Figure 17: Walsall Football Club - 2016

Figure 18: Cartoon, John Carrington and Michael Layton – 1993

Chapter Five

The Grim Reaper

(Stephen Burrows):

'We are all but one breath away from death'

So the saying goes, but you wouldn't know it in our modern world, where every aspect of death has been sanitized, and most people can go through the whole of their lives without seeing a dead body. Nowadays we tend to see murder and violent crimes purely through the eyes of a television screen.

It was very different, even in the relatively recent past, where for example in Victorian times, there was almost a cult of mourning, and death was always at one's shoulder, from war, disease, poverty, a low life expectancy or high infant mortality.

In the United Kingdom, the last seventy years have provided unprecedented peace. No war has touched our homes, diseases such as smallpox, tuberculosis and virulent flu epidemics have been almost eradicated, and people now rarely die in factory accidents.

The result is that at heart none of us really believe that we will ever be going through the crematorium curtain, and our society does everything in its considerable power to shield us from that inevitability in all its manifestations. Ironically, horror- films and books, and zombie films have never been more popular, but we never see a dead or maimed body 'in the flesh'. For those who don't like what they see they do of course have the choice to press the 'off' button.

That is, of course, until one becomes a police officer. Two of the first tasks a probationer on a '999' response shift was encouraged to experience were conveying a death message and viewing a post-mortem - an introduction to death.

The following comments are in no way meant to glorify a very personal subject but they are an effort at telling the reality of a part of policing which is not routinely exposed. No car chases, catching criminals, saving people, or other types of excitement and heroics – just dealing with pain and sadness.

On response duties in particular, death is monotonous in his regularity of appearance, just the method and condition of the corpse change. It is like watching all of the *'Final Destination'* films replayed on a loop.

***

Let's deal with post-mortems first. Any fan of *'Silent Witness'* knows all about them of course, but is that realistic? In essence yes, but you know you are watching an act, using sight and hearing only. The camera decides where you look, you smell nothing, and you can ask nothing, you are not there in person.

I have met some strange people in the mortuary, all of them thankfully alive, and the dead have stayed dead. The pathologist performs the actual examination, but the body has to be prepared and then cleaned up afterwards. These unpleasant, but necessary tasks are carried out by the mortuary technicians. I have seen these characters singing, humming and whistling as they work, opera playing loudly in the background. I have seen them eating their lunch whilst sat with the bodies. They tend to have an interesting philosophy and a locker full of really good jokes. I have however, never seen a body treated with anything other than respect as a difficult and necessary job is done.

If you die whilst being treated for a terminal, or long-term illness, and a doctor will certify the cause of death without a post-mortem, then one is not normally carried out, and the body is released for burial or cremation.

If however, you have the misfortune to die in other circumstances, then a post- mortem is usually required to determine the cause of death to satisfy the requirements of a coroner.

The coroner for an area will decide whether an inquest is required, and a post- mortem report will always form a significant part of the inquest evidence. Inquests have recently become a 'backdoor' means of public enquiry, but their proper legal purpose is to determine,

- Who has died?

- When they died?

- How they died?

They are not criminal courts, but if a verdict of 'unlawful killing' is returned, then the police usually investigate. If there is already a criminal investigation running, the inquest will open and adjourn, pending the result of police enquiries.

A 'standard' post-mortem can be conducted by any pathologist. They will determine cause of death and the body can then be released to the funeral directors. If the police deem the circumstances to be suspicious, then the services of a Home Office Forensic Pathologist are required.

This individual is highly trained to find and preserve forensic evidence of the cause of death to support prosecution. Unlike on the television, they do not investigate; they are classed as being an 'expert witness' and that is the limit of their involvement. There are no Quincy's, Kay Scarpettas, or 'Silent Witness' pathologists in the UK. This is pure invention, a device to dramatically conjoin the twin public fascinations of forensic examination and murder 'whodunits'.

The attendance of a police officer at any death is a crucial step in determining whether it is suspicious and the course of action required.

The smell of the mortuary is something that you never forget. Once you've experienced it, you always recognize it, and can always identify the smell on others. It seems to cling to clothing for hours afterwards. There is always a chemical undertone, think formaldehyde, but the aroma of a dead body is unique, and of course is worse the older and more putrefied the body becomes. The trick was to breathe through your mouth, and to apply a touch of 'after shave' or perfume to the back of one hand, to get occasional relief by means of an unobtrusive sniff. It was simple but effective.

Disposable overalls and overshoes are now available, but back then you simply wore your uniform, or suit in the case of CID officers.

Officers were known sometimes to make a rapid exit from the post-mortem to be sick, and some even passed out at their first 'PM', much to the amusement of the pathologist and technicians.

A forensic pathologist will usually attend the scene of a suspicious death, with the body in situ, in order to form a view of what has occurred, and to assist in deciding what the most propitious lines of examination might be. Sometimes they can come up with a hypothesis at the scene that sounds unlikely, but these people possess a huge level of expertise.

For instance, I once attended a scene where a young man in his twenties lay dead on his back, bare-chested, with a knife sticking out of his chest. There were multiple stab wounds in the chest, and abdomen, which at face value one might have assumed was a case of a frenzied attack and murder.

However there was no sign of forced-entry at the premises. A forensic pathologist was summoned to the scene. He inspected the body, the wounds, the knife, and the scene. I remember my incredulity when he announced, "I think this might be a suicide". Enquiries then revealed that the man was depressed, a drug-user and had attempted suicide previously. There was no indication of anyone else being involved. The crucial piece of evidence came from the post mortem. The angle of all the wounds clearly indicated that they were self-inflicted; it was indeed a suicide.

A pathologist normally begins a post-mortem by making the famous 'Y'- shaped cut. The ribs are sawn and the sternum removed.

This allows access to the main organs which are removed, inspected, dissected and, if required, samples taken for further analysis.

A cut is then made around the rear of the cranium and the skin and hair is peeled forward, usually being laid over the face, to protect it, but presenting a rather disconcerting aspect to the viewer!

A small circular saw is used to remove the top of the skull, allowing inspection of, and sampling of the brain without disturbance to the face. It all sounds a bit unreal but it is a delicate art designed to maintain the dignity and appearance of the body whilst ensuring that the investigative process is thorough and detailed.

In standard post-mortems this is usually sufficient to ascertain cause of death. In cases of suspicious death however, the process is likely to take longer and many more samples will be taken appropriate to the circumstances and suspicions. For example, if poison is suspected, a range of samples will be sent for analysis.

In most cases the organs are returned to the body cavity, the skin sewn up and the cadaver stored to await authority from the coroner for the release of the body to loved ones. It is then handed over for the funeral directors to work their magic.

If the body relates to a murder investigation, it will probably be retained for some time until the coroner directs that it be released. This is to cater for the possibility of a requirement for a second post-mortem where, for example, someone is arrested and the defence legal team requires an independent post-mortem.

The coroner is in effect, in legal custody of the deceased until satisfied that all enquiries requiring the body are satisfied. Occasionally a body is released and suspicions surface later, which is where one sees exhumations ordered by the coroner at the behest of the police. These cases are in fact extremely rare, but again make for good fictional television.

The retention of the body of a loved-one causes great tension between family and investigators and has to be carefully handled. If a defendant has not been identified it is likely that a body will be retained for a considerable time to await a charge in case a second post-mortem is required. It is always a difficult balance between the needs of a family to achieve the closure of burial, and an investigating officer who has a duty to bring the murderer to justice. In law, the state 'owns' the body until the coroner releases the body, a situation that of course families find very difficult to accept.

***

Officers on 999 response duties attend most 'sudden deaths', usually summoned by an ambulance crew, who are often the first attenders, and discover the deceased person. The phrase, 'sudden death,' seems to be used by the police for all deaths and always amused me, as death is nothing if not 'sudden'.

To a seasoned police officer, attending deaths can become dangerously routine, but one must always remember that each one is individual, and that the effect on families is almost always traumatic. It does not help that death is rarely dignified and comes in many guises, and locations, some of which can be blackly amusing.

For instance, a surprising number of deaths occur on the toilet as the act of straining can place a weakened heart under pressure.

One of the most difficult deaths I ever attended was a man who had dressed up in his wife's underwear whilst she was out. He had clearly been masturbating in the bathroom, had a heart attack and fallen into the linen basket head first, striking his head in the process. When I first entered the bathroom all that could be seen was a pair of legs wearing high heels protruding from the basket.

Any sense of amusement had to be quite properly stifled as the shocked and grieving family was downstairs and required assistance to start managing the processes which needed to be carried out. This type of unusual demise required a coroner's report and therefore photographs had to be taken and clothing seized. I am pleased to say that we managed to deal with things very discretely and to preserve the dignity of the deceased and his family.

Another report that is dreaded is usually captioned with the words, *'I haven't heard from my relative for weeks, I've been round and can't get any reply.'*

I once had a couple come into a police station front-office with just such a tale. There was no-one else available so I went to the address with them. It was a winter's evening and therefore dark. I opened the letterbox and my nostrils were assailed by that tell-tale 'mortuary smell'. I could see a pile of unopened post. It didn't take a detective to work out that this was not going to be a happy ending. I decided to break the news there and then and advised the couple to remain outside whilst I investigated further.

I noticed a small window at the side of the premises was ajar and managed to get it open. It was well above floor level so even with a torch and standing on a dustbin I couldn't get a clear view of what lay inside, other than it was clearly a bathroom.

The only way I could get in through the window was backwards, feet first, and the room was completely dark so I could not see what I was doing, and had to feel my way with my feet. As you can imagine, this was done in a very 'ginger' fashion, bearing in mind that I knew a decomposing body was somewhere inside. I was entering a toilet feet-first with the possibility in my mind that the body may well have been sat on it!

To my relief the bathroom was empty and the power was working, so I was able to turn lights on as I followed my nose. In true horror-story style I discovered the deceased in bed in a room full of flies. I estimate that he had been dead for around three weeks. This is not a pleasant stage of decay as the body bloats, turns green and liquefies. The later, 'mummified' stage is much better for the finder!

I opened the front door and relayed the bad news, once again I managed to prevail upon the couple to stay away and leave the arrangements with me. I suggested they found a hotel for the night, which they did.

I arranged for an undertaker and was not surprised to see that the two men who attended were almost 'gagging' as they virtually 'poured' the body out of the bed and into a body bag. It was necessary to watch in order to preserve 'continuity' of evidence regarding the body's journey to the mortuary and I had to follow the van to the mortuary and witness the lodging of the body there. This is normal evidential practice where there is an, 'unexplained', death, and whilst I was pretty certain this was natural causes, which indeed it turned out to be, that open window meant that the premises were insecure so every angle had to be covered.

Another regular manifestation of death is the suicide. People find many ways to take their lives, some intricate, some bloody, some not. All require an inquest and therefore, photographs need to be taken, evidence seized, and a full coroner's report prepared.

One of the prime times for suicides is Christmas and many a festive day on duty has been celebrated by attending the suicides of lonely and desperate people. Most support mechanisms for the lonely, vulnerable and disturbed are shut over the holidays, so the police tend to be the initial responders.

Some of the most common methods of suicide I have dealt with relate to:

• **Hanging:**

Strangulation frequently also results in a broken neck as well. Sometimes applying pressure around the neck has a sexual purpose only, which unfortunately can go wrong, if the victim is unable to release the pressure. The police wisdom handed down through the ages mandates that the section of rope with the knot in has to be preserved for the coroner. I was never actually sure what this achieved unless a 'knot expert', could be sure that it had been tied by the deceased.

- **Cutting wrists:**

  Often seen as a 'cry for help' and survivable if found quickly. The scene when found is dramatic, especially if an artery has been cut and has described a *'Jackson Pollack'* in blood on the walls, and ceiling, or the body is sat in a bath full of bloody water.

- **Exhaust fumes from a vehicle with the engine running:**

  Carbon Monoxide is deadly. The oddest one of these I ever attended was on a Christmas afternoon. The deceased had managed to lie at the rear of the vehicle right by the car exhaust pipe in a garage and ingest the fumes until he died.

- **Pills and poisons:**

  This method is also often a cry for help. The tragedy is that a cry for help using Paracetamol can have an unfortunate twist. Unless the stomach is pumped rapidly the liver can be damaged beyond repair resulting in death sometime later, even though the original attempt is survived.

- **Jumping from height:**

  'Jumpers' can cause massive disruption, especially if they are on motorway or rail bridges. The advent of trained police negotiators entails roads and sections of streets being closed to keep the public away. I have regularly witnessed frustrated onlookers exhorting someone to jump, accompanied by colourful invective.

Thankfully few people actually jump if they are still on the edge by the time negotiators arrive. The situation was somewhat different in the 80s, and the response officers just had to do their best. I recall once being called to a man sat on the edge of a wall on the top floor of Moat Lane Car Park in Digbeth, late one evening. It was freezing cold and I spent about two hours trying to persuade him not to jump. By the end of that period I was 99% sure he was attention-seeking, and told him that we were all going back to the police station for something to eat and a cup of tea. He could either come with me, or wait until I returned in an hour or so. I told the officers to start leaving the scene and he came down. I admit that my fingers were crossed behind my back!

- **Jumping in front of a train:**

The disruption to rail services and thousands of travellers is often immense, and the effect on train drivers for example is traumatic. Impact frequently leads to body disruption spread over an extensive area which all has to be searched and the body parts recovered. The guiding principle for all recovery, and emergency services, is that respect for the human body is paramount and is to be dealt with in the most dignified manner possible.

- **Drowning:**

Immersion in water speeds decomposition and can make effective body recovery more difficult. It is fact that many an officer has tried to lift a body from a canal by a limb and found themselves left holding an arm or leg.

***

Moving on from the act of death itself, one of the worst tasks an officer has to perform is the delivery of the death message, which was a 'bread and butter' task for the response officer, but one which you could never take for granted.

Picture yourself, in full uniform, knocking the door. A police officer is frankly not a popular occupant of a doorstep because everyone automatically assumes trouble is at hand – usually correctly. Police humour suggests that that an opening line such as, 'Are you the widow Smith?' may assist in conveying the message, but in reality the officer knows that heart-wrenching trauma is about to ensue. The recipient of the news will always associate the bearer with the news, no matter how compassionately it is transmitted.

The officer has to be prepared to offer comfort, advice, and to locate friends and relatives to support. For a short time they are at the centre of the worst moment of another human being's life, and then they must withdraw, rebuff any temptation to become personally involved, and attend the next job, perhaps a pub fight.

Such incidents are literally like 'walking on glass' and unwanted comments such as 'I know how you feel' will often draw angry responses – how can anyone know or feel another person's individual grief?

It is very difficult to keep emotion at bay in some circumstances, and certainly, the incident I recount remains clearly imprinted upon my memory, even now, well over twenty years later.

I was an inspector in charge of a response shift and was summoned to a road traffic accident. The motor vehicle is the biggest cause of death and life-changing injury that affects the general public. That same public, sanitized from seeing the results of accidents, continues to speed, drive recklessly, fail to maintain their vehicles, use mobile phones, and enjoy other distracting mobile activities, drive under the influence of drink or drugs, race each other, I could go on. They then moan and enquire why the officer isn't 'out catching burglars', when caught. That is, until one day an officer is on the doorstep with the message about their beloved family member.

The accident I attended was between a truck and a twelve-year-old schoolboy in his uniform. School had finished for the day and he had run out into the road, colliding with the truck and been killed instantly. The driver was distraught and could have done nothing to prevent the collision.

There the boy lay, skull shattered, a totally wasted life. It was an incredibly upsetting scene. I have children who were a similar age at the time and I could picture them lying there and imagine how I would feel. I decided to convey the news myself.

As I approached the house door I could smell food, the boy's tea being cooked. No doubt he usually burst in, full of life and starving, homework to do before fun could be had.

Mom was a single parent with a younger daughter. I will not go into more detail other than to say that her life changed forever, at that extremely distressing moment that I will forever embody in my mind.

This was not the end of the matter though. Identification of the body was required. Care for the young girl was arranged - she was of course in trauma at the loss of her elder brother.

I conveyed mom to the mortuary.

There I watched as she saw her only son lying dead on a slab. She asked if she could hug him and I said, "Of course", but had to advise her not to lift his head from the slab as it had been hastily reconstructed for her benefit. It is important for loved ones to be able to say goodbye. Sometimes the state of the body makes that very difficult. They also have a thirst for knowledge - they need to know what happened and why. Making things up like 'it would have all been over very quickly', don't help and could come back to bite you at inquests.

My duty shift that day did not improve. Once I had conveyed the mother into the arms of relatives I returned to the police station to eat my sandwiches. The next job was a suicide....

***

In such situations police officers have to learn their own 'coping mechanisms'. For seasoned detectives, part of that coping, after attending a post-mortem at Newton Street, in Birmingham City Centre - behind the Juvenile Courts, was to spend some time putting life back into perspective in the police bar at Steelhouse Lane Police Station. Alcohol helped, but in truth was merely a short-term fix. The smell on their suits would signify where they had just come from.

As individuals we are all 'wired differently', and what works for one officer will not work for another - there are some things that cannot be taught.

One of the key issues was that you could not, and must not, embrace another person's grief. To do so would strip away your ability to investigate thoroughly and impartially.

It was not about being tough; it was about doing your job.

Chapter Six

Early Mornings – Late Nights

(Michael Layton):

On the 27 September 1993 I started work as a detective chief inspector based at Willenhall, in the Black Country, which is home to a relatively small market town, and suffered from a cholera epidemic some hundred years prior to my arrival.

There were also numerous council housing estates, where a number of extended families lived, as well as domiciled members of the traveller community.

The market place, which was mentioned in the population census for the first time in 1851, was home to market stalls on Wednesdays, Fridays, and Saturdays. A large memorial clock was unveiled there in 1892 and is a prominent feature.

The locals were creatures of habit and tended to use the same shops and same pubs. For the most part they were decent 'hard working' people who were straight talking and honest. It was a place where everyone tended to know each other's business which was useful for us.

The police station in John Street was a tired-looking building, with two floors, situated near the town-centre, and close to a pub called the 'Ring O Bells' which took its name from the fact that the bells of the nearby parish church of St. Giles could be heard from there. It had a front office for the public to visit, and a small cell-block which was accessed from the rear. There were small offices for the management team, as well as CID, and also housed uniform staff that were a mixture of local beat officers, and response teams.

On the first floor was a small canteen and a club with a bar. Police social clubs were common in those days, normally attended by a dedicated core of regular officers and police pensioners. They were managed by committees which would include a chair, secretary, and treasurer but were quite incestuous by nature.

I arrived at 8am in the morning and started the process of introducing myself to staff locally, as well as paying a visit to Walsall Police Station to meet other senior officers.

My opposite number at Walsall was a DCI with many years' service and a local man. A larger-than-life figure he saw himself very much as the deputy to the divisional detective superintendent. Conversely as a *'Brummie'* I was something of a foreigner in an area where the community were referred to as *'Yam Yam's'* so I knew that it would take a while for me to be accepted, and for a while I was happy to accept the 'pecking order'.

I made friends quickly with the station cleaners and the canteen lady – if you wanted to know what was going on in a police station they were the people who would know.

As well as Willenhall, which borders with Darlaston, I was also responsible for the area of Bloxwich, and they were both high-crime areas. The police stations were somewhat old and dilapidated. In 'posh' terms they could be described as having 'character' but having worked in similar buildings before I liked them.

Darlaston is close to the boundary with Wednesbury, and is

steeped in history going back to the Middle-Ages. A place called *'The Bullstake'* is a focal point in the town-centre which derives from the fact that bulls – and occasionally bears – were baited there. The sport continued long after it was made illegal in the 1840s, and in 1875 sixty-five residents successfully objected to a proposal to erect a cast-iron gentleman's urinal on the site.

Situated in Crescent Road, the police station was built in the late 1890s. On the day of the official opening the workmen who had spent the morning putting the finishing touches to the building were invited to return for the afternoon ceremony. One of them got drunk at lunchtime and for some reason on his return assaulted a high-ranking police officer and was arrested. He was the first person to be put into the cells that he had helped to build. Because it was a special occasion he was however later released when he was sober.

Bloxwich has its origins dating back to the Anglo-Saxon period, and was a Royalist area in the English Civil War. It was heavily developed between World War I and II for council housing. Most were constructed around Blakenhall Heath, as well as Harden, and Goscote, whilst the Lower Farm, Beechdale, and Mossley Estates were added in the following twenty years.

The old Bloxwich Police Station was built in Elmore Green Road in 1884, classed as public buildings, together with two reading rooms. It was close to the High Street and a church which is now known as All Saints. In the grounds of the churchyard is an ancient cross which is thought to have been erected in the thirteenth or fourteenth century. The police station was closed in 2000 during my period as OCU Commander for the area, and demolished to make way for a brand new building which was opened on the 26 September 2002 by the Princess Royal. In the reception area of the new station is a picture of me proudly shaking hands with Princess Anne.

Social deprivation was high in most areas, with Bloxwich being the busiest in terms of policing. Dealing in the supply of controlled drugs was rife, as were offences of burglary and vehicle crime.

Only the month before, a search warrant had been executed at the home of Kevin Griffin aged thirty-three-years, unemployed, from Wilkes Avenue, Bentley, and amphetamine with a street value of nearly £5,000, cannabis resin worth £1,200, and smaller quantities of LSD, ecstasy, and herbal cannabis were recovered. Some of the cannabis had been cut up in blocks and split into bags ready for sale. In his defence when questioned he claimed to have been pressurised into becoming a dealer after his own brother had himself been sent to prison for possession of controlled drugs with intent to supply. He later followed his brother for a second time when he got two and a half years imprisonment.

In order to successfully execute drugs warrants, speed of entry was vital to secure the drugs before they were flushed down the nearest toilet. To achieve this door rams were frequently deployed to smash the doors of premises down.

Dave Faulkner eventually retired from the police service in 2008 and recalls the history and use of what became known as 'Nigel's', *"We used to use sledge- hammers frequently when I was on the drugs squad but in 1991 Derek Hopkins decided to develop a ram. He discovered a foundry in Great Barr and they made a ram which was about four feet long with nine-inch plates at each end. It had a six inch wide shaft with handles that ran all the way along it so that two people could carry it on either side. It was painted in black enamel.*

At that time Chris Eubank and Nigel Benn were successful boxers and Nigel was known as the 'Dark Destroyer' so we named the ram after him. Eventually hand- held rams for one person were developed but the name 'Nigel' stuck.

One day we took the ram to some flats in Walsall. It was a Saturday morning and we normally tried to avoid weekends, but we had good information that drugs were there so we came in specially to do the job.

We took 'Nigel' up the stairs and four of us got on it and hit the door with some real force. The door literally catapulted inside and down the hallway of the flat just as the target came out of the bathroom. It hit him full on, split his head, and knocked him out. We recovered two kilos of amphetamine and dealt with our prisoner, after he had paid a visit to the local hospital. The 'Dark Destroyer' had lived up to its name!"

***

Domestic violence was also common, and drunken and anti-social behaviour routine, and frequent. It was a very busy area with lots of challenges and I was really looking forward to the opportunity and to start making a difference.

After an uneventful day I left work for home just before 7pm and had plenty of time to think on the motorway on the way home. Junction 10 of the M6 was to become a familiar sight for me for the next few years.

To add to the mix at this time the police service as a whole in the UK was agonising over the recommendations of a report submitted to the government by Sir Patrick Sheehy, who had recommended wide ranging restructuring in terms of pay scales for officers, and the rationalization of a number of ranks. It effectively reduced the starting pay of a new recruit, by up to £5,000, and the Police Federation claimed that pay rates had been compared to, *'supermarket check-out operators, Mothercare assistants, insurance clerks, building society and bank tellers, and electronics assembly line operatives'.*

In their view the review failed to acknowledge the 'unique nature' of a police officer's role and the debate looked set to continue. Unfortunately for me it also gave the 'barrack room lawyers' plenty to focus on as they spread 'doom and despondency' and inevitably would make it harder to motivate staff, some of whom would see less financial incentive as well as reduced promotion prospects.

As was my habit I called into the office on my day off on Saturday 2 October 1993 and whilst I only stayed for an hour, I wanted word to go around that I was not a 'nine to five' person and that my movements would not be predictable. I could see that the staff were unsettled by my appearance and I did the same the following Saturday - whilst most people were watching the football I was watching the staff!

My previous experience told me that the positive people would come to value the additional support and the interest in them that I was able to offer, whilst the idle few would be kept on their toes.

I spent the next few days trying to speak to staff on a 'one-to-one' basis. They were a very mixed bag of individuals, with very few young in service. One of the detective sergeants was extremely experienced and was a prolific informant handler. His team of detective constables and attached officers were also very active and knew all of the local criminals. Another detective sergeant had extensive knowledge of the area, and an eye for detail, but he was not prone to smiling much!

On Wednesday 13 October 1993 I briefed the press in relation to an arson attack that had occurred the day before. An 11,000 volt electricity MEB Sub-Station, in Fryers Road, Bloxwich was set alight by vandals who stacked a car tyre, paper, and a plastic road cone around some cables and set fire to it. Serious damage was prevented by the fire service although power was cut for a short time to some local factories. In truth the culprits had put their lives at serious risk in a wanton act of stupidity.

The local reporters from the Walsall edition of the Express and Star routinely rang before 10am every day, and the Walsall Advertiser at least once a week. I made a practice of being as open with them as I could be as long as they were objective in their reporting. We needed the press as much as they needed us but there were lines not to be crossed and if, on rare occasions, I felt that our trust had been abused, I simply made myself unavailable to take phone calls for a few days and they struggled to get the right stories to fill their columns.

In order to try to get the staff motivated and working at the same level I arranged a CID office meeting at 2pm on Tuesday 19 October 1993 and used the conference room at my old NCIS office. I delivered 'chapter and verse' to the assembled group, as to how I wanted them to deliver performance, and watched their body language with great interest as they tried to digest my delivery. After a couple of hours I took them all for a drink in a local club and again used the time to understand the groupings and allegiances that existed.

On Monday 25 October 1993 the force announced the results of Operation Plato, a week long operation which had led to the recovery of stolen property valued at £59,000, heroin valued at £3,000, and one hundred and twenty eight persons being arrested.

Six days later the detective superintendent announced the commencement of a similar six month initiative to be run in the borough.

On Tuesday 26 October 1993 I cancelled an annual leave day and went into the office for 5.45am to oversee a burglary operation where we had a number of suspects to arrest, some of which were from positive 'Fingerprint Identifications' found at the scenes of crimes.

Where possible we always tried not to immediately disclose forensic evidence at the beginning of interviews because we knew that this would result in them being more cautious in the future. It also gave them time to come up with a cover story to negate the forensic recovery. Where denials were made it was always important to get them to confirm that they had never been anywhere near the crime scene and fingerprints from the same hand on both sides of a piece of broken glass were the 'icing on the cake'.

I briefed eighteen officers from Willenhall CID, and the Divisional Crime Support Unit, and at 7am six arrests were made – two aged sixteen years, and the others aged twenty three, twenty one, twenty, and seventeen years, at a number of addresses in Willenhall and Bloxwich. Nobody put up any resistance and they spent the day being interviewed about a number of burglaries.

On Tuesday 2 November 1993, I was out again at 5.15am for a briefing at Walsall Police Station for 'Operation TOM', part of a force-wide initiative aimed at arresting people involved in MOT fraud. Fifty CID officers from across the borough, supported by another fifty traffic officers, and members of the Operations Support Unit, made twenty five arrests in the Walsall area, and the offenders were lodged in the cells at Willenhall, Walsall, and Darlaston.

A number of them were later charged and bailed to a special court sitting at Aldridge Magistrates Court in November. A number of forged MOT certificates and excise licences were recovered as we searched for printing equipment. Across the force as a whole five hundred officers made one hundred and ten arrests, with almost the same number still to be arrested and further forged documents were recovered.

On Thursday 11 November 1993 I was committed with an aggravated burglary and dealing with an informant.

Four men, wearing masks, went to an address in Rutherford Road, on the Beechdale Estate in Bloxwich. They were armed with pick-axe handles, and proceeded to smash up a car valued at £4,000, as well as ripping up the fence at the home of fifty-three-year-old Derek Field. Whilst he was terrified, he escaped uninjured as up to a dozen people became involved in the disturbance, which was said to have been part of a long running dispute. With additional help from the Operational Support Unit five arrests were made and we needed help to try to unravel what was behind the attack.

I was out again at 6am on Tuesday 16 November 1993 when we went out for more suspects. As usual the Express and Star reporter rang me before 10am. The headline on the front page in the edition on that date read,

'Six Quizzed about Raids after Swoop' - Six men were arrested today when police investigating a series of burglaries mounted a dawn swoop on homes across Walsall. Nearly thirty officers were involved in the raids on five separate homes at 7am.

Detective Chief Inspector Mike Layton said the operation followed break-ins in Willenhall and Bloxwich. Detectives are also questioning one of the arrested men about an alleged arson threat on an elderly woman's home. Detectives and uniformed officers joined the divisional crime support unit to carry out the swoops. Arrests were made at four of the addresses. All six men being questioned are being held at Willenhall Police Station. Some were expecting to be bailed pending further enquiries and others to be charged later today.

Mr Layton said two men aged 21 and 22 were arrested in

connection with a series of burglaries in Willenhall Town Centre. A 17 year-old youth and a 21 year-old man were being questioned about several raids on factories in the Bloxwich area. A 23 year-old man was being quizzed over an alleged theft from a van and a 23 year-old man had been arrested in Bloxwich for allegedly threatening to damage a woman's house by fire. Mr Layton said police are still searching for three men who were not found during the operation.'

On Wednesday 24 November 1993 a lock-up unit in Woodall Street, Bloxwich, was searched and thousands of parts stripped from about thirty vehicles were recovered with a value in excess of £100,000. There were twenty complete dashboards, of which eighteen were believed to be from Metro cars stolen in the Walsall, Willenhall and Bloxwich areas, over a period of twelve months.

In one case the owner of a car stolen just three days earlier, was able to identify just the dashboard of his vehicle due to the fact that there were sweet papers in the ashtray which the owner's wife always folded in a distinctive way. A twenty- five-year-old man from Wednesbury was arrested.

On Monday 6 December 1993, at midday, eleven officers from Willenhall CID, and the Divisional Crime Unit, executed a drugs warrant at a house on the Mossley Estate in Bloxwich. Cannabis and amphetamine valued at £150 was recovered together with drugs paraphernalia. Three people aged seventeen years, twenty two years, and twenty eight years were arrested on suspicion of supplying controlled drugs.

Many of those we arrested were 'lifestyle criminals' who had known no other way of life and a number of them were driven by drugs dependency.

More burglary prisoners came Tuesday the 7 December 1993 as I started to get the staff into some sort of 'battle rhythm' and getting out of bed at 4am became a more familiar, if not very popular, feature of the officer's lives.

On that date we made eight arrests in total, during raids which took place between 7am and 9am, and involved sixteen officers. We also recovered hundreds of pounds worth of stolen property in relation to offences committed in the Willenhall and Bloxwich areas, including a quantity of biscuits stolen in a burglary on a Bloxwich shop.

A seventeen-year-old youth was questioned in relation to a burglary at Willenhall Comprehensive School, whilst a fifteen-year-old was arrested over an attack on a vehicle in the school grounds. Three youths aged fourteen-years, sixteen- years, and seventeen-years were detained in relation to burglaries on local factories, and an eighteen-year-old was arrested after failing to appear in a North Wales Court on a theft charge. Two other men aged nineteen-years, and twenty-years, were arrested over cheque frauds.

The cells at Willenhall Police Station were full for the day and I was happy.

In the build up to Christmas we did another coordinated sweep for burglary suspects on Friday 17 December 1993, in the Bloxwich area, and dealt with an allegation of rape. The local criminals were starting to feel our presence, as we made life uncomfortable, and at the same time increased the flow of newly recruited informants.

On Thursday 23 December 1993, at 11am,I attended a serious robbery in Fryers Road, Bloxwich, which kept me occupied for most of the day. A sixty-three- year-old female employee, from Genex Engineering, had gone in her car to collect the Christmas wages, which were in a briefcase. She had just returned to the factory when two men jumped out of a car and pulled her out of the driver's seat. There was a struggle during which she fell to the ground and the briefcase containing £17,000 was taken from her.

The victim, who suffered minor cuts to her head and back, was treated at the scene by ambulance men, and was extremely shaken by the incident. A total of four offenders made off in a brown Ford Sierra Estate car which had been hired, using stolen documents, from a car hire firm in Brownhills. They were actually about to return it after the robbery when they spotted a police car parked outside the premises and made off, eventually abandoning the vehicle in Ramsey Road, on the Beechdale Estate.

***

Ivan Kelsey started working as a civilian Enquiry Office Assistant in April of the previous year, at Willenhall Police Station, and recalls a Christmas story which to the best of his recollection took place in the early hours of Christmas Eve, 24 December 1993, *"Mark Buck was quite a sensitive, thoughtful, and effective police officer. He was also quite short, having taken advantage of the recent lowering of the height needed to become a police officer and many of his long-*

established team-mates towered above him.

'Bucko' as he was called, was often on the receiving end of so called police humour, and sometimes found himself getting a telling off from the unit inspector for things that weren't really his fault. The inspector was a mountain of a man, his shoulders were huge, his hands like pint-jugs, he was six foot six tall with jet black swept back hair, but despite his size, he was softly spoken. No-one dared to argue with him.

Bucko had the radio call-sign 'Mike 32' and I would often listen to him on the radio whilst I was in the front office, as he dashed from job to job. During these periods I would find myself with arms full of print-outs from the teleprinter machine.

The teleprinter was the latest technology, recently replacing the 'tikka tape' machine, which was just a line of punched holes. The sad thing was that most of the messages were of no use to our command unit.

Strathclyde Police loved the technology and diligently sent messages about every car stolen in Scotland, just in case in they should happen to travel hundreds of miles to pass through Willenhall!

The big chance for Bucko's fortunes to change came on Christmas Eve morning. We were again on nights, and the weather had set in cold and snowy.

Willenhall looked serene and hushed under a blanket of about six inches of snow that had been falling steadily, since about four in the afternoon of the previous day.

The officers had been in 'firefighting' mode, meaning that they only went out to dire emergencies. The town had been less busy than you would normally expect in the evening before, due to the snow, and once midnight had passed, and the pubs emptied, it fell into a beautiful silence.

Christmas Eve was a big day for the local butchers and up in Bloxwich it was no exception. They had worked into the early hours cutting up meat and preparing turkeys for the rush to stock up on fresh meat that would ensue. They would finish their work around 2am and return to their shops around 5am to start the last push.

It was in that small time period that local Bloxwich criminals had planned their move. About 3am a call came into the front office, "Mate, there's some blokes breaking into the butchers over the road".

Taking the note to the control room behind the front office I was not sure if the officers would go out, given how deep the snow had become, but by now they were bored with playing gin rummy and pontoon, and eagerly accepted the challenge to get to Bloxwich before the offenders got away.

With a sudden burst of blue lights and sirens, the "Zulu" fast response car and two pandas set off, as did Mark Buck, from the much closer police station at Bloxwich.

I listened into the radio transmissions whilst checking the bail signing book. On arrival the front door was open; and a trail of blood from the fresh meat indicated that the offenders had stolen a good quantity, and made good their escape. There was nothing more that could be achieved and Bucko was assigned to stay at the shop until the owner turned up in a couple of hours, whilst the other officers returned to the station to get a warming cup of tea as it was now well below freezing.

Bucko believed more could be done so he secured the shop door as best as he could and set about following the foot-prints in the snow. After a few yards other purple tracks made it hard to see which were the offenders, except for the odd spot of blood dripping from the meat. At the bottom of the street however the trail turned to the curb and stopped.

It was apparent that the offenders had got into a car and Bucko made his way to Harrison Street, where there were fresh tyre tracks in the snow down the middle of the road. He could see a light on in a house near the end of Chantry Avenue, there was a car outside with very little snow on it, and when he got to it the bonnet was clear of snow and still slightly warm. Small drops of blood led up to the door.

Bucko passed his findings on to the radio controller but instead of receiving praise he got told off for leaving the butchers shop unattended and was ordered to return to it immediately.

Despite this Bucko could not resist the temptation to sneak down an alleyway which would bring him to the rear of the suspect's house. Stealthily and slowly he opened the rear gate, a dog barked in the distance. Bucko could see a light and a crack in the curtains. He slowly walked to the window through the virgin snow. Looking

---

inside he could see a table piled high with meat; he could see the hands of the offenders clutching tins of lager, four of them.

The radio in Willenhall front office crackled into life, this time in a whisper. "Mike32 I have got four offenders and the stolen meat in sight". This time the reaction was very different, I could hear the chairs in the parade room scrape across the floor as officers got to their feet and dashed out of the station.

The four men were arrested and brought into custody at Willenhall police station. The meat was recovered and returned to a very grateful butcher, who had just arrived back at his shop.

Mark Buck never received any formal recognition for his efforts, but he received something he would value much more and that would stay with him forever - the respect and admiration of his fellow officers. Never again was he singled out for rough treatment, and he went on to become a well-respected officer."

***

On Monday 27 December 1993, at 6.40pm, a house was broken into in Field Road, Bloxwich, when a large quantity of electrical goods were stolen. Two hours later a suspect vehicle, a Ford Fiesta, was spotted by uniform officers in Goscote Lane and was chased by two police patrol cars to nearby Severn Road, where the three occupants jumped out and ran off. One police vehicle was damaged when it swerved to avoid hitting one suspect, and hit another vehicle.

All three aged seventeen years, twenty-three-years, and thirty-years, were eventually detained and property from the burglary found in the vehicle. One of the prisoners became violent when being transported to the police station, and smashed the passenger window of a second vehicle. They were detained in police cells overnight and I oversaw the investigation the next day. It was a really good piece of work by the uniform officers and we had some great 'thief takers' on the sub division, whose local knowledge was second to none.

On Wednesday 29 December 1993, at 8.10pm, a man walking his dog raised the alarm, when he heard the sound of glass being smashed, and alerted the resident caretaker at Beechdale Junior and Infants School. A window had been smashed to gain access to a staff room, and adjoining storage area, where a fire had been started.

Thousands of pounds worth of damage to books, school materials and paper was caused as well as plaster falling off the walls. Fire crews spent an hour bringing the blaze under control, which would have been much worse had it not been noticed so quickly.

Five youths, aged between twelve years and fifteen years, and wearing white tops were disturbed by the caretaker's wife, standing in the shadows of the building, and they ran off when challenged. We had experienced a spate of arson attacks on the estate and now with a positive line of enquiry I did a media appeal for the public to come forward with information on the five suspects.

The residents of the Beechdale Estate, like many in the area, were a fairly tightly-knit community with their own sense of identity. I was fairly confident that we would get some names before long.

In her New Year message to the community, at the end of 1993, Chief Superintendent Pat Barnett highlighted the fact that, between January and November 1993, a total of eighty three police officers had been assaulted in the Borough of Walsall.

***

Crime as a whole in the UK in 1993 was big business with property valued at £10,000,000 being stolen on each and every day. In the West Midlands alone there had been more than a hundred per cent increase in the value of property stolen, from £117,000,000 in 1988, to £237,000,000 and less than one third of this property was ever recovered.

***

Walsall was a tough area to police and the dangers that police officers routinely faced were highlighted again just three weeks later in an incident during the early hours of a Monday morning as two finance company agents were trying to repossess a vehicle in Penderel Street, Bloxwich. Four police officers were in attendance, to prevent a breach of the peace, but this did not prevent the disputed owner confronting them. Minutes later the situation deteriorated still further as a sixteen-year-old youth, at the address, appeared in a house doorway, and started firing an air gun at the officers, who were forced to take cover. After a standoff the youth was arrested.

There was just time for one more early morning set of raids on Wednesday the 5 January 1994.

I briefed seventeen uniform and CID officers and just after 7am six arrests were made at addresses in Bloxwich. Two youths aged thirteen, and fourteen years, were detained in relation to the arson attack at Beechdale Junior and Infants School, the previous Wednesday, whilst a seventeen-year old, and a nineteen-year old were detained over a theft from motor vehicle. A twenty-year old was arrested for burglary, and a twenty-three year old was arrested and bailed pending further enquiries into an attack that took place at a Willenhall nightclub on New Year's Eve.

On Friday 7 January 1994 I was tied up with CID, and uniform staff, dealing with a robbery and prisoners.

During the late afternoon three men entered the Cheltenham and Gloucester Building Society, in Bloxwich High Street. They ordered cashiers and customers to lie down on the floor claiming that they had guns. They escaped with £20,000 in cash, and made off in a stolen Montego motorcar which was then abandoned in Parker Street, Bloxwich.

Amazingly the three robbers, all in their twenties, then stopped off at a pub and drank a pint before ordering a taxi.

Just after 5pm, twenty minutes after the robbery, the taxi was flagged down on Wednesfield High Street, by PC Andy Hayburn after details of it were circulated.

The three men tried to make good their escape but PC Hayburn gave chase and arrested one offender, who ran into the arms of other officers coming from the opposite direction.

A second man threatened PC Alan Coleman, an ex-military-police officer, with an axe handle, in a shop where he was also threatening to shoot the shop assistant. PC Coleman duly knocked him out with one punch.

The third suspect was arrested by other officers and all three were taken to Willenhall Police Station.

Speaking to the media I highlighted the fact that at the time of stopping the offenders the officers had no way of knowing whether they were actually armed or not and in the circumstances had acted very bravely.

Simon Evans aged twenty-four years, Mark Wright aged twenty-four years, and Ian Middleton aged twenty-five years, all from Birmingham, were subsequently charged with robbery and stealing a motor vehicle, and the third also with possessing a firearm.

Two of them were residents of the area I used to cover as a detective constable in Ladywood in Birmingham.

When jobs like this happened officers would simply drop their routine enquiries and everyone would get their 'teeth into the job'. It was always nice to be part of a good team effort and in this case the score was '3-0' to the police.

I then had to leave my team in the hands of an Acting DCI who used to like to go to the gym in his lunch-break every day. He was an extremely strong and fit individual as well as being a real gentleman. We could not however have been more different in terms of personalities and I hoped that the progress we had made would not unravel. As it turned out he was a great 'safe pair of hands' and remained true to the spirit of what we were trying to achieve. Years later when he retired he did some work as a 'film extra'.

***

I left school at the age of sixteen years with five GCE '0' level certificates in English Language, English Literature, Economic and Social History, Geography and Physics, and a 'CSE' certificate in Mathematics. It was not a very impressive academic record but the reality was that I hated school and couldn't wait to leave.

During the course of my three years as a police cadet with the British Transport Police they made several efforts to get me to enrol at Mathew Boulton College of Further Education in Birmingham but I 'played fool' and each time missed the enrolment dates.

I was however the top - scoring student in the examinations for my initial training course as a police officer so had shown that I could study if I wanted to, but it was just something that simply did not appeal to me.

I initially passed my sergeants promotion examination very quickly but then sat back for several years before passing the inspectors promotion examination. I had never considered trying to do a degree at university and didn't want anything to get in the way of my love of operational policing.

As soon as my substantive promotion to detective chief inspector had been confirmed however I was nominated to attend a Junior Command Course at the Bramshill Police Staff College, in Hampshire, between the 17 January 1994 and the 4 March 1994.

201

It was a mandatory course to be completed, and as such not something that I could avoid. By the time I actually attended it had been renamed the Leadership Development Programme and I duly became a member of Syndicate L, on course number 1/94, one of six syndicates, which were part of a course attended by seventy - one officers in total.

Putting more detail on Steve's earlier description of Bramshill, the estate in which the college was situated had existed since the days of the Domesday Book, more than nine hundred years previously, when records were first made under orders from the new Norman King, William I. Bramshill Police College was clustered around a 17th century Grade 1 Listed Jacobean mansion, which was built in 1605 by Edward, Lord Zouche of Harringworth, and took twenty years to complete. It was set in three hundred acres of parkland, including three lakes, and inhabited by a rare herd of white fallow deer, rabbits and other forms of wildlife.

It had been used for higher police training in the UK since 1953, until being sold off for development in 2014, and as you drove in though the main entrance you could not fail to be impressed by the stunning views.

For me though the jury was out as to whether the standard of academic delivery would live up to the setting as I had previously attended a short course at the college in 1992 and found it be a 'dire' experience. The library boasted eighty thousand books on the subject of policing in Western Europe, plus three hundred and fifty periodicals and specialist publications. How many I might get to read remained to be seen!

***

We were required to wear uniform for the course, which was quite a unique experience for me, and I lined up for the course photograph with nine other members, and the syndicate director, who was a superintendent from Merseyside on a secondment. The other officers came from Lancashire, the Metropolitan Police, the Royal Ulster Constabulary, Hampshire, Derbyshire, Suffolk, Nottinghamshire, Hertfordshire, and Cambridgeshire.

The syndicate director was a pretty 'laid back' individual, which belied a hard edge, who took his time with everything. He was so relaxed that, despite the fact that there were only twelve of us, it took two days for us to finish doing personal introductions.

It was normal practice for students and instructors to negotiate a 'contract' for the duration of the course which would articulate how we would respond to our study environment. As adults we collectively refused point blank to enter into any formal arrangement but the syndicate director 'took it on the chin' and eventually gave up trying to persuade us.

My other fellow students also turned out to be equally relaxed but with more than a smattering of university degrees amongst them. At least one of them, a very relaxed but extremely bright individual, went on to become an Assistant Chief Constable, even though he was missing from the course for most of the time, whilst yet another became a Head of CID.

It was easy to lose touch with reality in such a 'hallowed' institution but we quickly bonded as a group and determined to get through the process with the minimum effort possible. I was required to produce a *'Record of Achievement'* and an Action Plan, whilst on the course, which was based on eight core competencies. We were also required to use evidence based on several sources of information, including a detailed Career Development Centre extended assessment process carried out on the second day of the course, and which lasted all day.

We started at 10.30am and whilst I was tired from a late night in the bar I listened to *'Tubular Bells'* on a tape before starting just to push any nerves to one side.

We were given some guidance notes, prior to the exercise, which concluded by saying *'Remember the results are only a snapshot of you on one particular day and it is important that you keep it in perspective. Relax as much as you can, be yourself, and if you feel that you have not performed particularly well in an exercise put it behind you and move onto the next. Who knows you may look back on the process and find you actually enjoyed it!'*

Whoever wrote those words must have been 'living on another planet'.

The day included group discussions, numerical and decision-making tests, a letter writing exercise, and a problem solving exercise which required the production of a detailed paper.

As a group we had already pre-determined not to 'do each other's legs' and whilst this was frowned upon by the teaching staff we made sure that everyone got a chance to speak, and got our points across without making it look too orchestrated.

Everything was timed to the minute just to add to the stress of the occasion.

We also had some 360-degree feedback from colleagues and I had seven responses from people who I either worked for, or who worked for me.

One of the anonymous feedback forms had said that, *'I did not always remain tolerant in the face of conflict and difficulty'* but I took that as a bit of a compliment. Yet again in another report I was described as giving the appearance of being somewhat *'laid back'*.

As a result of a media interview exercise it was suggested that I should be put forward after more training as a Force spokesperson. I thought that this was highly amusing as I made no effort to soften my broad Birmingham accent which I took great pride in.

***

I was proud of my origins and when directed to write an 'autobiography' on the course I wrote,

'I was born on the 9 August 1952 in the Lozells area of Birmingham. This is an inner-city area adjacent to Handsworth, which is well known nationally for having its fair share of problems. The address that I first lived at was at the back of 8 Wheeler Street, Lozells, which was in fact a three-storey residence behind an Asian shop. The house had a cellar, and an outside toilet with a rear yard. Grass was a luxury we did not possess and I vividly remember that the only green to be seen there was the colour of the paint on the fence. Bath nights consisted of a tin bath which was usually housed

on a hook in the kitchen and was strategically placed in front of the coal fire in the living room as required. I have always taken the view that 'you are what you are' and I am comfortable with that sentiment.'

I concluded the autobiography by saying, *'I have always felt that autobiographies were something which were completed by people who had either reached, or were reaching the end of their era in either a private or career capacity. I do not feel that I have yet reached that stage and perhaps should finish on the note....to be continued.'*

***

We politely declined to play any 'group' games in class and reviewed our day-to-day progress in the student bar with other syndicate members every night, where I was introduced to malt whiskies and copious bags of crisps. I also nominated myself as a 'welfare representative' for the Course just to show willing.

I was encouraged to keep a personal diary of events for the duration of the course and whilst this was somewhat alien to me I attempted to maintain a record of my feelings as we progressed – it was certainly not a technical document, and as Bramshill was supposed to be the 'icon' of higher police management training, some of my thoughts would not have been appreciated.

***

On Wednesday 19 January 1994, back in Walsall, a drugs raid at a house in Gretton Road, Aldridge resulted in the recovery of cocaine and heroin valued at £4,500 and the discovery of a body. Stephen

Wigley, aged twenty-six-years, was believed to have died from a suspected drugs overdose. He was single and unemployed, and believed to have been visiting friends at the time of the incident. Two persons were arrested and charged with burglary, and drugs offences, and a three month operation to crackdown on drugs dealers was announced.

**

On the course I assisted in arranging three social evenings, to which we invited members of the Senior European Detectives Course, who came from numerous parts of the world. It was great fun and although I have never been a big drinker it did not inhibit me from enjoying the spectacle of 'grown men acting like children' as the evenings wore on. They usually finished with everyone standing on chairs, glass in one hand, and singing songs at the top of our voices as officers from countries like Sweden and Iceland tackled such songs as, *'On Ilkley Moor Bah Tat'*, a traditional Yorkshire song.

**

On Saturday 29 January 1994, I went into the office, on my day off, following an assault on one of my CID officers, just to give some moral support.

There was a continual flow of work coming into the office, and on Monday 31 January 1994, yet another crime was added to the list, as a thirty-five-year-old sales assistant, from Victoria Wine Store, in Bloxwich Road, was attacked and robbed of her handbag, which contained £2,000 in takings. Mrs. Mandy Degville grappled with her attacker, who had long 'dreadlocks', but finally the shoulder strap broke on the bag, and he made good his escape with it, in a car stolen from Birmingham. She felt very bitter that despite her cries for help no-one had come to help her.

***

On Tuesday 8 February 1994 I wrote in my diary, *'Restarted at 2pm and got some work done AM. The role of the middle Manager, command leadership and management delivered by two academics. Well-presented again but a difficult afternoon. The briefing room is very warm and I suspect most people's minds were elsewhere. Charismatic leadership interesting perspective. 9pm Wine Tasting Evening with European detectives course. The equivalent of thirty - four bottles of wine were consumed up to 1.30am. An excellent evening where strangers took several steps towards becoming friends. An impromptu sing-song developed with Chris and Dave B leading events. First-class'.*

***

On the same day a police officer, who was the brother-in-law of one of the officers in my syndicate, was stabbed to death in London. Sergeant Derek Robertson was attacked whilst responding to an armed robbery at a post office in New Addington, South London. A thirty-two-year-old man was subsequently convicted and sentenced to life imprisonment for his murder.

My diary entry for the 9 February 1994 read, *'Half way through the course....At the end I made a note in relation to the murder of the officer and reflected, 'An occasion for sadness but a necessity to move on which is a function of most police officers –*

reality !!'

***

On Monday 14 February 1994 I managed to escape from the course for a day as I had a number of commitments in-force, including an appointment with Phil Thomas, the ACC Crime, to discuss my future once major changes had been completed in the police service.

It was a positive meeting and I expected to remain in the CID on the 'H' Division. All the senior officers were receiving 'one-to-one' interviews and not everyone was coming out of the process feeling good about the outcome so I was thankful for 'small mercies' as I drove back to Bramshill on a very cold evening.

On Tuesday 15 February 1994 I wrote – *'Focused module on counselling. One of the best presentations yet on the Course. 9.15pm Beer Tasting Evening with European course. Drinking analysis 223 cans to begin with. 153 left at 2200hrs, 124 left at 2300hrs, 96 at 0001hrs, and 95 at 0100hrs. (128 drunk). A pleasant evening which developed into a good sing-song. Finished at 0100hrs.'*

I decided to focus on trying to develop my skills in respect of dealing with stress amongst staff, and attended a module on 'counselling skills' which highlighted how much people can feel threatened by change.

More importantly I learnt a lot about dealing with pressure from the RUC colleague in my syndicate who I came to respect greatly for his quiet fortitude in relation to his work in Northern Ireland. I knew that the area that Roger was working in was very active in terms of terrorist activity, but he never made a 'big deal' out of it.

During the course of my studies I learnt that the BBC had issued guidelines, containing no less than eighty-six sub-sections, and one of them covered Northern Ireland.

One part defined the IRA and read *'The Irish Republican Army. It is illegal north and south of the border (and in GB too) originally called 'Provisional IRA' to distinguish it from the official IRA (now defunct), it is acceptable to call them 'The Provisionals' but never the 'Provos' nor 'PIRA'. We should not give 'pet names' to terrorists. Likewise the general section defined the southern part of Ireland as 'The Republic of Ireland' though the 'Irish Republic' was acceptable. Some people call it the 'Irish Free State' or 'Eire'. The former is wrong, the latter is Gaelic and inappropriate and we should not use them. Don't use the 'Twenty Six Counties' for the Irish Republic or the 'Thirty Two Counties' for all of Ireland. They express a political view. Great Britain is not the mainland for Ireland. To say it offends Loyalists and Nationalists north and south of the Irish border all at once'.*

What a complicated environment to work in!

We had a number of outside speakers on the course, some of which were excellent, and thought provoking. One of them was Dr. Carey, the Archbishop of Canterbury, which was good but spoilt by being stage-managed for the production of a video, and a series of annoying questions from the college commandant who made his presence felt.

Social standing and rank was reinforced at every stage

throughout the course and you had to know your place in the 'pecking order.' This was even reinforced for meal times when every course had a particular area to sit and eat in the dining room and the directing staff sat on slightly more splendid tables at the end of the room, a bit like in the *'Harry Potter'* films.

On Wednesday 16 February 1994, in the evening, seven of us had a walk down to the nearby *'Shoulder of Mutton'* pub where we ate £7.50 pence worth of chips between us. That would have been a lot of chips to eat in those days although we burnt a few calories off as we walked along the 'pitch black' roads to get back to the college and just in time for a last drink in the more casual 'students' bar.

On Sunday 20 February 1994 I was back in the office again, but this time to lend some support in relation to an assault involving one of my detective sergeants.

On Wednesday 23 February 1994 I had a free day and made arrangements to meet an old friend by the name of Nigel, who I had previously been on another training course with. He was a constable in the Hampshire Police and at one time had served on the Isle of Wight. He was a really genuine and warm person and we maintained infrequent contact. I met him at nearby Hartley Witney and we had a steak together in a local pub.

He could be quite funny and whilst we caught up on each other's news he spent some time providing me with lurid details about 'specimens and sperm counts' as he described how he and his wife were trying to conceive. It was nice seeing him again but at the end of the day I didn't feel that we had very much left in common any more, except perhaps our love of the job. We had both been very ambitious in the early years but Nigel was content not to progress further, whilst I had always been a 'restless spirit.' I wished him the very best and we went our separate ways. It was to be the last time that we would ever meet.

Later that evening we attended a 'European Evening' with the European Detectives Course who wanted to express their thanks for our efforts. It was a pleasant evening and although I kept off the drink I ate far too much. I did however avoid eating the shark and the goat's testicles that were offered up with much humour from our hosts.

The following day I was notified that I would be moving to a new role in Walsall in due course. By the end of the last week I was starting to wilt and was desperate to get back to work. I had visited the office at weekends, on no less than seven occasions, whilst on the course, so I was up to date with what had been going on.

I had not realised just how many management theory models there were as I grappled with the likes of *'Belbin's Typology of Team Roles'*, *'KAI Adapters and Innovators'*, *'My best team role – a self-perception inventory'*, and the *'Scaling of Life Change'*, which dealt with tests for stress levels.

I did this test myself and scored 99, which was well below the threshold of 150 to 199 that increased your likelihood of illness by 40%. I even learnt the concept of *'mind mapping'* and actually adopted its principles.

In stark contrast we had an outstanding presentation from RUC officers on Thursday 3 March 1994 which thoroughly moved me.

They showed a number of short films that were designed specifically to appeal for support from the public to tackle terrorism. Headed *'Don't Suffer It – Change It – Call 0800 666999 on the Freephone Confidential Hot Line'*, they featured different scenarios.

In one the words were flashed on screen, *'we can stop the Killing, We must stop the Killing, Whose Father, Mother, Brother, Sister, Daughter, Son, Friend, who will be next to pay the price? Call the Confidential Hot Line before the Terrorists Destroy You'* - and all this with the somewhat haunting music of the tune *'Danny Boy'* playing in the background.

In another a scenario was played out, where the wife of a terrorist, who was in prison for murdering a man, accidentally bumped into the wife of his victim in a street. In that moment neither of them knew each other, nor would they ever know that their lives were entwined together, as they smiled and apologised to each other, and went on their way. Both of them had lost the men in their lives, one buried, and one looking through the bars of a prison cell. It displayed brilliantly the futility of terrorism.

In the third the film captured the life of a convicted terrorist who had a young son who he was unable to see grow up whilst he was in prison. On his release he stopped being a terrorist, not realising that his grown-up son had by now followed in his footsteps.

The young boy in the street, that he never had time to play ball with, had grown to be an angry young man with a machine gun. The son that he never really knew properly finished up being killed, and the final shots were of the father attending his funeral, and walking away from the grave, a lonely and broken man.

A pair of black gloves placed on top of the coffin signified his para-military involvement, and all enacted to the tune, *'Cats in the Cradle.'*

The use of powerful music was extremely impactive and literally tugged at the 'heartstrings.'

The music and those powerful messages remained with me throughout my service and I asked 'Roger' the RUC officer in my syndicate to forward me some copies of the videos which he duly did.

***

I determined to get to know the workings of the press and media better, and produced a fourteen-page report as part of my 'Action Learning Phase'. I subsequently visited the Express and Star newspaper head office in Wolverhampton, and this was to stand me in good stead in later service as I came to understand the 'Power of the press' and the 'Power of knowledge.'

In one Birmingham newspaper I had identified that whilst robbery and assault offences accounted for 6% of crimes they occupied 46% of newspaper coverage. In those days the newspaper industry was self-regulating using a Code of Practice enforced by the Press Complaints Commission and covering eighteen ethical aspects.

Little did I know all those years ago how much this issue would become such a problem with the rise of 'hacking.' I learnt all about 'moral panics' that could be created by the press clustering negative issues, and the power of 'opinion formers' within the community.

All in all I had done some learning, although I doubt that I had fully realised that at the time, and I got through the process, relatively unscathed, with a really positive end of course report.

The course finished on Friday 4 March 1994 and my feedback overall was very positive, although not for the first time my lack of formal academic qualifications was raised. I made it clear that I had no intention of doing a degree course and that was the end of the conversation.

I drove out of Bramshill that day having left some very good friends behind but feeling much better than when I drove in - now it was time to get back to doing some police work.

***

On the 14 March 1994 'Roger' wrote to me from Northern Ireland and enclosed the videos I had requested. His letter also referred to the murder of WPC Tracy Ellen Doak, who was murdered by the IRA in 1985, and was a close friend of his wife's, having been police recruits together.

At 9.53am on the 20 May 1985 WPC Doak, aged just twenty-one-years, and three colleagues, were carrying out escort duties, and had just moved off in a police car from the old Customs Post at Killeen, Newry, County Armagh, when a bomb placed in a trailer near the road exploded.

She and her colleagues, Inspector Billy Wilson, Constable Ronnie Baird, and nineteen-year-old Reserve Constable Stephen Rodgers were all fatally injured. The police vehicle, a Cortina, was blown to pieces by a 1,000-pound bomb which was detonated by the IRA by remote control.

Tracy was planning her wedding at the time of her murder, and hundreds turned out for her funeral. Her coffin, carried by six police pall bearers was draped with a 'Union Jack' flag with her police hat placed on top, and the procession moved slowly into a church where a plaque on the wall now commemorates her memory, and the fact that she lost her life in the 'execution of her duty.'

A documentary programme about Tracy's murder was subsequently produced for a Remembrance Day, and featured interviews with her father, her mother, and her sister.

In deeply sad circumstances, her father described receiving compensation to the tune of just £560 for the loss of daughters life, from the Northern Ireland Office, and commented that if he had 'sold an animal at market' he would have received more, and how could such an amount compare to the loss of human life and the loss of a loved one.

Visibly distressed he described how his family's life had changed immeasurably. Despite being advised not to, he insisted on seeing his daughter's body in the mortuary in Newry and was profoundly affected by the experience, despite being a police officer himself.

Surrounded by memories, with even Tracey's clothes still in

a wardrobe, her sister Amanda described how they used to play the piano together, and that her favourite tune was *'Miss you Nights.'*

Showing great dignity her mother described how Tracy had insisted that she was going to have a Chris de Burgh song *'In a Country Churchyard'* played at the start of her wedding, although she had agreed to remove the last verse because it was sad.

In the event this was the music that was played at her funeral procession instead.

I still have Roger's letter, and the video, which twenty years on remains as powerful and thought provoking as it was then. What this programme did remarkably was to transform the anonymity of a few seconds of media headlines, of just one murder of a police officer in Northern Ireland, into a deeply personalised tragedy for those concerned.

Part of his letter referred to mortar attacks by the IRA at Heathrow Airport using similar tactics to those deployed in Northern Ireland. In fact, on the 11 March 1994, for the second time in two days, four mortar rounds were fired at a plane parking area at Terminal 4. Thankfully they failed to explode but maximum disruption was caused as police closed off the area,

Roger also confirmed the fact that the deaths continued 'ad nauseam' and mentioned that a policeman had recently been murdered at the greyhound stadium in North Belfast. In fact on the 10 March 1994, John Haggan, aged thirty-three-years, an RUC officer, was shot dead by the IRA whilst off-duty at the Dunmore Greyhound Stadium off the Antrim Road, in North Belfast. At the time he was with his pregnant wife.

By 1996 the Royal Ulster Constabulary had paid a terrible price with records of almost three hundred police officers murdered in the preceding twenty years.

The last part of 'Rogers' video depicted the work of the 'Disabled Officers Association' which was formed in 1984 and tried to raise money, through charitable events and voluntary subscriptions, to support the needs of eight thousand men and women, some just short of death who had lost limbs, sight, or hearing, in terrorist attacks.

One such charity event was an annual raft race completed in the sea in the small seaside town of Portrush, on the North Antrim Coast.

Whilst most of those entering came from Northern Ireland, there were teams from Scotland, and other parts of the UK, and in the video a West Midlands Police officer, David Withey, called for more mainland support for the event. The event had the support of the then Chief Constable, Sir Hugh Annesley, who promised a warm welcome to participants.

What was so striking was that even in the face of such huge adversity the officers were determined to live their lives in the best way that they could. Even the officer shown being supported into a wheelchair by his wife, having lost both of his legs completely, had a look of sheer determination on his face.

***

My first day back at Willenhall was Monday 21 March 1994, and I was in the office for 7.40am and glad to be involved in operational policing again. In the first week I was tied up with a number of robbery enquiries, and a British National Party event in Bloxwich, which had some limited support amongst local residents.

The BNP were a far-right political party formed as a splinter group from the National Front by John Tyndall in 1982.

On the same day figures announced in the local press revealed that the Walsall Division as a whole had the second highest detection rate in the Force, and that crime overall had dropped by 4% on the previous year.

We had detected thirteen offences of possession of controlled drugs with intent to supply, and cleared up 399 car crimes out of a total of 653. Unfortunately though, there was always another crime around the corner to take the shine off the figures.

On Wednesday 23 March 1994, at 5pm, a robbery occurred at the Staffordshire Building Society in Bloxwich High Street, as a lone robber, wearing a mask, pointed a gun at a female cashier and demanded cash. He got away with £1,500 in cash and then calmly disappeared amongst the shoppers even though the premises were within walking distance of the Police Station.

On Friday 25 March 1994 I went to Lloyd House to view my personal file before the majority of it was computerised. I was allowed to take a lot of the paper content before it was due to be shredded. The documents were part of my life and I wasn't prepared to let them be destroyed. Boxed up, they moved with me for more than twenty years.

On Monday 28 March 1994 we had a visit from the Mayor of Walsall who was shown around by the sub-divisional commander and introduced to staff. It was good for relationship building particularly with local political parties who could be particularly fractious with each other. This behaviour occasionally spilt over into relationships with the police as we tried to steer a middle course between competing influences.

On Friday 1 April 1994 we had a breakthrough on the Fryers Road robbery and I sent officers to Blyth in Northumberland to interview two men from the Walsall area who had been arrested for a similar offence.

A twenty-one year old was later charged, whilst a second man was released on bail pending further enquiries. Locally we made two arrests and charged one person with an offence unrelated to the robbery, and police bailed the second. We had some way to go evidentially but believed that we were 'fishing in the right pool.'

On Monday 4 April 1994 the Walsall edition of the Express and Star carried an all too familiar story, '*A 19 year old man was stabbed nine times in a street fight in Bloxwich. Peter Gunter was in a stable condition in Walsall Manor Hospital today with six stab wounds to his chest and three to his legs. DCI Mike Layton of Willenhall CID said his injuries were not thought to be life threatening and he was recovering in hospital today. He was stabbed after a row broke out in Elmore Green Road at 11.15pm on Saturday. A twenty two year-old Bloxwich man was today helping police with their enquiries.*'

On Saturday 9 April 1994, just to remind us that we were living with the threat of terrorism, the IRA carried out gun attacks on soldiers manning checkpoints in County Fermanagh in Northern Ireland, just minutes after a three-day ceasefire had ended.

On Wednesday 13 April 1994, fourteen officers again raided three houses in the Goscote and Leamore areas of Bloxwich and recovered hundreds of pounds worth of electrical goods, mountain bikes and furniture in another dawn swoop. Five people, including two females were arrested.

On Thursday 14 April 1994 the Express and Star again carried a story that was a reminder of the lengths that local criminals would go to steal,

'A plucky pensioner put two robbers to flight with her walking stick but still had four hundred pounds she had saved for bills stolen from her Bloxwich home. The brave 79 year old rapped one of the thieves on the back. She struck him as he searched her handbag at her home in Drake Close. But both he and another teenager managed to flee from the house in the direction of Bloxwich High Street.

The woman, who does not want to be named, was today praised for her courage. "She is a plucky lady, and it is just a shame that her efforts could not prevent her being robbed", said Detective Chief Inspector Mike Layton.

"This was a very nasty incident involving a woman who is disabled and has to walk with a stick", he added. The youngsters had tricked their way into her home by saying they were council gardeners. One kept her talking while the other searched the house. When the woman saw him kneeling beside her handbag she challenged him and hit him on the back with her stick and they both fled from the house.

Today the victim said the £400 was needed to pay gas, electricity and water bills. "I don't know how I will be able to pay them now," she added. She said that although she had been very frightened she hit the taller of the two teenagers in the hope they would both flee empty handed. "He must have been so hard he didn't feel anything", she said. Police are searching for two white males aged 17 or 18 one of whom had short fair hair and was about 5'5". The other had brown spikey hair and was wearing a blue anorak. The incident happened at 11am on Tuesday morning.'

On the same day three men were arrested, and stolen property, including computers, garage equipment and cars worth £30,000 was recovered following searches of houses in Willenhall, Wednesfield, and Ashmore Park.

The arrests followed burglaries at PDH Industrial Estate in Neachells Lane, and they were all subsequently bailed pending further enquiries.

On Monday 18 April 1994, at about 1pm, uniform officers from Willenhall were called to Frank F Harrison Comprehensive School, in Leamore Lane, when a gang of youths poured across the school grounds, wielding wooden stakes, and attacked two Asian schoolboys.

As two police officers gave chase across playing fields the attackers climbed over a motorway fence onto the hard shoulder of the M6. Motorway Police were called to provide assistance and three arrests were made. At that stage it was not known whether this was a racial attack, but on occasions right-wing activity had surfaced in the area.

On Tuesday 19 April 1994 the newspaper covered a story relating to the recovery of £50,000 worth of stolen property from a house in Birchills. The house was described as an 'Aladdin's Cave' and included the entire contents of a chemists shop, as well as china, pottery, door handles, car parts, camera equipment and antiques. It took a van four trips to carry all of the property away. The raid was led by Detective Sergeant Mick Swinnerton, who sadly is no longer with us. He worked for me at Bloxwich, and his team of seven officers made three arrests that day.

On Wednesday 20 April 1994 a traffic operation was run in the Coalpool area of Walsall. Many of our regular criminals drove around in uninsured, or un- roadworthy cars, and they needed 'wheels' to be able to ferry their ill-gotten gains to 'safe houses' or receivers of stolen property. If we could disrupt them by prosecuting them for road traffic offences we could potentially stop them from committing more serious crimes.

On Tuesday 26 April 1994, eleven teenagers, the youngest of which was only fifteen-years-of-age, were arrested for offences of burglary, attempted burglary, going equipped to steal, and trying to steal from motor vehicles.

Some of the offences had occurred in Walsall, and some in Darlaston, where members of the business community were 'up in arms' about the level of crime in the area. This was the environment we operated in on a daily basis and it was relentless.

***

On Thursday 28 April 1994 I commenced duty at 8am and it was to be the start of a very long and particularly sad day.At 6.20pm I was called to Victoria Street in Willenhall regarding a suspicious death. I finally booked off duty at 11pm but was back for 8am the following day to attend the post mortem and to deal with the media. The enquiry was given the operational name 'Tanfield' and another twelve hour day followed.

The events which unfolded were told in the Walsall edition of the Express and Star on Friday 29 April 1994 as follows.

'The body of a baby boy was found lying next to his unconscious and blood stained mother by relatives who burst into the bathroom of a house in Willenhall. Detectives this afternoon launched a murder enquiry after a post-mortem revealed six month old Christopher Southam had drowned. Police are waiting to speak to his twenty eight year old mother Tracey, who was found last night with "appalling" cuts to her body.

Mrs Southam, who had been receiving treatment for post-natal depression is seriously ill and unconscious in hospital. Officers were called to the terraced house in Victoria Street at 6.10pm by

Mrs Southam's brother Kevin Walker and brother-in- law.

Mrs Southam and Christopher were found lying side by side in the ground floor bathroom by the two family members who broke in through a back window. They battled to save Christopher with instructions on mouth-to-mouth resuscitation from an ambulance service operator but failed to revive him. Mrs Southam, who married her 28 year-old husband Kevin last year, was taken to Walsall's Manor Hospital. She was suffering from "appalling" cuts to her body and was in intensive care today. Her condition was described as 'poorly but stable'.

Detective Chief Inspector Mike Layton said "We are treating this as a murder enquiry. At this stage our enquiry is very localised. It is a tragic situation and our sympathies go out to the family." He said a post mortem was carried out this morning by Dr Ian Rushton, consultant paediatrician and pathologist at the Birmingham Maternity Hospital.

Mr. Layton said that he was satisfied that the cause of death was drowning. A murder squad of eight detectives had been set up and officers were hoping to speak to Mrs Southam when doctors allowed. A next-door neighbour who did not want to be named said, "The family came round last night and broke in through a back window to find Tracey and Christopher. She had been suffering from post-natal depression." Other neighbours in the quiet residential street described the couple who moved in less than twelve months ago as "very pleasant and quiet". One elderly resident living opposite said, "It is a real shock. She looked in a really bad way when they brought her out of the house"...'

A follow up article next day on Saturday 30 April 1994 read, *'A seriously ill Willenhall woman found lying beside her dead baby son was still unconscious and on a life support machine this afternoon. Detectives were at the bedside of Tracey Southam waiting to talk to her about the death......Detective Chief Inspector Mike Layton said, "We are still keeping an open mind. We are continuing our investigations but we are in limbo until we have spoken to Mrs Southam. She is unconscious and on a ventilator. Her family are still very distressed and their priority is to get her well again"...'*

A further article on Monday 6 May 1994 concluded, *'The seriously ill mother of a baby boy found drowned at their Willenhall home may not be well enough to talk to detectives for another week officers said today.......Detective Sergeant Dave Haffenden of Willenhall CID said she had since regained consciousness but was not well enough to talk. "We are in the hands of the doctors and it is unlikely to be this week before we will be able to speak to her"...'.*

As it was during that week that a decision was made to move Mrs Southam to St. Matthews Psychiatric Hospital in Burntwood, Staffordshire, for further treatment. I remained on the enquiry for several days working between Walsall and Willenhall, trying to keep my day job going, whilst fulfilling specific lines of enquiry, which included making enquiries at Walsall Manor Hospital and liaising with medical staff.

On Friday 6 May 1994 I met with HM Coroner in Walsall, and attended the opening of the inquest into the death of six - month old Christopher Southam, at the coroners court, which was adjourned.

**

On Monday 9 May 1994 I commenced an operation code named 'Zandra' and briefed staff at 6.45am the following morning. Local criminals were affecting the quality of life on the Manor Farm Estate and in particular were committing numerous offences of vehicle crime. We set up covert technical equipment with the support of local residents, some of whom showed courage in providing witness statements.

We gave these witnesses 'panic alarm' buttons to give them a greater level of confidence in the police and followed up with an arrest phase using special constables, and local beat officers, during which fifteen arrests were made, and three stolen mobile phones recovered.

On Thursday 12 May 1994 seven of them appeared at Walsall Magistrates Court and were remanded on conditional bail.

Mark Parker, aged twenty-three-years, of Pimbury Road, was charged with stealing a Mercedes motor car, valued at £13,000, and a mobile phone. Lee Perry, aged eighteen-years, of Chaucer Avenue, was charged with theft and receiving stolen property. Paul Wood, aged eighteen-years, of Keats Road, was charged with theft from a car and criminal damage. Peter Saunders, aged twenty-one-years, also of Keats Road, was charged with stealing two car cassettes and a handbag. Lee Bonser, aged eighteen-years, of Howe Crescent, was charged with theft of a car radio, vehicle interference, and going equipped to steal. Shaun Ward, aged twenty-two-years, of Haley Street, was charged with going equipped to steal, stealing a Ford Escort motor vehicle, theft of a radio and receiving stolen goods. A fifteen-year-old was charged with criminal damage, causing a breach of the peace, and driving without a test certificate.

Those that were charged had very proscriptive bail conditions applied and on the 13 May 1994 we followed it up with another traffic operation and executed a number of outstanding warrants. Some of the defendants subsequently received custodial sentences, and when seen in prison admitted numerous further offences.

***

On the same day I was engaged at St Mathews Hospital regarding Operation Tanfield and met with one of the Doctors to discuss Mrs. Southam's progress.

***

On Monday 16 May 1994, at about 4am, the licensee of the *'Brown Jug'* pub in Sandbeds Road, Willenhall, disturbed burglars who had broken into the bar area by smashing a side window. They had loaded up bags with cigarettes, cash and confectionary, but left in a hurry on being confronted. As the licensee gave chase one of the burglars turned and fired what was believed to be a pistol at him. Whilst the use of firearms in such incidents was relatively rare, what was unusual was the fact that having jumped out of bed the licensee was actually completely naked as he ran after them!

***

At 3pm on Wednesday 18 May 1994 I was back at the Manor Hospital for a second post-mortem on Christopher Southam, which this time was conducted by the Pathologist, Dr. Scott. I have been to a number of post mortems throughout my police service and each one is different, but you have to move your mind-set from that of dealing with a person to that of dealing with a body that no longer has a 'spirit'. In order to ensure that you do your very best in terms of an investigation you have to stay absolutely mentally alert and fully focused.

At the Manor Hospital we had the facility of a viewing area, distinct from the area where the actual post-mortem was being carried out, but nevertheless in very close proximity enough to be able to hold a conversation with the pathologist, and to be able to view organs.

Any death is tragic but the death of a child doubly so in my opinion. The forensic examination of a body, however small, is usually critical in providing clues which have to be translated into evidence and that was our job. Time for reflection could, and would, wait. This did not mean that I was not touched by the experience but I had learnt not to take on other people's grief.

I was now focused on establishing the clinically defined medical state of Tracey Southam, and in particular the offence of 'Infanticide', or infant homicide, which involved the intentional killing of a child under the age of twelve months in accordance with the Infanticide Act 1938. Such cases often involved 'extreme emotional disturbance' on the part of the person committing the offence.

***

Also on Wednesday 18 May 1994, in a follow-up to Operation Zandra, my officers joined up with local CID officers to search premises in Pershore Road, Edgbaston. Fifty mobile telephones, which were believed to be stolen, were recovered and two men were arrested and taken to Willenhall for questioning.

At 1am on Friday 20 May 1994, Bloxwich High Street was again the focus of police attention when Inspector Julian Whiting and PC Dave Turner approached a seventeen-year-old youth seen standing in a bus shelter. As they walked towards him he bent down and as he stood up he pointed a black and silver gun at the officers.

Instinctively the inspector grabbed the gun and disarmed the youth, who was arrested and later questioned about a shop burglary on the High Street. At the time the officers had no way of knowing that the pistol was in fact an imitation.

***

On Monday 23 May 1994 I was again at the Coroners Court for the inquest on Christopher Southam, which had previously been adjourned.

***

On Tuesday 24 May 1994 the divisional detective superintendent highlighted the fact that, between February and April, forty seven arrests had been made for drugs offences, and that drugs including LSD, heroin, cocaine, cannabis and ecstasy, valued at £52,000, had been recovered. The operation had been prompted by the death of twenty-six-year-old Stephen Wigley after a suspected drugs overdose at the beginning of February, whilst I was away. A special confidential drugs hotline, which had been set up, had produced more than two hundred calls.

***

On Wednesday 25 May 1994 I was tied up all day with Tracey Southam. In a deliberately low-key operation she was brought from hospital, and processed at Walsall Police Station where she was formally charged with the murder of her son.

She appeared at Walsall Magistrates Court, on the same day, and was remanded on conditional bail until the 20 July 1994, on the proviso that she continued to receive medical treatment at St. Matthews Hospital. I did not let the media know beforehand, as I wanted to avoid the possibility of any press photographers loitering outside the police station or courts.

We had a job to do but there remained a strong sense of sadness throughout the day.

***

On Saturday 28 May 1994, I highlighted in the media the success of the Crimestoppers initiative which had been launched as a Freephone line 0800 555111 just twelve months previously. More than one hundred and twenty five calls had been made resulting in twenty five arrests for robbery, assault, theft and burglary. Whilst rewards were on offer many callers were attracted to the idea of providing information anonymously.

***

On Wednesday 1 June 1994, the funeral of Christopher Southam took place.

I have never forgotten the death of this child, not least of which because of the fact that in reality there were really two victims involved in this incident. Tracey Southam's family remained dignified and supportive to her throughout the following court proceedings and showed incredible strength and fortitude.

At the time of this child's death the mobile telephone company *'O2'* was also running a television advertising campaign which showed a small baby swimming underwater. Whilst clearly this was entirely coincidental every time the advert came on the TV I was reminded of this incident.

Those were my moments for quiet reflection.

***

On Thursday 2 June 1994, I oversaw the investigation into a serious wounding at Dave's Discount Store in The Square, New Invention, Willenhall. The twenty-one- year-old checkout assistant had just served a man to some cigarettes which he had paid for. As the assistant handed him his change however, without warning, his attacker pulled out what was believed to be a craft-knife, hidden in his shirt cuffs, and slashed at the assistant who said, "It just came out of the blue. I have never seen him before... and never had trouble. I didn't see the knife, and I didn't realise I had been cut until he had fled."

He was left with a six-inch wound that needed nineteen stitches and stretched from behind his left ear to his cheek. His attacker was 6' tall of muscular build with distinctive ginger hair and it seemed to be an attack without motive. I have witnessed craft-knife injuries before, which used to be the favourite weapon of football hooligans, and whilst they produce 'paper-cut' type wounds the blades penetrate several layers of the skin causing severe bleeding and intense pain.

On Sunday 5 June 1994 it was my weekend to perform senior CID officer duty cover and I worked all day. I was later recalled to duty in relation to a sudden death which had occurred in Aldridge and the following morning I was back at the Manor Hospital Mortuary for the post-mortem.

On Monday 6 June 1994 I did a press appeal in relation to a large fight which had occurred just after midnight at the Forest Community Centre, in Hawbush Road, Leamore, in Bloxwich. Dozens of wedding guests got caught up in fighting as a mass brawl, involving up to twenty people, spread into the bar of the community centre. One man was treated at the Manor Hospital for bruising after being struck by one of the attackers, some of whom were believed to be 'gate crashers.'

Fifteen officers, and a dog-handler, were needed to restore order and in describing the incident and appealing for witnesses I said "It must have been quite frightening for those who were caught up in it. There was damage as chairs were thrown and windows broken. One of the men ran into the bar pursued by six or seven others who then set upon innocent people. There were children and old people sitting in there sent running for cover. The staff at the premises did their best to control it. Two women bar attendants coped quite admirably and did their best to calm things until the police arrived."

A twenty nine-year-old man was arrested and bailed pending further enquiries.

On the same day the actor Mark McManus, otherwise known as *'Taggart'* in the television detective series, died in hospital at the age of sixty-years from pneumonia. He played the role of a 'hard-nosed' but committed senior CID officer for whom the police service was his life. He must have had brilliant advisors and the character was eminently believable. The police service had its fair share of real 'Taggarts' but few of them became as famous.

Bloxwich High Street was yet again the focus for attention when the staff at the Rose of Bengal Restaurant made an urgent call to the police asking for help with the words, 'Come Quick', at 11.30pm on Thursday 9 June 1994.

The first two officers on the scene Sergeant Steve Ayres and PC Roger Bowness received cuts and bruises as they were assaulted by a group, who had been out on an 'all-day stag do.' Windows were smashed in the pandemonium, which started as a dispute over the bill, and five arrests were made before order was restored.

In those days police officers took such incidents as 'par for the course' and generally gave as good as they got. If an officer shouted for assistance colleagues would drop everything, wherever they were, whether that meant piling into a car from the police station, running on foot to the scene, or putting 'two tones' and lights on to get through traffic in a car. You simply got there as quickly, and as you safely could, and would never leave your colleagues in a violent situation, for one second more than could be avoided.

***

As part of multi-agency efforts aimed at combatting the drugs problems in the Borough, Pelsall community worker, Gail Edwards, appealed to the public to get involved with drug awareness sessions. Having arranged two workshops at a residents association, where not one parent turned up, she urged them to raise their awareness before it was too late. We had already highlighted instances of dealers offering drugs at school gates, and seventeen of the forty-seven people dealt with for drugs possession in the previous weeks had been aged under sixteen-years-of-age. Some of them were as young as fourteen-years, and three of them were actually charged with dealing.

Further workshops were advertised at T.P. Riley, Shelfield, and Manor Farm Schools, and on Monday 13 June 1994 I participated in a drugs initiative event sponsored by the Walsall Education Authority, and gave a talk, this time in one of the packed school halls.

***

On Monday 20 June 1994 Steve Burt was appointed as the new detective inspector at Willenhall and pledged that 'lawless members of society would be dealt with quickly and effectively'. Steve had worked in Walsall five years previously on the CID, and was familiar with the area, so I had no doubt that he would be up and running quite quickly. Whilst he was to work with me at a later date for now we would be 'passing ships' as I prepared to move again.

Now I was ready for the next phase of my time in Walsall.

Figure 19: Willenhall Police Station - 2016

Figure 20: Darlaston Police Station - 2016

Figure 21: Walsall Police Station - 2016

West Midlands Police   **INCIDENT REGISTER**

1. REPORTING OFFICER: EVERY DISCERNING DETECTIVE	PERSONAL NO. 999	2. OFFENCE THEFT (OF XMAS FUNCTION)	

3. STATION REPORTED WALSALL	STATION DEALING WALSALL	CONTACT TEL. NO. 01922 439146.	4. PERSON REPORTING (Title) DC	TIME 0.7.0.0

FORENAME(S) I NEED A

5	TITLE DC'S FORENAME(S) OF DCU	SURNAME DRINK.	DATE 13.12.95

SURNAME

ADDRESS DCU

VICTIM	ADDRESS GREEN LANE, WALSALL POST CODE	GREEN LANE WALSALL POST CODE	YEAR 95 DIV S SUB H O

CRIME NUMBER X X X X

CONTACT TEL. NO. DAY 999	EVENING 999	DAY 999	EVENING 999	GRID REF (CASTLEMAINE)

6. SCENES OF CRIME: INFORMED – YES/NO. VIA. SOCO REGISTER/CONTROLLER/OTHER (specify) ....
PRESERVATION OF SCENE: INSIDE. ITEMS OF SPECIAL INTEREST PRESERVED – YES/NO
OUTSIDE. BROKEN GLASS COLLECTED & PRESERVED – YES/NO. FOOTWEAR IMPRESSIONS COVERED – YES/NO. OTHER (specify)

BEAT   AREA

7. VICTIM: D.O.B. ALL AGES   MALE ✓   FEMALE ✓

WHITE EUROPEAN ✓ DARK EUROPEAN ✓ AFRO-CARIBBEAN ✓ ASIAN ✓ ORIENTAL ✓ ARAB ✓ UNKNOWN ✓

INITIAL

8. INJURY TO VICTIM: FATAL ☐ SERIOUS ✓ SLIGHT ☐ THREATS ☐ NONE ☐

WEAPON _____ FIREARMS _____

CRIME SCREENER ☐
INPUTTER ☐

9. MO BETWEEN TIME 0.9.0.0 DATE 11.12.95 AND TIME 1.4.0.0 DATE 11.12.95

MAIN FILE NO.

LOCATION ALDRIDGE SOCIAL CLUB _____ BUILDING TYPE BAR

KNOWN OFFENDER BELIEVING WORK WAS WHAT
DETECTIVES WERE PAID TO DO, DECIDED
WITHOUT CONSULTATION, TO CANCEL SOCIAL
EVENT CAUSING EXTREME DISTRESS AND FEAR OF
DEHYDRATION BY ALL HARD DRINKING DETECTIVES
IT MATTERS NOT THAT HEAPS OF MONEY WILL BE SAVED

MINUTES

D.C.I. LAYTON
F.R. please
as a matter
of urgency!

MONEY NOT NO HANGOVERS
10. PROPERTY STOLEN £ HANGOVER RECOVERED £ SAVED DAMAGED £ _____
(inc. description)
(a) IDENTIFIABLE ☐ (b) NON-IDENTIFIABLE ✓   NO NEED TO (c) RECOVERED ✓   LIVER. (d) CRIME PROPERTY NO. ☐

a) SEVERAL HEADACHES UPSET STOMACHS.

11.	VICTIM	PLACE	OFFENDER	PRISONER (CHARGED) – REFER WC 201
ALCOHOL RELATED:	☐	☐	☐	PRISONER (47(3)) Yes ☐ Refer WC 200S
DRUGS RELATED	☐	☐	☐	SUSPECT Yes ☐ Refer WC 200S

12. WATCH SCHEME MEMBER: NEIGHBOURHOOD ☐ VEHICLE ☐ OTHER (specify) _____

Figure 22: Crime Report. 'Theft of Xmas Function' – 1995

Chapter Seven

'999'

(Stephen Burrows):

'999 response', is the 'bread and butter' of uniform policing. This is where everyone starts their career as a police officer. Whether they be detectives or chief constables, 'fliers' or 'plodders', it was rare that one didn't return to 'the shift', at some point throughout what was the traditional thirty years' service.

This is the job portrayed on *'The Bill'*, *'Z Cars'*, and more recently, a plethora of 'reality' TV programmes. These follow officers on response duties as they mop up the damage caused by drink, drugs, anti-social behaviour, mental illnesses and vulnerability, inadequate parenting, inadequate education, social disenfranchisement, people who cannot handle their emotions, and any other of the many social-ills and failures that drive criminality, or require a police response.

The 999 response crews are the 'thin blue line' incarnate, often under- resourced, full of probationary officers with under two years' service, working unsociable shifts, and having to deal with everything that is thrown at them. Often they have little time to assess a situation that can have life-threatening implications for themselves or the public involved. At all times they have to act within the law whilst at the same time developing a 'sixth sense' and acting on pure instinct.

In this chapter I have tried to provide some insight into what it's like working 'the shift' whilst acknowledging that I cannot possibly do justice to the huge number, and variety of incidents, that the response crews attend. Personally, I must have attended many hundreds, if not thousands of 'response jobs' and can only give a small 'snapshot' flavour of the variety and differences in 'seriousness' those spanned.

The public's expectations are that a 999 call will result in a police officer appearing within seconds to assist. What is not well understood is that:

- A significant number of 999 calls are trivial or bogus, thus requiring the separation of the 'wheat from the chaff'.

- Other calls, tasks and information are received that have to be assessed and responded to in some way. These hugely outnumber the 999 ones, but often relate to, or result in, serious incidents, and each one has to be assessed on its merits.

- Covering a geographical area twenty-four hours a day, three hundred and sixty five days a year, spreads resources very thinly and requires four 'shifts' of officers. Thus there were, in reality, a relatively small number of officers on a particular shift at any one time – and they would be further depleted by dealing with prisoners, court, the dreaded paperwork, and numerous other tasks that removed them from patrolling the streets. These basic principles will still apply to today's modern policing.

- The demand for 'fast response' policing is impossible to satisfy. Shortage of numbers, the avalanche of calls, especially since the advent of mobile phones, traffic jams, officer numbers and distance all play a part. It was very common for an officer, having booked on duty, to finish up going from job to job throughout a duty shift, often without a break, and then with a requirement to catch up on the paperwork later. Officers do not get paid for the first hour of retention on duty. This used to be half an hour, and was amusingly known as 'The Queen's half hour' because Her Majesty is the 'boss' and police officers are not employees but 'Agents of the Crown'. Having said all this, somehow we coped, albeit not always in a perfect fashion!

***

In a previous chapter I dealt with the impact of death on response duties. Another mainstay is the 'domestic dispute'.The handling of these incidents has changed beyond all recognition over the years as realisation has dawned upon society that the mental and physical abuse of, mainly, but not exclusively, women, often resulting in murder, torture or very serious assault, was and is, widespread.

An understanding of the fact that seemingly minor precursor incidents and support for victims can disrupt the path to these serious outcomes has now resulted in a sophisticated set of guidance and legal powers with the welcome addition of support mechanisms and organisations for victims.

This was not the case in the past. Every shift contained 'domestics' calls, and the sheer volume experienced brought home to every officer the scale of this hidden problem. This was clearly linked with historical male attitudes towards women and how they should be 'controlled' and kept 'in their place'. I can still clearly recall my disbelief as a young officer as I was sent from domestic incident to incident, dispensing advice upon relationship management to people often twice my age and more.

Unless an obvious injury was involved, we were 'discouraged' from getting too involved. Domestic disputes were regarded as 'civil matters' rather than criminal ones warranting police action. I suspect this was also because the 'powers that be' knew that turning over the 'domestics' stone would result in an avalanche of work that would stretch resources, and so it has proved. There must be many thousands of incident logs from the 80s period with the closing line, *'civil matter - both parties advised'*.

Officers were, and are, also extremely wary when attending these incidents. Firstly you are entering the abuser's 'home ground'. They know the layout and where potential weapons are kept. Secondly you became acutely aware that you were the stranger entering a complex situation that may have been evolving for years, with the interplay of control, and institutionalized abuse sometimes well hidden. It was also amazingly common for the victim who called for police assistance to suddenly become totally uncooperative, or even to turn on the officers.

Many cases never made it to court due to the victim refusing to attend, often through a misguided notion that there was still love behind the abuse. Finally, there were often children involved, and victims would remain in an abusive relationship simply to keep the family unit together. All in all it could be an incredibly complex, and dangerous environment to blunder into, wearing a uniform and bearing authority.

I will recount just one incident as an example of how a domestic dispute can escalate into a serious incident:

I was a shift inspector at Harborne Police Station when I was informed that a 'siege situation' had developed in Quinton.

There had been an ongoing marital breakdown with associated abuse, aggravated by drink and drugs issues. There were two children from the relationship, a girl aged eight-years, and a boy aged fourteen months.

A domestic dispute on the evening in question had escalated to the point where the mother had been assaulted, and the house 'smashed up'. She had left the premises without the children, intending to report the assault to the police, however at the police station she had changed her mind and decided not to press charges.

She re-appeared at the station sometime later, stating that on her return to the house around midnight she had discovered that her husband had nailed the front door shut and boarded up the windows. She had eventually persuaded him to let her in via the garage and found the fourteen-month old asleep. When asked as to the whereabouts of the eight-year-old girl, her husband informed her that he had 'thrown her out'.

The mother had enquired with relatives but failed to find the girl. She was now back at the police station stating that her husband was in an 'agitated state' and had made threats to harm himself and the fourteen-month-old boy. She also exhibited bruising consistent with an assault.

She was extremely concerned because the father was drunk,

and a drug abuser, and in her opinion the child's safety was compromised in a number of ways.

Another complicating factor was that father was a known drugs-dealer, violent, and known to keep weapons including a Samurai sword just inside the door, and in the stairwell, just in case hostile drug-dealing rivals came calling with bad intent. She confirmed that he had swords, knives and baseball bats inside the house.

The man was also extremely anti-police and had assaulted officers in the past.

These were the days before negotiators and the lot of the response Inspector was to take charge and resolve situations like this. I was also the custodian of 'Timmy Mallet', a large and much beloved shift sledgehammer used to open things in such situations - this was before the development of specialist door opening equipment and teams.

The mother was ensconced safely at the police station, having agreed to make a statement, and I went with other officers to the address.

I was in no mood for compromise that evening and had already decided that the early rescue of the child was of paramount importance. We had a legal power of forcible entry to save life, and to effect arrest, and I was prepared to use it.

The front door was clearly nailed shut and boarded up, as were the downstairs windows. I remember standing on the front step and shouting a number of times, without getting any response, whilst knocking the door for around five minutes – still no answer.

I then announced loudly that I was going to start demolishing the door if it wasn't answered - still no reply. Having taken these entirely reasonable steps I ordered the PC in charge of 'Timmy' to break the door down. He gave the door a few good thumps and suddenly an upstairs window opened and a head appeared.

I had anticipated invective and defiance, but what I got was innocence personified, as if some benevolent OAP had been aroused from their slumber.

He tried some delaying tactics but I made it clear in no uncertain terms that if he didn't let us in the door was going to be smashed down, and that this wasn't the moment for a discussion.

I think that he could sense that this was only going to end one way and he finally relented and soon the garage door was opened. He appeared as the full picture of innocence and was promptly arrested for assault before he could utter another word. His reply after caution was the oft heard, and often true, "I don't know why you're bothering; she'll only drop it tomorrow".

I uncrossed my fingers and inspected the house. The fourteen-month-old was found upstairs safe and well and the eight-year-old was found at the offender's brother's house, again safe and well. Inside I noted that the door was indeed nailed shut with wooden batons fixed across the inside, there was a large sword in the bedroom, and a screwdriver on the stairs.

Cue a sigh of relief and one 'babby' back with mum. ***

The first chapter dealt with public order in terms of larger scale disorder and riots. There is another dimension to the term however, that occupies much of a response officer's time. This falls into two main categories, fights in pubs and other licensed establishments, and keeping the streets in order, more often required in the city-centre than in the suburbs.

Pub fights were common and it could be quite daunting to approach a 'hostile' pub full of drunks, and glasses, unless mob-handed or 'back-up' was nearby.

One day, early on in my career, I was double-crewed in a vehicle when we were sent to a pub in Acocks Green. It transpired that a barman had been assaulted by means of a bar stool being smashed over his head when he refused to serve a drunk and aggressive customer. It was a nasty assault, certainly bad enough for 'wounding with intent' - a serious offence.

Usually this type of allegation would have been recorded and passed to the CID for investigation, by which time the offender would have sobered up and could be arrested, either first thing in a 'dawn swoop', or by arrangement to attend the station with a solicitor, commonly known as a 'brief' – all much more civilized!

The bad news on this occasion was that the barman knew the offender very well, and where he had gone. The news did not improve as the barman informed us that the offender was celebrating being released from prison that day, together with his family and friends, all of whom had been drinking and were 'lively'. He was also confident that they had moved on to a pub on Warwick Road, Acocks Green which had a reputation for hosting a difficult 'clientele'.

A few checks on the radio quickly revealed that our offender was a violent armed-robber who had just been released from a seven-year sentence - this was getting better and better!

We informed our radio control room that we were attending the named pub to affect the arrest and requested 'back up' to be in the area. This was regarded as one step down from an, 'assistance call'. It meant trouble was likely and an officer dealing with a situation wanted colleagues to know where they were and to be making the area 'just in case'.

'Urgent assistance required' meant that it had 'all gone off at Haydock', and that an officer was in immediate danger of assault, injury or worse. An 'assistance call' mandated that every officer on duty would drop whatever they were doing and make the scene as fast as possible to rescue a colleague in trouble. It was the 'panic button' of its day. To this day, when the public see lots of police cars arriving at an incident it is usually due to an 'assistance call'.

The pub in question was an ugly 60's brick-block building with a large car park at the front. My colleague and I both knew that we were likely to be putting ourselves into a difficult situation but this was one of those moments where duty demanded that we took action so we gritted out teeth and entered the pub. It could not be entertained that the police would not affect an arrest because it might be difficult. The local criminals needed to know that we would enforce the law whatever the situation.

The pub had a single large lounge area in an 'L' shape. There were about fifty people inside. As we entered beer mats started spinning towards us and 'oinking' noises began. It was clear that there would be little or no support from the customers - quite the contrary!

My colleague did in fact know the offender, a local man, then in his thirties. A scan of the room revealed him to be sat in the corner of the 'L', in a large alcove surrounded by around fifteen family and friends.

We had discussed tactics prior to entering, and had decided that speed would be the key. We had a stroke of luck in that the offender stood up as we approached, having no doubt guessed what was coming. I formed the impression that he was about to start 'grandstanding' in front of his associates.

My colleague rattled off the arrest wording in about two seconds flat and we grabbed an arm each, put a restraint hold on and began walking the man out on his tiptoes - cue uproar!

Wife and mother were present. In my experience male drunks and fighters were straightforward and usually fairly easy to deal with, often shaking a hand when sober and released next morning. Not so with the women. First of all they fought dirty, and as a male officer it was awkward trying to restrain them. Worst of all they seemed to have a knack of appealing to all males present to assist them, often by hanging onto an arrested person, pleading their innocence, that they had a 'babby' that needed them, and any other pulls at the heartstrings that might come to mind.

In this case the female opinion present seemed to think that, having been released from a significant sentence, it was entirely appropriate to get drunk, assault people and go on a rampage through the local drinking establishments. We were 'bastards' for intervening in the celebration.

Their excitable pleas thus had the predictable effect of mobilizing the onlookers as we pulled, and pushed, the offender out onto the car park followed by an angry crowd. I think that both of us managed to get off an, 'assistance call' by the time we got outside.

Our pugilistic friend took one look at the police car, and having clearly decided that a swift return to prison was in prospect, he embarked upon a violent struggle. I can remember us falling to the ground, fortunately with me on top, and holding him down, whilst my colleague stood between us and the crowd outside the pub – a crowd who were clearly intent on joining the fray.

I recall looking up from the ground to see a forest of legs and began to anticipate an early hospital appointment.

At that moment, as in all the best movies, the 'cavalry' arrived with a screech of tyres and brakes, in the form of a van load of officers who had turned out from Acocks Green police station to rescue us. These fine fellows included a number whom I had never seen outside an office but who proved surprisingly effective at restoring order, especially as they seemed to know a lot of the potential troublemakers by name – ample proof that local knowledge can be very effective.

Thus, our ex-convict re-entered the justice system on the day of his release and two officers lived to fight another day!

***

Public-order patrol in Birmingham City Centre did consist of disorder in pubs and clubs, but much less so than in the suburbs, probably due to the strict door policies and larger number of doormen, who were called 'bouncers' by everyone in those days.

In 'town' the disorder was on the streets, usually at 'chucking out' time, or in and around the various 'kebab houses' and other fast-food outlets where the revelers felt the need to obtain distinctly unhealthy food fortification for the journey home on the night service bus. Some didn't make it that far as copious amounts of vomit would frequently be evident on pavements as dawn broke.

After a while on the 'F' Division, covering Steelhouse Lane and Digbeth, you could sense when a night was going to be lively; there was a palpable tension in the air. The key to preserving order was to keep the upper-hand by having a low tolerance of any disorderly conduct and being able to get numbers of officers to an incident fast before it spread. Luckily the Division was physically the smallest in the Force and could be traversed quickly, even on foot.

This no-nonsense approach was very effective in keeping the city-centre under control, certainly during the six years I spent there. During that period I heard a number of comments from miscreants indicating that they preferred to drink out in the suburbs or even other counties due to the fact that they could not put a foot wrong without being arrested.

There was almost a respect there, and we got to know a number of regulars who would shake our hands and apologise the morning after their standard evening out of drink, curry or kebab, and a scuffle.

The method we used to maintain order was simple and effective, but these days I doubt would be possible due to the morass of paperwork and prisoner rights surrounding any arrest. Steelhouse Lane police station had an impressive array of cell space because it was actually a wing of the 'Central Lock Up', a Victorian mini-prison where prisoners were held awaiting court. Thus there were a lot more cells than in a usual police station and an 'overflow' capacity if required.

We couldn't afford to have officers removed from the streets for hours dealing with prisoners, so for minor disorder such as pulling flowers out of displays, a regular and annoying event, swearing at, and giving the 'v sign' to passing police, being drunk and incapable or drunk and disorderly, or being abusive and threatening to passers-by, the offender would be properly arrested and put in a cell for the night. The officer could return to the streets whilst the detainee 'slept it off', and in the morning a bleary-eyed, disheveled and rueful offender would often either be given a caution, or a verbal ticking off and released.

This was a 'win-win' solution. We did not lose officers from the streets for hours doing paperwork for court and trouble was prevented from escalating by removing the troublemakers for a night. The arrestee was punished with a night in the cells.

Earlier, I mentioned the night buses. We loved these vehicles.

As if by magic, large congregations of potential trouble would vanish as the bus wound its way off to the suburbs with its cargo of the comatose, drunk, skirmishing or shouting passengers. Our only issue was maintaining order at the ranks of bus stops as the last bus was awaited.

One row of bus stops in particular was a regular trouble spot, namely those outside Rackhams at the top of Corporation Street. This location was blessed with nothing in the way of fast-food establishments or bars, as Rackhams occupied the whole frontage. Large groups of the post-pub crowd would mill about and they often got bored with waiting and enlivened their evening with a spot of disorder to bring a good night out to a satisfying end.

Thus it was that one night I was summonsed to a particularly logistically challenging policing incident at that very location.

A report came in of a burglary at Rackhams, the window had been put in and items stolen from the display. 'Supervision' was requested by the initial officers in attendance.

Upon arrival I noted that the window was shattered and the contents of the display were spread across the pavement. An extremely full bus was parked directly outside the yawning hole in the window.

An officer advised me that whoever had done the burglary was on the bus and that a load of biscuits in tins from the display had been taken.

I boarded the bus, a single-decker, and around forty pairs of bleary eyes stared back at me. Many of the owners of the eyes were holding biscuits, some with them half-eaten and frozen in the act of the next bite. Biscuits and the tins were strewn around the bus. Clearly a case of mass 'munchies' had taken place.

The driver was unable to assist as to the identity of the initial burglars, but he knew that they were on the bus. I addressed the passengers en masse, a large number of whom were clearly finding the whole episode very amusing and were no doubt confident of having strength in numbers.

Like a schoolteacher asking a class to volunteer an offender, or else face class punishment, I asked for the burglars to come forward or for innocent passengers to identify them. There was no response other than further amusement.

I could see that to an alcohol affected group the incident appeared trivial and funny, but actually burglary is a serious offence and a large plate glass window would be expensive to replace.

The amusement began to fade as I explained that eating the stolen biscuits amounted to handling stolen goods and as just about everyone on the bus seemed to have imbibed, I had reasonable suspicion to arrest them all. I offered one more chance to give up the offenders but I knew it was unlikely that anyone was going to come forward in front of the whole group and so it proved.

This was a potential stalemate and I knew that the police could not be seen to lose. There was nothing for it but to arrest the whole bus load, which I duly did and directed the driver to Steelhouse Lane, which he did with obvious enjoyment. I would imagine that being the night bus driver was not the happiest of duties and he seemed to relish his customers getting some 'comeuppance' for once. I can remember him telling his control via radio that the bus had been 'arrested'.

At the police station a reception committee of officers directed the passengers into the cell-block waiting area, whilst the driver was taken off for a witness statement to be obtained.

Luckily, because Steelhouse Lane was the custody block for Birmingham City Centre, it was geared towards handling large numbers of prisoners, especially on Saturday afternoons when shoplifters and football hooligans in large numbers were prone to visit.

Thus, there was a very long and secure corridor where prisoners could be queued, before entering the custody office to give their details and be given their rights prior to being placed in a cell. This was known as being 'placed on the sheet' or custody record, or simply being 'sheeted'. This was the point of no-return for a prisoner. Once 'on the sheet' the arrest had been accepted by the custody officer and a cell was the next port of call whilst enquiries took place.

I once again addressed the queue, which was now looking much less cohesive. The concerns of actually being put in a cell and charged, coupled with a desire to get home, were having an effect.

I offered that anyone who wished to speak to an officer privately would be removed from the queue and that their accounts would be compared to other's. If we identified the offenders they would all be turned into witnesses and released without charge. If no one co-operated, they would all be placed in cells and individually interviewed which would certainly take all night. I also told them somewhat 'tongue in cheek' that we might have to take clothing for examination for glass fragments.

Within minutes people started to relent, and much to my relief, within an hour we had cross-referenced accounts and identified the burglars, who were later charged.

***

On response duties, one truly did not know what would come next. One night, together with a colleague, John Webster, I took 'parade' as we were the patrol sergeants for that tour of duty.

In those days, prior to the advent of centralized custody blocks and control rooms, there were three main sergeant roles on a response shift.

- **Custody Officer**: In charge of the cell-block and responsible for 'sheeting' prisoners, their rights, welfare and managing the custody side of an investigation and charge decision.

Footnote: As an amusing aside I once came on nights as custody officer at Steelhouse Lane on a Saturday – a day notoriously busy for prisoners. I relieved a very harassed sergeant who explained the 'bending' he had received, putting around forty shoplifters on 'the sheet'. He explained that he had managed to clear them all out, leaving me with an empty block. After he had left I decided to check the cell conditions after such a busy day. On reaching the very last cell I found it locked and upon peering through the hatch found a forlorn and sorry looking lad of about fourteen sat on the bed. It transpired that he had been arrested with a large group for shoplifting but due to the overwhelming volume of prisoners had been 'lodged' pending being put on 'the sheet'. Basically he had been forgotten in the earlier chaos. It took a bit of sorting out but fortunately his parents were very understanding and thought his incarceration a good lesson!

- **Sergeant Controller**: The sergeant in charge of the incident logging computer and radio, controlling officer deployments. A very busy role requiring incidents to be assessed and graded, deciding how and who to respond, managing the incidents on control and resulting them.

- **Patrol Sergeant**: Outside supervision of any incident requiring it, and management of shift paperwork and administration. Thus the patrol sergeant and inspector took 'parade'. The name of this ritual event belies its origins. It was once an actual military-style parade whereby the inspector would inspect the ranks drawn to attention in respect of their uniform and general condition. Pocket notebooks would be produced and signed to the effect that they were up to date, a serious business, as these were relied on in court and the notes therein were supposed to be entered as close in time to an actual incident as possible. Officers were routinely asked in the witness box by solicitors as to when they had made their notes up. Another ritual element of parade was the production of 'appointments'. This was still being celebrated into the late 80's at Steelhouse Lane and involved officers on parade holding aloft their truncheon, and handcuffs, to prove that they were properly equipped for patrol. Officers carry so much equipment now that they would need a box each to put it all in.

'Parade' eventually became another name for the briefing session prior to a shift leaving the station on patrol for a tour of duty. It was accompanied by cups of tea, usually made by the newest probationer, sometimes biscuits and cakes and, on early mornings, a symphony of flatulence known as the 'dawn chorus'!

***

On one night shift, (10pm-6pm), I read out observations for a Ford Cortina, which was said to have been involved in armed-robberies at several off-licences that day where a shotgun was seen.

I have always had a good memory for registration numbers and because I had read it out, this particular one stuck in my mind as I left the station to patrol the city- centre, with John, in the plain white non-liveried car we were using.

As we drove along New Street there was a car parked on the double yellow lines outside Pizza Hut, hazard-lights flashing. I immediately noticed, much to my disbelief, that it was the same registration number. We pulled in about fifty yards ahead whilst I double-checked via the radio; it was indeed the same vehicle. We requested more officers. Within minutes, a male appeared from Pizza Hut and got into the driver's seat

Whilst I was doing this the car pulled away past us and made several right turns off New Street, bringing it up alongside Pizza Hut in a side road, Ethel Street, where it was caused to stop by a marked car we had summonsed. We pulled in behind, blocking it in.

We approached the vehicle on foot from behind, as did the other officers from in front. The engine was still running. One officer opened the driver's door and requested the driver to get out and hand him the keys, which he did without complaint, other than a comment in the 'what's the problem' vein. He was then arrested on suspicion of robbery.

Another officer reached into the rear seat and came out holding a double- barreled shotgun wrapped in a plastic bag. Further inspection of the foot-wells revealed empty spirit bottles and socks stuffed with loose change to form makeshift 'coshes'. The driver was drunk and alcohol clearly brought out his better side because he was strangely co-operative. He was handcuffed, searched and a knife was retrieved from his pocket. When asked where his friends were, he replied that there were three of them 'having a pizza', indicating Pizza Hut. He also helpfully described them, including their clothing whilst explaining that he had just 'dropped them off'.

Luckily this had all taken place just out of sight of the restaurant. By now lots of officers were in attendance and we entered Pizza Hut 'mob-handed'. It took but a moment to identify the other three offenders stood at the serving bar all extremely drunk and filling their plates – clearly enjoying their post-robbery pizzas! They surrendered without a fight and were arrested and handcuffed. I subsequently recovered a flick-knife from the pocket of one of them.

They were all taken to 'The Lane', CID came over from the sub-division where the robberies had taken place and we continued our duty tour. The offenders received nine-year sentences and a number of us were proud to be subsequently awarded Chief Constable's Commendations from the Chief Constable, Geoffrey Dear.

The robbers seemed to have successfully robbed the first off-licence, consumed rather too much of the proceeds, and gone on the rampage, drinking as they went. At some stage it must have seemed like a really good idea to finish the evening off with a nice pizza, using the same vehicle containing the shotgun and proceeds of the crimes, and with a final master-stroke, parking on double yellow lines on the busiest street in Birmingham with the hazard-lights flashing. It was a very costly mistake for them.

I gave evidence at Crown Court in this case. Despite the overwhelming prosecution evidence they all pleaded 'not guilty', no doubt because they had 'previous', (convictions), and knew they were 'on a bender', (looking at a good stretch inside). I can remember the look of incredulity on the judge's face as the defence barrister alleged that we had lifted the defendant's fingerprints from the custody block desk and transferred them to the robbed off-licences, a 'fit-up' in other words.

After the jury delivered the 'guilty' verdict he left no one in the courtroom in any doubt as to his views as he castigated the defence for wasting everyone's time, and public money, by concocting this desperate allegation in the face of such overwhelming evidence. It was a satisfying end to the case, and an illustration as to the lengths that a defence team will go to, something I experienced many times in my service.

***

Another mainstay of response in the city-centre was the defusing of 'bombs'.

Memories of IRA bombings, especially the terrible events of November 1974, were, and still are, seared into the collective memory of 'Brummies'.

Every shop and office building had its evacuation plan, and 'suspect packages' were frequently reported. It was a regular occurrence, unfortunately exacerbated by the forgetfulness of citizens in respect of their belongings. Thus it was 'meat and drink' for response officers to attend and assess such packages.

Officers were well-trained in how to handle genuine bomb incidents, including evacuation, the setting up of cordons, and the summoning of army bomb-disposal units. A black sphere with a smoking fuse would have been simple to assess, but it was never that easy.

Officers were very aware of the disruption and economic loss a bomb-scare caused, with roads closed and hundreds of people milling about – a combination of evicted office workers waiting to be reunited with their belongings and 'gawkers' with nothing better to do. The poor response officer in the city-centre soon became 'trained' in 'bomb disposal'.

This took the form of assessing the 'package' and taking a personal gamble if it appeared innocuous in form and circumstance. I, along with all the officers on city-centre response have defused numerous Christmas presents and forgotten briefcases by such means as poking them with a truncheon, gingerly unwrapping them or booting them up the street whilst retreating in the opposite direction. We never lost anyone, and the fact that I am writing this is a testimony to my own 100% success rate!

However, in the late 80's there was an Animal Liberation Front campaign in the city-centre involving the placing of genuine incendiary devices in various stores.

These took the form of cigarette-box sized devices containing a time-fuse and combustible material. They would be secreted in flammable material on a store shelf with the intention of causing an overnight conflagration.

They were actually very crude devices, and not very effective, but the publicity for the *'ALF'* was however extensive. We got very used to attending incidents and became quite conversant with the power – or lack of it, of the devices.

One day I was called to Rackhams where an 'unexploded' device had been discovered on a shelf. It was the usual size and I was not too worried about it. It was gingerly manipulated into a fire-bucket containing sand, and carried it out to the rear loading bay near to St Philips Churchyard.

We taped the pedestrian walkway off and I remained awaiting the arrival of a bomb-disposal team who had been summoned by Control and were en route.

Having by now become skilled in 'defusing', I waited with increasing boredom to see how the experts would handle the real thing. Eventually they arrived, donned their protective equipment, approached the bucket and peered inside. I wondered whether a robot would be employed, or perhaps a controlled explosion.

Imagine my disappointment when one of the team appeared with a second bucket, full of water, picked the device up and dropped it in. Job done! - I clearly had a lot to learn about bombs....

***

My next tale of response actually involves 'event policing'. As with 'public order mobilisation', the shift was the first port of call for resources to police any city-centre event including marches, parades, demonstrations and even the 'Birmingham Super Prix'.

So it was that I found myself as sergeant on nights policing the Olympic Committee Conference, held at the then new International Conference Centre, (ICC), in Broad Street. The meetings took place in the ICC and the delegates, who included Princess Anne, resided in the Hyatt hotel opposite. A secure and sterile site around both locations was established and security was enhanced by virtue of the bridge link joining the two buildings.

The Olympic Committee was deciding where the next Winter Olympics were to be held and the hopeful cities had arrived bearing many gifts, as is the way with such jamborees. Exhibition displays were set up and no doubt much 'glad-handing' and false bonhomie was in evidence during daylight hours.

We were under the command of the able and pleasant Inspector Richard Hockaday, an unusual surname that was somewhat amended to reflect later events. As we were the night security cover we had little contact with the delegates, or exhibitors, other than for an hour or so as they were packing their stands up in mid- evening. In fact, for most of the time we roamed through the vast, soulless spaces of the ICC like a band of uniformed vampires seeking prey.

Most of the officers were actually seeking souvenirs, and there was a vast supply of 'freebies' on offer from the exhibitors, ranging from tat such as key-rings through cuddly toys to the pinnacle, the 'star' acquisition, a Stetson hat from the Canadian delegate stand.

These hats were supposed to be gifts for Olympic Committee members only and naturally became the target of 'freebie envy' and the sole mission of one officer, who had a habit of going missing from his post, only to be found cultivating the nice young ladies from Canada. He stoically withstood the resultant 'dressing downs' and eventually emerged triumphant, holding a coveted hat aloft.

We were there for a week, in the dead of night, no other human beings within the security 'bubble' after around 10pm, and boy were we bored. Once all the free gifts had been acquired we resorted to riding up and down in the glass-fronted lift of the Hyatt Regency Hotel but that soon waned as an occupation and people-watching in the hotel did little to relieve the boredom.

After the first two nights, Inspector Hockaday and I discussed the boredom issue and its pernicious effect upon police officers – usually it meant they got into mischief. He was an experienced 'gaffer' and secured the use of a room with a large screen, and a video, so that we could watch films in two-hour shifts whilst the security cordon was preserved by others.

During the boredom a number of 'choc-ice' ice creams that had appeared to be 'on offer' went missing from a freezer in the ICC. It then transpired that these were not 'freebies' after all. It was a genuine miscommunication and the ICC staff were very understanding.

In the tradition of police humour, a 'spoof' crime report subsequently did the rounds for 'theft of choc-ices'. The reporting officer was recorded as 'Inspector Chocsaway', and that nickname stuck for some time afterwards.

***

It was just another quiet Sunday on response but I was about to encounter one of the most serious offences, coupled with the oddest set of circumstances one could imagine.

Rape - just the word evokes a multitude of emotions. It is a heinous crime, having little to do with sex and everything to do with the exercise of power over another. It is the worst kind of assault, apart from murder. Many would say worse than murder in terms of its impact upon the victim, and the consequences for the rest of their life.

The investigation of rape has changed beyond all recognition over the past three decades. There have been countless words of advice and guidance produced by experts of all kinds, many of which have found their way into the procedures of the criminal justice system.

Thus we now have, for example:

- Anonymity of victims.

- Specially trained officers dealing with the initial report.

- Specially trained police surgeons to collect evidence in such a way that the victim does not feel further violated.

- Excellent support services, many of which are run by volunteers, supported by the National Health Service, and which include immediate and appropriate medical and counselling capability.

- Special procedures at court to assist vulnerable victims. The circumstances that follow hail from the 1980s. Despite this, they provide a superb case study of the difficulties in prosecuting rape successfully. This case also provides a clear example of just how far the police have journeyed, especially in the treatment of what must by any standards be classed as a vulnerable complainant. However, this case is also recounted because it provided the most interesting Queen's Counsel advice that I ever saw in my whole service, and one which I remember well to this day.

There is no intent to trivialize this crime in any way, but the circumstances of this particular instance were summed up by the QC in one sentence, *'This is a truly bizarre case which is fraught with difficulties for the Prosecution.'*

It was a quiet Sunday morning on 'earlies', which in those days was a 6am to 2pm shift. I was in charge of a 999 immediate response unit in Birmingham. As an experienced supervisor, I had become attuned to having the radio chattering away in the background on the desk, alive to certain key words or phrases that crashed into one's consciousness. Examples were 'found body', 'need assistance,' and the always concerning, 'I'm about to put the door in Sarge'.

Another one was 'kidnap,' and that was the trigger word that Sunday morning.

A distressed sounding female had dialed 999, claiming that she had been kidnapped and was being held prisoner in a flat. This sort of call on a Sunday morning, following the Saturday night before, was not that unusual in the city, and on the majority of occasions resulted in either no trace, or a downgrading of the original report.

On this occasion my one ear on the radio heard that the panda car attending could see a partially-naked female waving from a balcony of a flat in a tower-block, before disappearing inside and not re-appearing – it was time for me to attend!

By the time I arrived the officers had located the flat on the ninth floor and were in conversation with the female through the locked front door. She informed us that she couldn't get out because her 'captor' had hidden the keys and was fast asleep!

It was the first intimation that this was not going to be a straightforward affair.

As we chatted I did not get the sense that this was the sort of incident that ended in a siege, hostages or violence. She described the man as old, and she did not actually seem afraid of him. She just wanted to leave the flat.

She informed us that he did not seem to have any weapons. He was clearly quite happy to go to sleep and leave her roaming around the flat and onto the balcony. These were not the actions of a determined kidnapper.

Policing is full of decisions that have to be made on minimum information using common sense, experience, and gut feeling and this was one of those moments. These days, thoughts would immediately run to cordoning off the area, evacuating the surrounding flats and calling in trained negotiators, but this was the 80s, and a time when there was room to make a decision without reverting to guidance and procedure. Besides, evacuating a tower-block in these circumstances was not an easy undertaking on a Sunday morning when all I had was about six officers to call upon.

Rather than smash the door down I made a decision and persuaded the female to go and wake the man up and to get him to the door.

A few minutes passed, during which I confess to having my fingers-crossed behind my back, and then a male voice was heard. After a short prevarication, during which I threatened to kick the door in, the sound of keys in the lock was music to my ears.

The door was opened by, to my then young eyes, an ageing man, at first glance looking more likely to be engaging in a round or two of dominoes than kidnapping women and holding them prisoner. Behind him I could see an obviously much younger female.

The first rule in such a situation was to separate the participants and to attempt to sift the truth out of two accounts. I remained with the male who appeared totally bemused by his morning thus far.

After a short while the female officer with the woman reappeared and called me aside. I was then informed that the woman was alleging rape and buggery as well as being held prisoner in the apartment. Once that allegation was made the preservation of forensic evidence and early complaint was the priority action to be taken, hence the female was taken back to Steelhouse Lane Police Station, leaving me to inform a still apparently confused and protesting male that he was under arrest for rape.

The majority of evidence in a rape allegation is found upon the bodies of the parties involved, and it is imperative to get them examined by a Police Surgeon as soon as possible, and to remove and bag up their clothes for later forensic examination.

Hence the male found himself ensconced in a cell whilst the Police Surgeon was summonsed to perform the necessary actions, with examination of the complainant taking first place.

The bedclothes were seized but there could be no dispute that the female was locked in the flat although an examination of the flat revealed no corroborative evidence.

This was already looking like a scenario of one person's word versus another's. In rape cases especially, the prospect of a conviction in these circumstances hinged, and still does to a great deal in fact, upon forensic evidence and the character and credibility of the accuser and accused.

The best possible scenario was for the accused to deny having sex and for forensic evidence to be discovered to destroy such a claim. The worst was a claim of consent that then left a court to decide whom they believed.

The law on rape has changed radically since those days and the giving of consent is now strictly defined, and cannot be assumed, or given, whilst drunk and the word 'no' can be taken as a denial of consent right up to the moment of penetration.

Secondly any sort of penetration, including digital, now constitutes rape, whereas back then it had to be penile penetration of vagina.

Returning to this particular case - the medical examinations took place and the Police Surgeon observed that the accused was 'hung like a donkey', a fact that was to feature prominently later. The Police Surgeon also gave me the bad news - he had found very little forensic evidence.

The complainant was adamant that she had been raped and buggered. There was a full and frank denial on the part of the accused and forensics was not much help.

A decision was made to charge the prisoner with abduction, rape and buggery and to seek legal opinion. Those were the days before the invention of the Crown Prosecution Service and the decision to charge was still in the hands of the Police.

We subsequently received very detailed written advice from

Queens Counsel. These people are the best and most experienced legal minds in the country and yet they were not generally devoid of a sense of humanity or humour.

Initially the QC dealt with the facts relating to the charges and how they stacked up in relation to the events and evidence. It made for very direct reading and got straight to the point in the unique manner in which legal minds see the world.

He confirmed that in his opinion there was no corroborative evidence of either rape, or attempted buggery. He took the view that the injuries to the complainant and her knowledge of the size of the defendant's penis were corroborative evidence of indecent assault, but not of rape or attempted buggery, in the absence of any admissions by the defendant.

With this in mind he added a count of indecent assault, but dropped the count alleging abduction, in view of the difficulty of proving intention to have sexual intercourse. Instead he substituted a count of false imprisonment, since the defendant had at least admitted in interview that he had locked the girl in the flat and hidden the keys.

The QC then went on to outline in some detail the difficulties that the prosecution would face in relation to the complainants circumstances.

He displayed some sympathy for the complainant, who was in a sense a rather sad case. She had sustained a serious head injury at the age of two-years, which had necessitated a brain operation; and she suffered from epilepsy, although this was largely under control.

She was educated at a special school and at the age of twenty-years was involved in a serious road accident which had left her with occasional blackouts and serious memory lapses. On the night in question she had clearly had too much to drink which was not the best basis for reliable testimony.

The QC also highlighted gaps in the chain of evidence in light of her lack of recall:

• How the defendant had got her into his flat on the ninth floor.

• The fact that the flat was on the ninth floor, whereas she thought it was the on the second.

• The fact that she could not remember how she got her injuries.

• That she did not recall how, or when, the defendant had undressed. The QC then highlighted problems with what the victim could remember adding some dry comments of his own:

• She maintained that she had been raped, and that attempts at least were made at buggery, and that the defendant had ejaculated. None of the scientific findings supported this contention.

• She described the defendant as having a huge penis that came half way down his thigh when in a relaxed position. Apparently, the QC observed, this was regarded as 'a rather large dimension' for the male penis. The fit such an organ may have induced in the complainant was a tight one, and indeed she maintained that the intercourse was painful and that she was very sore afterwards for quite a long time. Unfortunately the Police Surgeon, found no evidence of irritation or injury to the vagina, or even the anus, for that matter. Furthermore the victim had made no complaint to him of feeling sore in that area.

- On a brighter note though the QC pointed out that she was able to describe the penis, which, on the defendant's account, would not have been possible since he was at all times at least partially, if not completely dressed. The evidence therefore tended to support an allegation of indecent assault.

The challenge that any jury would have to face would be in trying to digest these facts, whilst at the same time considering the main elements of the victims account. In essence these were that she had met the sixty-year-old man at a nightclub, she had danced with him and let him buy her drinks. She had accompanied him in his car to a party at 3 o'clock in the morning and then driven back with him to his flat.

Apparently she had never called for assistance, or shouted out for help, and went with him to his flat. On the face of it they might not be construed as the actions of a reluctant party.

The QC also reflected on the response by the defendant when questioned as to how he felt when he woke up next morning next to the much younger woman. He maintained that he was still sexually active, but his reaction to this discovery however was simply to get up and make a cup of tea. With true British stoicism he clearly regarded this event 'as a crisis rather than a miracle'.

Returning to the facts of the case, the flaws in the defendant's account are then exposed.

Significantly the QC highlighted three things that went in favour of the prosecution. Firstly how did he sustain the bruise to his arm which was one of the few things the victim remembered doing i.e. striking him on the arm? Secondly, he had no explanation for her knowledge of the size of his penis; and thirdly, he could give no account as to how she had sustained her injuries or got the love bite to her neck.

It is worth stressing that '*throughout the web of the English Criminal Law one golden thread is always to be seen, that it is the duty of the prosecution to prove the prisoner's guilt* subject to the defense of insanity, and subject also to any statutory exception. If, at the end of and on the whole of the case, there is a reasonable doubt, created by the evidence given then the prosecution has not made out the case and the prisoner is entitled to an acquittal. *No matter what the charge or where the trial, the principle that the prosecution must prove the guilt of the prisoner is part of the common law of England and no attempt to whittle it down can be entertained.*'

Taking all the circumstances into account was this a case of an older man exploiting a vulnerable young lady or was she foolish, or willing, and later regretted it? How did someone with her vulnerability end up on her own at a nightclub? Was the defendant completely innocent?

We will never know the truth. All we had was the forensic evidence, such as it was, and two versions of events, a scenario often repeated in all types of investigations. The job of the police is to search for the truth, gather as much evidence as possible, from witnesses, the scene, forensic examinations, the accounts of the parties involved and then present it to the criminal justice system.

The English court process is adversarial, testing the evidence by cross- examination. In a serious case like this, it is up to a jury to decide guilt or innocence.

Having been privy to the facts and legal opinion, you might not be surprised to know that this case never went before a jury.

The defence subsequently offered a guilty plea to the charge of indecent assault; a plea that was accepted and a suspended sentence of imprisonment was handed down.

The unfortunate lady was spared a torrid cross-examination in the witness box, and of course a lot of time and cost was saved for the court officials and jury members.

Was justice served? The real world is not like *'The Bill'*, the truth does not always miraculously come to light, and cases are not solved in half an hour.

We just tried to do our best within the law and the rules – without fear or favour.

Figure 23: Inspector Stephen Burrows - 1992

Figure 24: Steelhouse Lane Police Station - 2016

Figure 25: St Phillips Cathedral, Birmingham - circa 1970's

Figure 26: Rackhams' service entrance & 'bomb disposal' site,
Birmingham - circa 1970's

Figure 27: Cherry St, Birmingham - circa 1970's

Figure 28: Union St, Birmingham - circa 1970's

Figure 29: Victoria Square, Birmingham - circa 1970's

Figure 30: Ramp to Birmingham Shopping Centre - circa 1970's

Figure 31: New Street, Birmingham – circa 1970's, 'armed robber's' vehicle was parked near bus

Figure 32: Commendation certificate, 'armed robbers' – 1987

Chapter Eight

The Sting

(Michael Layton):

On Monday 4 July 1994, I commenced duties as the designated detective chief inspector, (Intelligence), based at Walsall Police Station on the H Division. I was tasked with piloting a force project aimed at creating crime bureaus, and integrated intelligence cells. Given my background it was perhaps a natural move as I once again led a restructuring programme, leading to the selection and recruitment of up to forty staff. I was determined not only to make it work, but also to make some impact.

The three-month pilot was designed to be rolled out across the Force, with Brierley Hill, and Steelhouse Lane stations, being next to take the concept forward.

At Walsall the Crime Bureau was set up with the latest computer technology to cater with dealing with all recorded crime in the borough, which stood at 30,000 crimes per year. The system allowed for searches to be carried out on crimes recorded in the previous five years, which enabled better use of analysis and predicting seasonal trends.

Nine civilian staff, and six police officers, were placed on shifts to provide 24/7 cover, and to take phone calls from victims of crime, on four dedicated help-desk lines, and closer links were created with Victim Support and bodies such the Rape Crisis Centre. Detective Sergeant Roger Freeman, an experienced detective, who knew Walsall well, was one of the original police officers appointed in the Bureau and I was satisfied that he would provide a 'safe pair of hands.'

A further six police officers, and four civilian staff, formed the dedicated intelligence cell, tasked with gathering and analysing information and intelligence on crimes and criminals, and turning it into target packages with a view to increasing detection rates. We were to be the 'engine room' of the division, which would drive activity, and it was described as a major reform in the way we operated. The remaining operational CID would be managed centrally from Walsall and my new role put me in a pivotal position to determine what work they would take on.

The police service was becoming more and more aware of the benefits of technology in intelligence gathering and, during the same month, my old boss John Carrington announced that the regional NCIS office now held the names and details of five hundred major criminals, and seventeen targets of long term interest, on the NCIS database. He also pointed out that in targeting these people over the previous twelve months some fifty arrests had been made, and drugs and stolen property valued at £780,000 recovered.

On Wednesday 6 July 1994 the new structure was tested with the death of Leroy Reid, following a disturbance at 9.30pm in Mount Street, Caldmore. The circumstances of the death were initially unclear but at some point he had fallen to the ground and hit his head on the pavement. He died after emergency brain surgery to remove a blood clot. Initially Glenroy Reid, the twin-brother of the deceased, was charged with his murder, and following an emotional hearing at Walsall Magistrates Court on Friday 8 July 1994, during which at one point he shouted out, "But it was an accident." he was remanded in custody.

Detective Inspector Martyn Thomas continued enquiries and one week later Reid was granted bail whilst enquiries continued as to whether the death had occurred during a 'play fight'. He was however also facing other unrelated charges.

After two separate attacks on elderly and vulnerable victims, on Friday 15 July 1994 I highlighted the dangers of distraction burglaries and associated offences, and gave crime prevention advice in the press the following day.

In the first attack two men posing as Post Office officials tricked their way into the home of an eighty-eight-year-old woman in Bescot Street, Caldmore, and stole £900. Whilst one kept her talking the other made a search of the house and stole the cash.

In the second attack, which took place at 9.30pm, a sixty-six-year-old Sikh man was stopped by five youths, some white, and some black, in Palfrey Park, Walsall. They grabbed him by the wrists and threatened him with a knife. A total of £260 was taken from his wallet but in a struggle to try and remove his watch his wrist was slashed, and he needed three stitches to his injury.

Also on Saturday 16 July 1994, at 7.20pm, in a pre-planned operation, ten plain-clothes and uniformed officers stopped a motorist in Ford Street, Pleck, and subsequently arrested the thirty-seven-year-old driver. A quantity of ecstasy valued at £4,500, together with amphetamines, was recovered in his possession, in the car, and at an address in Walsall. I briefed the press on the outcome of the operation and made it clear that this was just the start of an ongoing effort to combat dealers.

***

On Wednesday 20 July 1994 Tracey Southam appeared at Walsall Magistrates Court at the start of committal proceedings to Crown Court.

***

On the 25 July 1994 I was obliged to return to Bramshill again, for one week, to submit the report on my *'Action Learning Phase',* and to attend a firearms exercise which involved having a working knowledge of two manuals, *'Staying Alive',* and *Staying in Control'.* I also had to submit myself to another six '360 degree' reviews, and deliberately chose some quite strong characters, who had been requested to provide feedback. It was supposed to be a bit of a 'then and now' exercise to see how I had developed as a manager during the intervening period, but didn't reveal anything startling.

On Thursday 28 July 1994 we attended a formal 'Dining in Night' which required dressing up in dinner suits. It was attended by special guests from 'the great and the good' and after formal speeches there was music, and plenty of alcohol consumption, as old friends caught up on each other's news. Needless to say nothing was done next day before we left for home.

***

Violent incidents were becoming depressingly routine with forty-seven instances of knives being used in attacks in the previous seven months alone. At 11pm on Tuesday 2 August 1994, Malcolm Rees, aged twenty-years, was walking in Ablewell Street when he was attacked by two men, who kicked and punched him to the floor. He managed to get to his feet and run off but his assailants chased and caught up with him again. He was kicked in the head, and then one of them produced a knife and stabbed him in the neck causing a two-inch-deep wound, which just missed the jugular vein, and could have had fatal consequences. Two Asian men in their twenties were later arrested and charged with attempted murder.

On Thursday 4 August 1994, a man entered the Bradford and Bingley building Society, in Digbeth, Walsall, armed with a pistol, and threatened three female assistants sat behind a counter with no protective screen. He demanded money and, after initially being handed some, he demanded more, and got away with thousands of pounds. Two years previously the same Branch was robbed by a man who got away with £3,000.

Following early morning raids carried out on Tuesday 9 August 1994 Detective Superintendent John Plimmer commented in the press, *'the burglary and robbery rate in Walsall has been going up and we intend to clamp down on it. Around £25,000 worth of property from people's homes has been stolen in burglaries over the past months and we are questioning these men about them. We want them to leave Walsall alone and this is the first of many operations to crack down on these people'.*

In an operation code named *'Newton',* more than twenty officers arrested fifteen persons, aged between eighteen-years and thirty-years, after executing warrants in Pleck, Darlaston, Bloxwich, and Walsall. Four other officers travelled to Coventry and arrested two men in relation to burglaries in Walsall. This was a follow- up to an earlier arrest-phase under the same operation - little did they know what we were planning.

***

At 12.35pm on the same day, the offence of burglary dwelling house was brought into even sharper focus with the discovery of the body of eighty-four-year-old Second World War veteran Clarence Haddon Cooper, at his semi-detached home in Alexandra Road, Palfrey. He was found after a Walsall Council 'meals on wheels' volunteer failed to get an answer at the house and alerted police.

Clarence Cooper died from asphyxiation after being stabbed twelve times, and had a handkerchief forced so hard into his mouth that his lips were bruised, and his tongue cut. He was found lying in bed, in a front ground-floor room, with his arms above his head, and covered by a quilt. The house had been ransacked, and burglary became an early potential motive after it was discovered that there been a break-in at the house only five days before.

It was a savage and senseless crime, committed against a vulnerable man, who used a walking stick. He had served his country as a bugler with the Staffordshire Regiment but after surviving violent conflict in North Africa and Burma, had died a slow and painful death in his own home.

I was about to go on annual leave two days later, for two weeks, and was not directly involved in the investigation, but many of my officers were seconded onto the murder investigation.

A team of forty-eight officers were involved in various

capacities, which included house-to-house enquiries, and over two hundred witness statements were taken. There were early indications that local youths had targeted Mr. Harper, and harassed him regularly, and there was a clear feeling from investigators that the answers to this crime would not be far from his door.

On Friday 12 August 1994 nine people were detained during raids, in Palfrey and Caldmore, and property believed to be stolen recovered. The nine were interviewed about the murder and outstanding burglaries in the area, as John Plimmer made further appeals for information. Six further arrests followed, with all being released on police bail pending further enquiries.

***

On Wednesday 24 August 1994 Tracey Southam was committed to Crown Court for trial.

***

On the same date four significant arrests were made in relation to the murder of Clarence Cooper, again in the Palfrey and Caldmore areas. They were not amongst those previously arrested and were also suspected of committing burglaries in the area. Detective Inspector Ian Dodd was now taking the lead on the enquiry and provided the press with an upbeat message following the arrests.

On Thursday 25 August 1994 two seventeen-year-olds, and a sixteen-year-old, were charged with the murder. All three lived not far from the victim. Ultimately they were tried at Stafford Crown Court six months later, together with a forty-eight year- old man from Manchester, who was also charged with 'conspiracy to commit burglary'. He was in a 'Fagin' style relationship with the other three accused.

***

During the previous six months, the 'H' Division, which covered the whole of the Borough of Walsall, had seen a slight increase in the rate of recorded crime. This went against force trends generally, which during the same period, had recorded overall decreases. Offences of burglary, and theft of property from vehicles, were giving cause for concern and there had been a drop in detection rates on my old sub- division, which included the Bloxwich area.

Between January and September 1994, there was a 13% increase in house burglaries on the 'H' Division, with a total of 2,758 break-ins, up by 363 offences over the same period in 1993. Each of those crimes represented a victim and often it was not the financial cost which affected them most.

Between January and July 1994 a total of 823 offences of burglary dwelling house were reported on the H2 sub division, of which only 117 offences were detected, which represented a detection rate of just 14.2%. Very little of the stolen property had been recovered.

We knew from intelligence that there were large-scale movements of stolen property going on in the area and having a border with Staffordshire police made it even harder to obtain a full picture. Professional 'receivers' were making a 'killing' and even 'car boot sales' had become magnets for people to get rid of their ill-gotten gains with very little fear of detection. Earlier in the year we had conducted *'Operation Round'*, to address this particular issue, and whilst this had produced some success now was an ideal opportunity to do something different.

***

On Friday 2 September 1994 I had an early morning planning meeting in Birmingham with managers who ran a covert unit, to progress issues relating to *'Operation Portdale'*, and four days later had a similar meeting with NCIS, as I wanted to make use of their facilities and to work in partnership with them in developing intelligence that we hoped to obtain.

The concept of the operation, which was to be the first 'sting' operation of its type outside the Metropolitan Police Force area, was quite simple. We were going to buy property that had already been stolen, from criminals, and in due course identify and arrest the offenders. We already had 'flyers' printed, and cards advertising for TV's, videos, mobile phones, and computers, together with a contact telephone number. Little would the criminals know that the person answering the phone would be one of three undercover police officers, who would be using a van kitted-out with technical equipment to capture all the transactions on video and audio.

A 'sting' operation had previously been defined as *'An independent long term undercover operation being by virtue of the manner in which it is established within the environment to attract members of the criminal classes to provide evidence or intelligence against themselves, or others of their fraternity.'*

250

In May 1994 the Metropolitan Police had completed a similar operation, resulting in the arrest of forty-two persons, and the recovery of stolen property valued at £125,000.

Police in Walthamstow had set up a second-hand shop and found that three- quarters of the property they purchased was stolen.

We had done some research and were satisfied that what we were proposing was legal. In May 1992 there was a stated-case before the Court of Appeal, Criminal Division that we felt that we could rely on.

In the case of *'R v Christou and Another'*, which occurred in 1990, in order to combat a high rate of burglary and robbery in parts of North London, a shop called *'Stardust Jewellers'* was opened in Tottenham, which purported to conduct the business of buying and selling jewellery on a commercial basis. Although unorthodox and novel in the UK it was said that similar operations had been mounted in the United States.

The shop was in fact a police undercover operation and was staffed solely by two undercover officers, using the pseudonyms *'Gary'* and *'Aggi'*, who purported to be shady jewellers willing to buy-in stolen property.

Transactions in the shop were recorded by cameras and sound recording equipment, the object of the operation being to recover stolen property for the owners, and to obtain evidence against those who had either stolen or dishonestly handled it.

Persons selling property were also requested to sign receipts which afforded the opportunity for the police to obtain fingerprints from the paper. Over a three-month period a substantial amount of stolen property was recovered, and some thirty men charged with various offences.

The two appellants were among those charged with burglary and/or handling stolen goods as a result of the operation. At their trial the defence challenged the admissibility of all the evidence resulting from the undercover operation but the trial judge ruled that the evidence was admissible. The appellants then changed their plea to guilty of handling stolen goods and were convicted.

They appealed on the grounds that the judge had wrongly allowed the evidence resulting from the undercover operation to be admitted since they had been tricked into expressly, or impliedly incriminating themselves, and that a caution under paragraph 10.1 of the Code of Practice for the Detention, Treatment and Questioning of Persons by Police Officers ought to have been administered before the undercover police officers engaged in conversations with the appellants.

It was held by Lord Taylor that the evidence obtained by the police, by means of the undercover operation, in which criminals were deceived into thinking that they were dealing with a jeweller willing to trade in stolen property was admissible at the appellants trial, since the police operation had not tricked them into committing an offence they would not otherwise have committed, and questions asked during the course of such dealings were not questions about an offence which required a caution to be administered.

Although the police had engaged in a trick which had produced evidence against the appellants, the trick as such had not been applied to them as they had voluntarily applied themselves to the trick and it had not resulted in unfairness. It followed that the appeals would be dismissed.

Another meeting in Birmingham followed on the 14 September 1994, as we approached the start date of a job that was to prove yet another big test. Authority had been given to run the operation by the Assistant Chief Constable (Crime) Phil Thomas, and the Head of CID, Detective Chief Superintendent Mick Jenkins so yet again we were in the 'spotlight' and with no guarantee of success.

**

At the beginning of October 1994 a spate of robberies commenced involving two West Indian males, using stolen cars, who attacked Asians in the street and stole gold chains from them.

**

From the 4 October 1994 I was responsible for the day to day control and management, of *'Operation Portdale'*, and I was able to gain a great deal of experience in the control of undercover officers, and to use the skills developed on other major Operations such as *'Red Card'*. It was not long before the thieves started to 'take the bait.'

In the early days we did some leaflet drops in four selected 'hot-spot' areas for crime in Mossley, Blakenhall Heath, Beechdale and Bloxwich. We kept a record of where the leaflets were posted but avoided the addresses of known criminals, so as to negate accusations of acting as *'agent provocateurs'* by counselling, inciting, or procuring the commission of a crime. The undercover officers were encouraged to find their own targets as too much information could prove to be dangerous for them.

Their cover stories or 'legends' were designed to show that they were from the Leicestershire area, and exporting goods to Eastern Europe. Therefore they would not have been expected to possess much local knowledge.

On Tuesday 4 October 1994 one of the undercover officers was out on his own, in the Bloxwich area, in the van, when he came across a well-known local criminal who took him back to his house and offered to sell a satellite dish and decoder, and said that he also had a Pioneer stacker system for sale, which had come from a burglary. They arranged to meet again on the following Friday.

***

On Wednesday 5 October 1994 a seventy-year-old pensioner suffered three puncture wounds to her face when she was attacked in her home in Pelsall between 11am and 12.30pm. Her attackers gained access to the house and forced her to go upstairs, where she was tied up. The experience left her in hospital, and feeling very distressed, but the reality was that our 'lifestyle burglars' rarely showed any remorse if caught, no matter what the age of their victims was.

***

On Friday 7 October 1994 the undercover officer purchased the satellite dish, for £30, and viewed the stacker system with a view to purchasing it later. At the time he was able to make a note of the serial number. During the course of a lengthy conversation, all of which was captured on audio, the suspect went on to admit three house burglaries. Enquiries subsequently failed to identify two of the offences, but one of them related to a burglary at a house in Clayhanger in Brownhills at the end of June 1994. The householder had returned home and disturbed three burglars in a vehicle in the process of stealing a microwave. A TV and video recorder had already been taken.

One of the burglars had been detained by the householder, whilst the other two had made good their escape. He had maintained 'the code of silence' and gone 'no comment' when interviewed and subsequently charged. Clearly our man was one of those who had got away.

This was an individual who couldn't stop talking and he went on to describe being involved in the theft of pedal cycles from the Cannock area, and criminal damage in London, whereby he alleged that he had been paid £150 to damage two vehicles.

At about 7.45pm on Friday 7 October 1994, the home of a widower, who lived with his three children, in Keats Road, Bloxwich was locked and secured. The following morning the owner returned home and found that the kitchen door had been forced open, and that two television sets valued at £700 had been stolen. One of the television sets was a twenty-one-inch Tatung colour TV bearing a serial number and with a number of unique identifying features.

On Tuesday 11 October 1994, during the course of purchasing a legitimate television set from a man in Bloxwich, two of the undercover officers were made aware that another man had apparently got two other TV's for sale, which were believed to have been stolen.

The officers were provided with another address in Bloxwich which they duly visited. They were then referred to yet another nearby house, in the same road, where they were shown a Tatung television set in an upstairs bedroom, which bore a serial number. The officers later offered to purchase the TV for £40, and eventually a price of £80 was agreed. In the interim the TV was moved between different addresses and we started to develop a better understanding of their methods. When it came into police possession on the 18 October 1994, the serial number of the TV had been removed, but otherwise was identical in every respect to one of the two stolen in the burglary.

As part of their 'cover story', the undercover officers always tried to get a receipt signed for the cash handed over. Where possible the criminals were encouraged to sit in the front seat of the van, whilst this was completed. Taped to the dashboard in front of this seat was a postcard of a naked woman, which always attracted admiring looks and comments from 'customers'. What they didn't know was that there was a 'pin hole' camera, behind the picture, and as 'M.Jones' signed his receipt we had a nice full-frontal facial picture of him.

***

On Wednesday 12 October 1994 a memorial service was held at St. Mathews Church in Walsall for Clarence Cooper. The circumstances of his death, and his previous military service, had touched many ordinary people in the community.

***

On the morning of Thursday 20 October 1994, a woman who lived in a 7th floor flat in a tower block in Bloxwich, left her home locked and secured.

Less than two hours later three undercover officers were in the Leamore Shopping Precinct, in Bloxwich, where they gave out some of their business cards. Almost immediately they were approached by a youth who asked them if they were interested in buying a video recorder. They were directed to a house some thirty yards away and shown in through the back door, where a female and a young child were also present.

In the kitchenette area they were shown a Goodmans GVR 6000 VHS video recorder. The youth put his own price on the video recorder, which the female undercover officer negotiated down to £60. We were in 'business' so could not afford to make it look too easy for them. I also had a fixed budget to spend and wanted to make the most of it!

The officers completed their purchase and were provided with a black bin- liner bag to take the video recorder away with them.

At 1.30pm the same day, the woman in the tower block returned to her flat to find that the front door had been forced open. A check of the flat revealed that a Goodmans GVR 6000 VHS video recorder, valued at £350, had been stolen. It was identical in every respect to the one purchased by the undercover officers, and on this occasion we had purchased the stolen property before the burglary had even been reported to the police.

Whilst this was good news we had to be careful not to arouse suspicions and because we were dealing with 'closed communities', we held back from getting statements from the victims identifying their property until the last moment, to avoid any loose talk that their property was in the possession of the police.

***

On Thursday 27 October 1994, Tracey Southam appeared at Stafford Crown Court where she pleaded not guilty to the murder of Christopher Southam, but admitted an offence of Infanticide. The pleas were accepted by the prosecution and the Judge Mr. Justice Ian Kennedy. Her husband and parents were present in court for the hearing.

In outlining the circumstances of the case Miss Estelle Hindley QC prosecuting said that Tracey Southam had married her husband the year before, and her pregnancy and birth had been a happy one. Miss Hindley said,

"In the first three months she was determined to be as good a mother as she could possibly be. She was described as being brilliant by her husband. But as the months passed she was described as an 'anxious mother' by her GP and was particularly worried about the baby's crying. As she became depressed her moods began to change, she was not feeding herself properly, and she developed irrational beliefs about her baby, thinking that the baby was rejecting her and crying because he did not love her. This ultimately resulted in her drowning Christopher and making a very

determined attempt on her own life with serious cuts to the body."

Mr. Richard Wakerley QC defending described the case as "truly a tragedy" and in sentencing Tracey Southam to three years' probation, with a provision for continuing psychiatric care, the Judge said, *"Because young life is precious, when something like this happens it has to be monitored by the court and your case is in every sense tragic."*

***

On the evening of Friday 28 October 1994, two of the undercover officers on 'Portdale' were on the car park of a pub in Blakenhall giving out 'flyers' when they were approached by a youth who said that he had a mobile telephone for sale for £40, which he implied was stolen. They were taken to an address nearby where they examined an NEC P3 mobile phone, which they purchased for £35. In this case he kindly signed the receipt using his real name!

We were subsequently able to confirm from the initial airtime provider that it had in fact been reported stolen but because it had been re-chipped, and its memory emptied by a company in Birmingham, known to the police, we were unable to confirm exactly from where it had been taken. We did however come up with a couple of Walsall connections which we would be able to follow up at a later stage.

Also on Friday 28 October 1994, the managing director of a construction company in Cannock secured his premises at about 7pm. The following morning the premises were found to have been broken into by someone smashing a 5' x 4' pane of glass. Property to the value of £25,000 had been stolen, which included two mobile phones, one being a Motorola and the other a Vodak, as well as a camcorder, contractor's equipment, and a number of air guns.

Later that same day, on Saturday 29 October 1994, a target, who was to become a major player in the operation, contacted one of the undercover officers on the dedicated telephone number, and offered to sell him a camcorder. He came from a domiciled 'traveller family' who were well-known in the area. Arrangements were made to meet up with him the following Monday.

At 3.30pm, on Monday 31October 1994, they duly met the target, who initially sold them the two stolen mobile phones for £60. Following a discussion, about a Sony camcorder, the target went to an address and returned to the officer's vehicle with it wrapped in a black bin liner bag, together with its accessories. They were then invited to go back to the address where they met a second person who we later identified. He negotiated a price of £200, and the deal was done with everyone going back to our van to complete business, where the two were duly videoed.

The camcorder in fact contained a tape when sold to the officers. When viewed it was apparent that it contained Christmas scenes, with the family of the managing director, interspersed by overwritten scenes taken by those unlawfully in possession of it. Our luck was holding.

On Tuesday 1 November 1994 a dwelling house in Bloxwich, was broken into and a Toshiba TV set, remote control, and satellite decoder stolen.

Also, on Tuesday 1 November 1994, two of the undercover officers met our 'traveller' target again, during which he indicated that he was in a position to sell counterfeit £20 notes for £8 each. He also implicated himself in the supply of controlled drugs, and gave information regarding the theft of ten camcorders.

From the information given we were able to subsequently confirm that he was referring to a burglary in June 1994, at a shop in Walsall, where the front display window was smashed, and ten camcorders valued at £7,000 were stolen.

He also mentioned about having some chainsaws for sale, and on Thursday 3 November 1994 met the two undercover officers again. This time he was in company with another man, who was a 'prolific burglar', who sold the officers a Kango hammer and transformer for £60. Both items were actually on rental from a plant hire firm in Rushall. There was a further exchange of counterfeit currency and a promise of a further TV for sale.

The burglar went on his way with a promise to meet up later, and the officers were then taken by the traveller to meet his uncle at an address in Bloxwich. He in turn sold the officers two chain saws, for £120, with a promise of more. The undercover officers queried with him as to whether they were in full working-order, and with the side door of the van open, and in full view of the covert camera inside, he spent several minutes turning them on.

Whilst the officers didn't want to give the impression that they would just buy anything it was nevertheless a clear example of the dangers they were prepared to put themselves in, as they stood one foot away from a man with a live chainsaw in his hands. They were promised a 'parcel' for the following week after a discussion about the price of 23-inch television sets which were on offer for £100.

Just to round the day off they were then taken to a further address in Bloxwich where the burglar, and a female, were present. He sold them a Toshiba TV set, remote control and satellite decoder for £100, which in fact was the proceeds of the burglary on the 1st November 1994.

Between the 5 November 1994, and the 7 November 1994, engineering premises in Bloxwich, specialising in lawn mowers, were broken into, and four lawn- mowers valued at £510 were stolen.

On Tuesday 8 November 1994 two of the officers went to meet the uncle again at the address in Bloxwich. On arrival they met yet another man who said that he had been tasked with showing them a 'parcel' that had been arranged. They were then taken to an address in Walsall, where they were introduced to another individual, who was also to become a significant target.

In the rear garden was a grey three-piece suite, which was offered for sale for £200. At the same time they were offered four lawn-mowers, which in fact were the ones that had been stolen from the burglary in Bloxwich. Again the officers queried whether they were in working order, and the response they got was that they 'thought that they had all been repaired', which pointed towards them knowing where they had been stolen from.

The officers then went with this target to some premises in

Darlaston where they were given an ITT television, a remote control, together with two Sanyo speakers and a Sony Hi-Fi system. All of the property was loaded into the van partly assisted by yet another individual.

We had hidden cameras running constantly in the van which covered every angle. In particular the undercover officers always encouraged people to help them to load up so that we could get good video footage of them holding the property. The rear walls of the vehicle were papered with pictures of 'Page Three' models which always attracted attention and meant that we got some good shots as they were scrutinized!

All of the video recorders were dated and timed for evidential purposes.

Each time the circle of criminality was getting bigger and more complex. We had infiltrated a team of professional thieves, burglars and receivers of stolen property, who were talking openly to the undercover officers, almost bragging about their activities.

Eventually the officers negotiated with the uncle by phone and purchased the four lawnmowers, plus the property taken from Darlaston, for a total of £215. They deferred a decision on the three - piece suite.

Further discussions took place at Darlaston regarding the availability of counterfeit clothing, perfume and cigarettes, which were being sold in packs of two hundred. They were shown samples as well as other clothing which were said to be from the proceeds of shoplifting.

They paid the uncle later in the day and he promised to provide a large quantity of televisions and videos, counterfeit one pound coins, and notes, more plant hire equipment, kitchen units and cigarettes. They were told that the suite that they had been offered was gone, but that another was available.

On Wednesday 9 November 1994 the uncle was seen again and this time he offered to sell them another suite for £125 which they purchased. We later identified the suites as having come from a furniture company, operating from an industrial park in Kingswinford. Enquiries revealed that they had suffered from a number of thefts.

He also said that he had six antique bikes, being four *'Penny Farthings'* and two *'Bone Shakers'* which had been taken in North Wales six months previously.

They went to see the Darlaston man again at his home and were shown a 'Penny Farthing' bike and a 'Bone Shaker' in his rear garden shed. The officers deferred the purchase to give us time to discuss tactics, as this would mean spending some serious money. Whilst at the house his wife also got in on the act by showing the officers counterfeit perfumes, aftershaves and Walt Disney videos.

The female undercover officer was able to have a good conversation with the wife when they met up again on Thursday 10 November 1994 at their home. Whilst he was out visiting yet another associate, to collect some counterfeit goods, she gave a detailed account of their counterfeiting activities.

Thirty minutes later he returned with two large boxes from

which the officers purchased counterfeit aftershave, 'Armani' jeans and 'Timberland' sweat shirts, also counterfeit, for £190. Somewhat perversely the target carefully checked the payment notes making reference to the fact that he had been involved extensively in the circulation of counterfeit £20 notes in the Walsall area.

Between 3pm on the 10 November 1994, and 1.30pm on the 11 November 1994, a maroon and white Kawasaki Jet-Ski was stolen from the front garden of a house in Bloxwich, which was valued at £2,000. Although the original crime report made no mention of a trailer being stolen a check with the complainant revealed that one had been taken. Only one had been stolen in the area that year.

***

On Thursday 10 November 1994 I held a meeting with the Crown Prosecution Service to discuss progress on the undercover job, (Operation Portdale). I was extremely pleased with how well things had gone but knew from experience that there was no room for complacency. We held regular monthly meetings and it was critical to have support from the CPS. Martin Denbigh, (Special Case Worker), gave us excellent support throughout.

***

The safety and welfare of the undercover officers remained my absolute priority and whilst there had been no confrontations, as in Operation Red Card, I was acutely aware that things could change quickly. One false move with their cover stories and they would be in danger.

I met them regularly well away from police stations, sometimes in pubs, and sometimes motorway service stations. One of my CID staff was also an experienced undercover officer and I used him in a 'liaison' role to make sure that they felt supported.

It was my job to look after them and I took the responsibility very seriously. We discussed tactics and sometimes disagreed on how to proceed but we had a mutual respect for each other's skills and always managed to find a way forward. On some occasions I put a 'back up' team behind them, using the Divisional Observations Team, who were able to monitor 'one way' transmissions from the undercover officers, who also had an agreed 'password' to indicate if they were in trouble. For the most part however they were operating on their own.

Clearly no-one, other than my team, knew of their activities and if they got into trouble they had been briefed to get away from the scene by all means possible. The undercover police officers knew fully the risks they were taking, and routinely displayed great bravery in their efforts to infiltrate criminal networks. At the same time they were operating under very strict, nationally approved guidelines, and knew that any slip ups might render any evidence they obtained as inadmissible, as well as run the risk of exposure.

Every day that they were deployed I was obliged to remind them of their legal obligations before they went out. At the end of each operational day they had to log, and hand over all of the property recovered, to an exhibits officer prior to it being forensically examined for fingerprints - even the bin liner bags were subjected to a fingerprinting process. Then they had to complete detailed witness statements, and prepare the van and technical equipment for the next day.

By the end of the operation we had more than four hundred exhibits. It was a hard slog and no-one went home until it was finished. We constantly battled with tiredness, and the prospect of long journeys to drive home in the dark, which led to the occasional bad-tempered outburst, but there was no other way to do things, and humour usually brought us back to normal.

The van itself, which was not registered to the police, was flagged of police interest, so that if anyone checked it an officer not connected to the enquiry would be informed. The 'flag' contained specific instructions that the vehicle should not be stopped. Two weeks before the end of the operation the vehicle was actually spotted in suspicious circumstances, by uniformed officers, who submitted a report to the effect that the occupants had been spotted engaged with the occupants of other vehicles, and that property had been seen to be exchanged between them. In the event that the undercover officers were arrested they understood that they would not disclose their identities and would go through custody procedures, until we could get them released without raising suspicions.

It was also important to identify the 'end game', as there had to be a limit as to how long we let our targets carry on committing crimes. Some of them were prolific, and we needed to balance the evidence we had, against the need to get them behind bars. We also only had an initial amount of £5,000 to spend on buying property so it was inevitable that we would eventually run out of funds.

***

Also on Thursday 10 November 1994, an anonymous phone call was received at Walsall Police Station saying that if we went to a particular address in Goscote we would find them selling forged £20 notes. Being unaware of this two of the undercover officers actually visited the address in the afternoon having been made aware that one of the occupants had two mobile phones for sale for £10 each.

The suspect was not at home but five days later they spoke to his sister who told them that the phones had been sold. Outside her home was a vehicle, which was of police interest for a theft from a warehouse in Cannock, in October 1994, where a male and a female with a child had been seen.

Running alongside the team of undercover officers, I was also managing a team of investigators, and intelligence staff, from the NCIS offices, who were busy confirming the identity of target suspects and preparing comprehensive files of evidence.

On Tuesday 15 November 1994 a further meeting took place with the uncle at his home address. The officers were eventually shown two Kango hammers, and a Bosch electric drill, in a case, which were covered by a blanket in the rear of his vehicle. They were then shown a 'Gen-Set' generator attached to the back of a flat back pick-up.

All of the property referred to was subsequently purchased for a total of £380, whereas its true value would have been nearer to £3,000. Whilst concluding their business a second pick-up turned up at the house with two occupants with whom they had done business. A check on this vehicle later revealed that, on the 5 October 1994, a male occupant had been seen to run off from a newsagent in Norton Canes after presenting a forged £20 note.

Again on Tuesday 15 November 1994, two of the undercover officers visited a road in Walsall where they had previously seen a blue Ford Transit van, with a white male occupant, who had allegedly been seen offering IBM computers for sale. They spoke to someone with a disfigured nose, who was known to us, and he referred the officers to a house in the road where they could find the van driver. It wasn't hard to identify this further suspect due to the fact that they were also provided with details of his next court appearance!

On Wednesday 16 November 1994, the officers visited the house and spoke to the suspect, who was another 'lifestyle' burglar. It wasn't long before he was providing them with details of a burglary he intended to commit on Friday 18 November 1994 where he intended to steal a drum kit, and a Panasonic 22 inch television that he offered to sell them.

The officers needed to be very careful in this situation because under no circumstances were they allowed to encourage the commission of a crime by acting as an *'Agent Provocateur'*. This target also revealed that he had recently stolen a Jet Ski and trailer, and sold it for £300.

***

Between 9.30am and 9.35am, on the 16 November 1994, a Vauxhall van belonging to a courier service was broken into whilst unattended in a street in Walsall. Two red plastic crates, containing Midlands

Electricity Board tokens, were stolen.

***

The officers met this particular target again on Thursday 17 November 1994, and he confirmed that he was going to commit a burglary, and would offer them the proceeds on the Saturday. He also talked about purchasing gold from a female with learning difficulties, as well as admitting to placing nails under the tyres of an unoccupied police vehicle, which was parked in a road at the time, with the intention of puncturing them. He disliked police officers and thought that it was highly amusing.

Also on Thursday 17 November 1994, the 'prolific burglar' who had met the officers with our 'traveller' made a phone call, in the morning, to say that he had some electrical goods for sale. The officers met him in the afternoon and he took them to a flat. Inside was an older woman who the officers took to be his mother.

They were taken into a bedroom where they were shown a JVC video recorder, and remote control, a Pye television and remote control, and a Phillips Stereo CD stack music system and remote. He also took out a cuddly toy rabbit from a cupboard and stated that he had previously had one thousand of them.

The property was placed in bin-liner bags, and taken to the officers van, and a total price of £220 agreed. By now he was totally relaxed with the officers and told them that he had left two other TV's at the scene of the burglary from which he had taken the other property. He also admitted breaking into a Tandy's vehicle and removing electrical goods.

That same day a Western traffic officer stop checked a VW Golf motor vehicle in Blakenhall. The vehicle was red in colour and contained three local criminals.

***

Normally the officers took their days off at the weekends but the proposed burglary meant switching things around a little. On Saturday 19 November 1994 they tried to make contact with the target but he fobbed them off although eventually made an arrangement by phone on the Sunday to meet up the following day. This was a pain for the officers because it meant one of them had to have the dedicated phone with them at all times, and to be able to record any phone calls. As the cover story adopted by the officers was that they did not live locally, they tried to avoid pressure to do short notice meets, so that they could get some time off.

On Sunday 20 November 1994 the 'traveller' left a recorded message on the dedicated phone, but by the time the undercover officer returned the call the goods had been sold on - we were not the only people buying and selling in Bloxwich.

On Monday 21 November 1994 they met the target who took them to a house in Walsall where they were introduced to an older couple, who the officers believed to be his parents. In the rear kitchen they were shown a Granada TV, a Hitachi video recorder with a remote, and in the lounge a Logic video recorder. The property was purchased for a total of £170. Whilst in the house they were also offered paint for sale at a cheap price.

That same day the officers met the 'traveller' again on the car park of a pub in Bloxwich, where he handed them a sample of an MEB electric token, with a face value of £1, and indicated that it was part of a large quantity which were available. He left them for fifteen minutes and then returned with a disc cutter which he sold to the officers for £65. On the cutter were details of a hire company. He then invited them to go with him to meet someone who had a mobile for sale.

They went with him to yet another address in Walsall where they met a 'new face' who was yet another regular to the cell blocks in Walsall. He offered a Motorola brick-phone to the officers which they purchased for £10. It transpired that the phone had been stolen in a house burglary in Bloxwich, that very day, where property valued at £800 was stolen. The house where they met was already of interest to us in relation to a female suspected of being involved in counterfeit currency offences.

On Tuesday 22 November 1994 they went back to the 'parents' address in Walsall and were shown eighteen containers of 'Brolac' paint which were for sale. The officers took one tin as a sample, on the pretext of having a potential buyer, and were warned by the targets father not to dispose of it in the Walsall area. It was offered at £7.50 pence per can with an alleged retail price of £30.

The same day the officers were flagged down by the 'traveller' again as they passed the same pub in Bloxwich which he obviously used as his 'headquarters'. He offered them a double video recorder and a camcorder to the future, plus some further MEB tokens. They left the scene but in the afternoon met him again on the pub car park on no less than three occasions with different suspects.

On the first occasion they purchased a Pioneer radio cassette, from an unknown youth, who had it hidden under his jumper, for £30. On the second visit another known youth came out of the pub carrying an Asda bag containing a Grundig Multi CD system which was purchased for £10.Finally, on the third meeting, another known person produced a Goodman's video recorder and remote, contained in a toilet roll bag, which was purchased for £45.

The recorder contained a videotape which on examination showed a television programme recorded the previous evening. Enquiries revealed that on the 22 November 1994, a burglary had occurred in Blakenhall where the Goodmans video recorder, and some jewellery had been stolen. Yet again we had recovered stolen property before the victim had actually discovered the break-in.

As a result of these latest incidents we identified that we had come across a team of three prolific burglars in the area.

On Wednesday 23 November 1994, a house was broken into in Bloxwich, whilst the occupants were out, and a phone and gold chain stolen. That same afternoon the stolen phone was offered for sale by the three targets to the undercover officers, again on the pub car park. One of them boasted about kicking the door in, as they split the £30 that they received between the three of them.

On Thursday 24 November 1994, one of that team of three referenced them into yet another team of three criminals who came from the Coalpool area of Walsall. This team was offering disco equipment for sale, and the officers were taken to the rear of a house where there was a caravan. Inside they were shown a portable TV, a Decca TV and a four-piece Akai stereo system, which were all purchased for a total of £80. It transpired that the property had been stolen from a vehicle in Walsall two days earlier. They were also shown four BMW alloy wheels which were allegedly stolen.

Later that afternoon the officers met the 'traveller' yet again on the pub car park and he took them to another local address where yet another persistent offender surfaced, who produced a blue/grey camera bag containing a Canon camera which was purchased for £70.

That same day a burglary occurred at a house in Bloxwich, and this camera was part of the proceeds.

Inside the house, in one of the bedrooms, they were shown a brown cardboard box containing MEB one pound tokens, and five hundred were purchased for £180.

The 'traveller' also showed them a Mitsubishi video recorder which they purchased for £50, and a gents gold wedding ring which they declined. Later in the day they were offered two large speakers, and further pieces of disco equipment which were in the bedroom of yet another house. They deferred buying it but as a gesture of good-will one of the targets handed to one of the officers a P3 telephone charger and lead at no cost. It had been another long but successful day.

Subsequent enquiries revealed that between 11.30pm on the 23 November 1994, and 8.15am on the 24 November 1994, a vehicle was broken into in the Cannock area of Staffordshire. Reported stolen from the vehicle was a total of £9,000 worth of disco-equipment and a portable telephone battery charger.

At 1.30pm, on the 24 November 1994, two white males were seen to steal four chainsaws with a total value of £1,400, from a local council depot in Blakenhall. They were seen to drive off in a red coloured Golf vehicle. Just prior to that, a similar vehicle was seen at a burglary in Mossley where a red-coloured 14 inch TV was stolen.

***

On the same date the Force announced that the new divisional commander for the 'H' Division would be Chief Superintendent Bob Packham, who would take over from Chief Superintendent Patricia Barnett, the highest ranking female officer in the Force.

Bob was very highly regarded and had just finished overseeing the force internal reorganisation. I didn't know him well at that point but with the activity that we were undertaking it was a good time to establish my credentials with him. He had worked in Walsall before and told the press that he was 'thrilled to be returning to an area that he knew, and was looking forward to making it a better place to live and work in.' As it happened he was in post for just six months before being promoted and moved again.

***

On Saturday 26 November 1994, a target contacted the undercover officers again by telephone and said that he had a mobile phone for sale on behalf of another party. On Monday 28 November 1994, the uncle contacted the officers and they visited him at his home address where they were offered two of the recently stolen chainsaws, plus the TV from the burglary on the same day, and a generator. After the price was agreed at £260 they kindly offered to load up the van and were routinely videoed.

In the afternoon two of the undercover officers visited the married couple with the Darlaston connections, and placed an order for £500 worth of counterfeit currency. A total of ninety five counterfeit £20 notes bearing three different serial numbers were subsequently handed over. During the discussions there were indications that they had recently purchased cannabis and cannabis seeds, whilst in Amsterdam, and that their major source for counterfeiting had suffered a setback with a police raid the previous week in the Aldridge area. We were later able to confirm that this had been carried out by CID officers from Birmingham.

'Uncle' made a further call and it was back to his address yet again where one of the locals sold them eight children's coats stolen from Woolworths. He sat in the vehicle with the officers, looking intently at the nude picture, and proceeded to tell them about a burglary three days before, where he had stolen a freezer and a Raleigh bike from a house. More significantly he went on to describe his involvement in a robbery at a petrol station in Harden, where two persons wearing balaclavas, one of whom was carrying a 6-inch long knife, had stolen cash and an electronic till. He just couldn't stop talking and all of it was recorded covertly on audio.

On Tuesday 29 November 1994, undercover officers visited a road in Walsall which was a well-known area for drugs dealers to operate in. It was within an extremely tight-knit community and extremely difficult for the police to operate effectively in. Whilst there they got into conversation with two men, who were sitting in adjacent jeeps, and were busy placing a herbal substance into twenty to thirty plastic bags, which were in the footwell of one of the vehicles. One of the officers purchased a poly bag containing £10 worth of cannabis bush.

Later that day they purchased another mobile telephone from one of the targets, for £15, and discovered that the disco equipment that they had previously been offered had already been sold on to someone else.

On Wednesday 30 November 1994 two of the officers paid another visit to the uncle's address. In the front garden, under the hedge, were a number of electrical tools, including a Wacker Plate Unit, which was covered with a piece of carpet. The items were purchased for £280. Part of this property was subsequently identified as having been stolen from the South Wales Electricity Board.

Later that day they met the 'traveller' in the usual place, on the pub car park, where he offered to supply £100 worth of cannabis bush to them the following day.

On the same date officers went to Walsall Magistrates Court to apply for search warrants for the home and business addresses of our proposed targets. Each of the warrants had to be individually applied for and scrutinised by the magistrates, and it was a lengthy process. All this had to be done in great secrecy as we were still in the live stage of the undercover operation.

The following day on Thursday 1 December 1994 officers visited the uncle again, at his home in Bloxwich, where they were invited into the lounge and made a purchase of ten pairs of Lacoste shoes for £150. They were subsequently positively identified as being part of a consignment of fifty boxes of Lacoste shoes stolen during the course of a burglary at business premises in Blackburn, Lancashire in June 1994.

They met the 'traveller' again on the pub car park, later that afternoon, and he said that he would provide 4.5 ounces of cannabis the following day, for £400.

On Friday 2 December 1994, as promised, the 'traveller' together with another unknown man, met the undercover officers on the pub car park. They all got into the back of the van where the covert cameras recorded them passing over 4.5 ounces of cannabis bush for the agreed amount.

The officers had already purchased a portable TV from another target, who was obviously storing stolen property at his girlfriend's address. This seemed to be a common tactic adopted by the local criminals who knew that they were less likely to attract the attention of the police. The 'traveller' himself said that he kept stolen property at his girlfriend's parents' house because it was not known to the police.

In the afternoon they were contacted by the Darlaston couple and on visiting their address were confronted by a room full of boxes of LA Gear training shoes, which were being offered at £12.50 per box. The officers made a down payment on the pretext of buying all of them. It later transpired that this property had been stolen during the course of a theft in Willenhall.

As we were only a few days away from executing search warrants we took a gamble that they would keep them for us and would be found later. They said that they had already sold one hundred pairs, and the lady of the house made a record of the transaction in an A4 book. They were running their illegal business activities as if they were keeping accounts. Promises were made regarding a consignment of stolen television sets which were going to come from an 'inside job.' They totally trusted the undercover officers and the sheer scale of their activities was breathtaking.

Our 'traveller' had proved to be a great asset and had unintentionally referenced the officers into several good criminals. He couldn't stop himself as he tried to impress them with his knowledge of what was going on in the area. I suspect that he had some difficult questions to answer later with his criminal associates.

We had accumulated a mass of evidence against a lot of individuals in a very short space of time and now we were on the home straight.

During the covert evidence gathering phase of the operation stolen property valued at £30,000 was recovered which included video recorders, stereo systems, TV sets, cannabis, and £5,000 worth of counterfeit currency, as well as a £1,000 worth of counterfeit goods. All this was achieved for an outlay of £5,214 spent by the undercover officers in purchasing the items.

***

We had already set the date for the arrest phase some weeks previously, and over the next four days there was a massive amount of activity aimed at making sure that our targets packages were as comprehensive as they could be. I had the experience of Operation

Red Card behind me and stuck to a successful formula in terms of planning.

For every target package we had an intelligence only element, an evidential element, including witness and police statements, a miscellaneous document package, copies of all exhibits, and photographs of the property recovered.

A detailed operational order was prepared by myself which was designed to leave nothing to chance.

***

On Wednesday 7 December 1994, a briefing took place at 5am with arrest teams at eight locations in Walsall. We had briefed a core group of senior officers the day before and they were required to give the briefings to the teams which had to be 'short and sharp' so that all of the officers would be in place and ready to execute their warrant at 6am. We couldn't risk losing prisoners, or evidence, by giving people the opportunity to phone each other, so it was critical that they were all ready to go at the same time.

We had fifty-three targets to go for, and fifty-three arrest teams. During the course of the operation we had prepared seventy-eight target packages on suspects, but in some cases we had not been able to positively identify the offenders, or build the evidence to the level required to have sufficient grounds for arrest.

We made use of the divisional incident room at Walsall Police Station and staffed it with intelligence operatives to assist with coordination. I went to Gold Control in Birmingham, with the divisional detective superintendent, who would be in overall command on the day with me being the nominated deputy.

All officers would operate on dedicated VHF channel 2, and a logistics officer would update each target's status as radio messages came in. Officers were advised to be wary of saying too much on the radio, as we knew that some of our targets had access to radio scanners, and monitored police patrols. That said, the constant flow of positive messages that flowed in from 6am onwards told us that the planning had paid off.

For each target we had a mixture of uniform and CID staff, who were given designated roles as arrest and interview officers, exhibit officers, and search/support. I knew many of the officers personally, and their strengths and weaknesses, and made sure that the best detectives were put with the key targets. It is difficult to say what makes a good interviewer and whilst training is all part of it, the reality is that some people just have a natural instinct for getting people to talk to them. Whilst we had a mass of evidence I wanted to squeeze everything we could in terms of other offences at this stage.

In one case we identified a target who was believed to be an active burglar, and indeed at the scene of one offence, where a photocopier was stolen from a church, his fingerprints were found on the inside surfaces of a locked filing cabinet, which had been forced open. The problem was that the fingerprints were classed as *'Non Provable'* in that they didn't provide sufficient 'points' to satisfy the evidential standard required by the courts. This could be frustrating, but this detail could only be used as intelligence, and the key would rest with a good interview.

Officers were instructed that during the first interviews with targets they would ask standard questions aimed at asking whether the individual had ever owned, or sold, a specific item of property. On the second interview, notwithstanding their first responses, they would be shown video evidence and asked to comment and confirm their identity.

A minimum of four officers went out for each target, but in some cases I deployed additional OSU search teams of eight further officers, knowing the scale of the property we were likely to recover, or where we believed that we might find additional suspects.

This was particularly so in the case of our married Darlaston couple and an associate. Our 'uncle' target could be an intimidating figure so he had the benefit of receiving a team of eight officers, as we were also looking for at least two unidentified targets that might have been staying at the same address.

We even had a large Cargo van with a driver on standby at Park Lane Traffic Headquarters in order to assist with the removal of recovered property. Two dog handlers were on standby in the event that we needed to deal with any dangerous dogs found in houses or to act as a deterrent should any target become aggressive with any of the teams. As it was *'the shock and awe'* style of the operation meant that most people came very quietly.

Throughout the day, in the final phase of the operation, forty six search warrants were executed at houses, pubs, and business premises in Walsall, Willenhall, Blakenhall and Bloxwich, involving more than two hundred and thirty officers, with more than sixty police vehicles. The pub used by our undercover officers as a regular meeting place, was amongst them, and whilst we were not that confident of recovering stolen property we had to try to stop criminals using it as a 'base' from which to conduct their activities.

Over fifty persons were arrested in total, and stolen property recovered in excess of £120,000, as well as a small quantity of drugs, nearly £2,000 worth of counterfeit currency, £10,000 worth of counterfeit goods, and £500 worth of alcohol, on which no excise duty had been paid, was seized.

In some cases it took us several hours to search properties, room by room, and to remove property, and we had three force photographers on standby to take photographs in situ.

All of the property recovered was initially taken to the old firearms range at Walsall Police Station and it wasn't long before the room started to fill up.

Prisoners were taken to pre-determined custody suites at Walsall, Willenhall, Aldridge, Wednesfield, Wednesbury, West Bromwich, Bilston Street in Wolverhampton, and Queens Road in Birmingham.

At each of the stations we deployed an inspector to give advice and to deal with any issues regarding the provisions of the Police and Criminal Evidence Act 1984 in areas such as search, and access to solicitors. Video equipment was made available at each of the stations, together with audio equipment, in the event that they needed to introduce material into the interviews under caution.

By 8am we had secured forty-seven of our targets, and carried on looking for a further eight persons during the course of the day.

Peter Wilson, a reporter, and film crews from BBC Midlands Today, went out with some of the search teams and showed coverage of two of the raids on TV.

At the first an officer with a sledgehammer struck a red-coloured half-glass door to an upstairs flat. The first two strikes took out panes of glass, and as he was encouraged on by colleagues with shouts of "Come on" his third strike took out the Yale lock on the door and it swung open. The officers, some of whom were in plain clothes but wearing checkered police baseball caps, surged in and quickly started searching the address whilst the occupant was arrested. Even the content of a suspicious looking light fitting in the living room was checked.

At the second address an officer using a more conventional red 'door-opener', known as a 'Nigel', took one swing at the door of a flat to smash it open as four officers rushed in shouting 'Drug Squad'.

At the end of the media coverage John Plimmer did a TV interview with a reporter, whilst I sat in the background taking a phone call. He said *"Anybody who thinks they can go into a public house or wherever and buy a television cheap, or a radio cheap, or audio set cheap, be very careful, extremely careful because we're in there with you. Even the criminals don't know who to trust."*

Events at another address were witnessed by Paul Hinton, (an Express and Star Reporter, who I came to know well over the years), Debbi Gardner, and photographer Tim Sturgess, who reported on what they saw in the following terms,

'It was a case of poetic justice when the long arm of the law caught up with two suspects at a house in the Delves area of Walsall.

DC John Shelley and Detective Sergeant Alan Shakespeare led a team of six officers in a 6am wakeup call at the smart three bedroomed house in the shadow of the M6. Just one neighbour's curtain twitched as the full force of the law – in the shape of a twenty-pound sledgehammer, splintered the front door.

The element of surprise was essential for the success of the early morning mission as officers raced up the street and surrounded the house. Seconds later four arresting officers, a TV camera crew and a Press photographer had bounded up the stairs and burst into the main bedroom. A startled husband and wife, with a babe in arms, were arrested in their bed in the full glare of powerful television lights.

Both faced possible charges in connection with a series of offences including handling stolen goods and burglary. Downstairs officers stumbled on a Christmas grotto of goods, all thought to be counterfeit. The haul included a stock of chart topping Power Ranger videos, Polo jerseys by Ralph Lauren, Georgio and Samsara perfumes and Armani watches.

Five minutes after his rude awakening, a hastily dressed man in his mid-twenties, shadowed by the two poetically named officers, was on his way to Green Lane Police Station for questioning. The mother of two followed later, but only after brewing up a pot of tea for officers as they carried out a thorough search of the house. By

6.30am the baby and a young boy were up and dressed and the TV was on. Almost an everyday breakfast scene.'

A picture next to the article showed Sergeant Graeme Pallister, who years later became a senior CID officer in Warwickshire Police, examining some of the recovered property at Brownhills Police Station.

As a precautionary measure, after the arrests were made, we put local beat officers out on the area looking for a rise in tension. The last thing that we wanted was a public-order situation developing on the area and from 6pm that day we deployed members of the force Operational Support Unit to the streets in a high visibility role. The acknowledged force experts in public order, they were trained in early intervention techniques and were extremely effective. As it was Walsall remained quiet and the criminals kept their heads down.

The three undercover officers were kept well away from any of this policing activity but I kept them updated during the course of the day - they had done a brilliant job.

As anticipated, we charged a number of those arrested with specific offences and kept them in custody to appear at Walsall Magistrates Court on the 8 December 1994. At 4pm that afternoon we held a full debrief with the arrest teams and morale was sky high. After the formalities, the bar in the police social club was opened and did some brisk business. It was a good day for the police in Walsall.

Others were bailed to appear at Walsall Magistrates/Youth

Courts on the 10 January 1995.

'Uncle' was charged with conspiracy to receive stolen property, and possession of a section 1 firearm, which was a gas propelled rifle, found at his address. Other power tools, and a generator, were also found when his home was searched and whilst he made admissions in relation to the events which had unfolded he denied any guilty knowledge of handing stolen property.

The 'traveller' found himself facing charges of conspiracy to dispose of stolen property and possession of controlled drugs with intent to supply. Found at his home was a scanner, which was used to monitor police frequencies, some electrical equipment, and a motorbike which was suspected of being stolen. He made admissions as to his criminal involvement.

The married couple with the Darlaston connection, faced charges of conspiracy to receive counterfeit currency and drugs, as well as conspiracy to receive stolen property. The male associate was charged with the supply of counterfeit currency, and handling stolen property. Work done by one of our intelligence analysts, on an association chart, showed that they were connected to at least twenty other people in relation to the counterfeit currency offences.

Amongst the numerous items of property recovered, during the course of searches connected to these three, was some further counterfeit twenty pound notes, cannabis resin and cannabis bush, as well as three antique 'Penny Farthing' bicycles which had actually been stolen in a burglary at Llandridod Wells in Wales on the 31 July 1994, with a value of £10,000.

They appeared in a press photograph the day after the arrest operation with DI Martyn Thomas standing in front of them and surrounded by other property. Critically we recovered the A4 book containing transactions, and two bank notes used by the undercover officers to purchase property, which had been marked beforehand. Another lawnmower that had been stolen in a burglary in Willenhall was also recovered. The two men made admissions in respect of their criminal involvement, but the wife denied everything.

Another target was charged with possessing cannabis with intent to supply, and our drug dealer from the jeep in Walsall was dealt with for offences of possession of drugs with intent to supply, and possession of a prohibited article namely a CS spray canister. Yet another was charged with receiving stolen property and cultivating cannabis. Others were charged with burglary and theft.

***

A total of seventy primary offences were cleared, and an additional one hundred and fifty offences later cleared following prison visits with some of those convicted. During the month of November 1994 thirty-five offences of burglary dwelling house were recorded, whilst in December 1994 following the conclusion of the operation only twelve were recorded in one of our 'hot-spot' areas.

The operation had been a major success, and put the local organised criminal community on the 'back foot'. We had not played by *'Queensbury Rules'* and they didn't like it. The divisional detective superintendent had made it plain in subsequent press releases that this operation was to be one part of a divisional burglary initiative and that other phases were planned in the New

Year. It was all part of the philosophy of reassuring the public, whilst at the same time keeping the criminals guessing. The power of the media was enormous and we 'milked it' for all it was worth.

John Plimmer, the Detective Superintendent, was renowned for his experience in dealing with the media, and used all of his expertise to best effect.

In keeping with the success of operation Red Card, none of the undercover officers were ever required to give evidence in the witness box at court, with solicitors and defendants accepting the sheer weight of the overwhelming evidence against them.

Before we provided any video material to either the Crown Prosecution Service, or defence solicitors, we did a mosaic of the faces of the officers who had provided direct covert evidence in relation to more than thirty of those dealt with, in order to try to protect their identities.

For those who went to prison the minimum sentence was three months, and the maximum was two years and seven months. They were not massive sentences but there was a clear message to criminals in Walsall that they needed to start 'looking over their shoulders.'

In the wake of Operation Portdale I developed a burglary strategy for the first three months of the New Year which would focus on three other 'hot-spot' areas and involve another ten short-term operations, some of which would overlap each other for maximum effect.

Operational names were generated randomly at Force

Intelligence, so we finished up with strange names like Abhac, Dacsland, Garlea, Earlslawn and Gandalph, although personally I liked names which captured the public imagination. Each operation would have an arrest phase, as well as a crime-reduction phase, and the media would be involved at each stage. The idea was to keep the pressure up, and to be intelligence led.

On the 19 December 1994, I submitted a report to John Plimmer, which was designed to supplement these operations, and made some further proposals relating to covert policing activities. Due to the increase in the use of 'scanners' I suggested creating a 'disinformation team' that would put out bogus information on police operations in a particular area.

Amongst other things I also suggested setting up a 'bogus lottery' whereby we would deliver fake 'winning' scratch cards to the addresses of known wanted targets and give them instructions as to where and when to pick up their prize – at which point they would be arrested.

Intelligence staff working on *'Operation Abhac'* had already identified twenty-three targets that could fit into this category. As part of a separate piece of research we had also identified a further thirty-nine targets that had intelligence updates on their records in the previous two months. This gave us a total of sixty-two targets to look at and as I liked double figures I was keen to get approval but it was not forthcoming at that stage.

Approval was subsequently given to doing a feasibility study in relation to setting up a bogus 'Car Boot sale' on land bordering Staffordshire.

In January 1995 I again started to get restless and I was acutely aware that if I wanted to reach the next rank I would probably have to do a spell in uniform. There was however to be no respite in the fight against crime at the start of yet another New Year.

***

On the morning of Monday 9 January 1995, two men tricked their way into the home of a couple, both aged ninety-years, in Leamore Lane, Walsall. One of the men distracted the couple by telling them that they had won a new carpet, and a hamper, in a raffle. He kept them talking for about fifteen minutes, following which they found that the back door had been unlocked, and hundreds of pounds in savings stolen from the house.

On Tuesday 10 January 1995, four men, armed with iron bars, and wearing black balaclavas, burst into the Co-Op Superstore in Shaw Street, Walsall, at 12.30am. They struck as twenty-one year old James Morgan was walking around the store checking stock. He was ordered onto the floor, and bound and gagged before being dumped inside a toilet. The robbers then proceeded to steal property valued at £20,000, comprising electrical equipment and cigarettes, before escaping. Mr. Morgan eventually raised the alarm two hours later after cutting himself free with a penknife he had in his pocket.

On the same date yet another drugs raid took place at a house in Palfrey, in the relentless fight against drugs, leading to the arrest of one man and the recovery of amphetamine sulphate valued at £500.

Again on Tuesday 10 January 1995, Walsall CID officers alerted French police in the search for a man who was believed to be the mastermind behind a gang who had been targeting vulnerable people in the Black Country, and used threats and intimidation to gain money for driveway resurfacing work, which was never done.

In one case an eighty-year-old woman had been forced to hand over £20,000, after initially being told that the work would cost just £35. The suspect was eventually tracked through the Channel Tunnel before being detained by French Police in Calais, and returned under police escort to Walsall.

***

On Wednesday 11 January 1995 twenty four of the Portdale defendants appeared at Walsall Magistrates Court, many of them facing multiple charges, and strict bail conditions.

***

On the same date, officers from the Divisional Crime Unit, raided a house in Willenhall, and seized two hundred ecstasy tablets, along with a substantial quantity of cannabis resin. The drugs had a street value of £10,000, and a twenty-six-year-old man was arrested.

On Friday 13 January 1995, racism reared its head again as drinkers watched an anti-racism band in the Wheatsheaf Pub in Birmingham Road. During an earlier incident two men were ejected by the London based folk group Blyth Power for shouting abuse. At 10.30pm two men were walking out from an upstairs room when they were attacked by three 'skinhead' youths wielding broken glasses. One of them had a smashed bottle pushed into his forehead and below his eyes. Both men needed thirty stitches to their wounds after being treated at the Manor Hospital. Their attackers made good their escape.

***

The following week youths broke down the door of seventy-three year old Lilian Tipton, and her seventy-two-year old brother Oliver Brewers' home in Walsall Wood, demanding drugs and money. When they found nothing they beat the disabled couple, leaving them terrified.

***

During the course of 1994 a total of six hundred and fifty people, classed as pensioners, were burglary victims, many of them falling victim to so-called 'bogus officials.' A further eighty five were the victims of street robberies.

***

At 2am on Thursday 26 January 1995 three burglars broke into the Master Snooker Club in Bridge Street, Walsall and caused damage as well as stealing £100. Officers from the Divisional Crime Unit were lying in wait and, having surrounded the premises, went inside and arrested a fifteen-year-old, and two men aged nineteen years, and twenty years.

***

On the 27 January 1995 I applied to become an operational uniform chief inspector when a vacancy arose. The truth was that I was judged to be a 'career detective' and I knew that it would narrow down my options when the selection process came. My application was supported by Assistant Chief Constable (Crime) Phil Thomas, when I met him on the same date, for my yearly appraisal, but no-one was in a rush for me to move.

***

On Tuesday 31 January 1995 we arranged a viewing at Walsall Police Station for people to come along with a view to identifying some of the property from Operation Portdale.

It was the end of a very busy month, and the start of an even busier one for the division.

***

On Tuesday 7 February 1995 forensic officers, and police search teams, commenced searching a house in North Street, Ryecroft, Walsall, following the arrest of a fifty- three-year old man on suspicion of rape and indecency some twenty years previously, the victim a young woman.

As a result of information received during that investigation, the files had been reopened in respect of sixteen-year old Dawn Falconer, who had gone missing on the 24 July 1978. The arrested man had lived at the address five years before and the following day human remains were dug up in the back garden. Home Office Pathologist Dr. Kenneth Scott attended and the remains were subsequently confirmed as being that of the missing teenager. Yet another murder enquiry was underway.

On Friday 10 February 1995, David Sharpe, an unemployed builder, appeared at Walsall Magistrates Court, charged with the murder of Dawn Falconer, who had been strangled.

He subsequently pleaded guilty at Shrewsbury Crown Court in 1995 and was sentenced to life imprisonment. During his trial the court heard that the discovery of the teenager's body was prompted by an episode of the soap-opera *'Brookside'*, where a body was found beneath a patio and a disclosure to the police from the killer's eldest son.

On the 1 February 2009 David Sharpe, then aged sixty-seven years, was found dead in his cell in HM Prison Wakefield, from natural causes.

***

At 9am on Monday 13 February 1995 workmen found the fully clothed body of a woman, in her fifties, half buried in mud on land off Darlaston Lane, near to work being carried out on the new Black Country Route. The body was believed to have been there for less than twenty-four hours. Search teams were once more deployed and senior detectives attended, as enquiries commenced to establish the cause of death.

***

At 2pm on Monday 13 February 1995 I attended a meeting with the community, and other agencies, at Pelsall Comprehensive School, to discuss drug related issues. Everyone knew that the availability of drugs in the Borough was driving up crime levels. As the number of addicts increased so did the levels of acquisitive crime as people looked at any means possible to pay for their daily habit. The introduction of so called hard drugs, like cocaine and heroin, would only make matters worse putting more pressure on the police, health, and social services.

***

Between the 27 February 1995, and the 10 March 1995, I put myself through a two week criminal intelligence analysis course, and sat alongside sixteen trainee analysts from the West Midlands Police, South East Regional Crime Squad, Sussex, City of London Police and HM Customs and Revenue.

The course was based on a concept developed by an American Company called *'Anacapa Sciences Incorporated'* which had been established in 1969 to service the needs of American government agencies, and industrial companies. In pioneering the development of new intelligence and investigation methods they had already trained people from hundreds of law- enforcement agencies.

Analysis was described as the process of developing meaning from collated information and from it to draw inferences. It was, and remains, particularly useful in the investigation of organised-crime, drug trafficking, and complex fraud cases. The process relied heavily on the use of the continuous 'Intelligence Cycle' which had a number of components to it namely Direction, Collection, Evaluation, Analysis and Dissemination, as well as something called the 4 x 4 system of grading intelligence, which placed a value on the source, and nature of the information received. There was however no magic 'crystal ball' within the process, and good 'old fashioned detective work' was still required.

In those days techniques had not become totally computerised and I found myself using rolls of wallpaper, and numerous marker pens, with which to complete complicated sequence of events charts. The easiest way of doing some of the work was to lay it all out on the floor and literally get on your hands and knees.

It was a tough course but we worked well in teams together and got through four practical exercises, all of which required formal briefings with findings to be presented to fellow students and the five instructors. At the end I felt better equipped to understand what analysts would be able to offer me in future. It also meant that I was less likely to be 'blinded by science'. The course director was in fact the principal analyst in the West Midlands, whom I had previously recruited when in FIB, but no favours were expected, or shown, and that was fine.

***

At the end of March 1995, I submitted a paper suggesting that we mount another covert operation but this time my suggestion was based on identifying sources of disposal of stolen property, through the use of newspaper adverts, and in particular the availability of *'Exchange and Mart'* type publications.

I proposed that we make selective contact with some of the advertisers using undercover officers, and in some cases, dependent on crime trends, actually advertise for goods ourselves to see if we could draw the thieves towards us. The idea was actively considered, and the Crown Prosecution Service saw no legal difficulties with the proposal - but events started to overtake me once again and the proposed initiative went no further.

***

On the night of the 1 April 1995 a particularly nasty attack took place at a family home in Bescot Road, Pleck, when a gang of four men, armed with a meat cleaver, burst in on a mother and her three children, who were watching television.

The gang, who were all described as Afro-Caribbean, forced the Asian family upstairs and used packing tape to tie their hands and gag them before ordering them to lie on a bed. Telephone lines were cut and the house ransacked before they made good their escape with a large quantity of jewellery, credit cards, and somewhat surprisingly a child's cricket bat. All of them were wearing masks, and it was a terrifying experience for the young family.

There was a common belief at this time, within the criminal fraternity, that Asian families were prone to keeping quantities of gold jewellery in their homes and this increased their chances of becoming targets. There was just no end to crimes being committed – it was relentless.

Figure 33: Operation Portdale 'wanted' poster – 1994

Chapter Nine

Murder and Mystery

(Michael Layton):

On the 4 April 1995, I was appointed as the Detective Chief Inspector (Operations), still at Walsall, on the H Division, but with responsibility for some fifty staff, including the pro-active Divisional Crime Unit, two Area CID teams and the Family Protection Unit.

The post also normally assumed responsibility for acting as the divisional detective superintendent when the post-holder was away, and for acting as an Investigating Officer when a serious incident occurred. In a personal review at this time I was described in the following terms by my detective superintendent, *'Whilst initially he may appear quiet and unassuming, he is an extremely determined individual who is not afraid to confront situations, or make contentious decisions.'*

At the beginning of this appointment I went on leave for two weeks and was out of the country for a quiet family holiday. It was not so quiet in Walsall.

On Sunday 9 April 1995, Manchester United was due to play Crystal Palace in an FA Cup semi-final at Villa Park football ground in Birmingham. There was said to be 'bad blood' between supporters from both clubs, after an incident in January when Eric Cantona, a Manchester United player, had delivered a 'Kung Fu' kick to a Crystal Palace supporter at Selhurst Park in London.

During the afternoon, before the game, fans from both teams gathered to drink in the 'New Fulbrook' pub in Weston Street, Walsall. Tension started to rise, culminating in up to one hundred fans pouring out of the pub into the street where, after a 'stand-off', bricks, bottles, glasses and lumps of concrete were thrown. The violence lasted for a matter of minutes but in that time one person lost his life, and another suffered very serious injuries.

Crystal Palace fan Paul Nixon, aged thirty-five years, was struck on the head by a brick, and as he tried to board his moving coach, which the driver was trying to steer away from the clashes, he stumbled and fell underneath the front wheels. He was crushed to death.

A second man, Dennis O'Leary, also aged thirty-five years, and also a Crystal Palace fan, was hit twice by missiles, and suffered serious facial injuries which required facial reconstruction. He needed to wear a head-brace for a month.

Walsall South MP Bruce George, who later attended the scene, commented in the media, *"I think it is what I would refer to as the barbarism of Britain – a general deterioration in patterns of behaviour where a football match can provoke such intensity of hostility."*

I came to know him quite well over the coming years and always found him to be a strong supporter of the police.

The uniform officers who initially arrived on the scene faced a huge task in terms of trying to contain the situation, deal with the casualties, preserve the scene, and to stop potential witnesses and offenders leaving the scene. Three arrests were made initially, although they were later released without charge. Details of more than one hundred people were obtained, and an incident room opened with Detective Superintendent John Plimmer in charge.

On Thursday 13 April 1995, an inquest was opened by the Walsall Coroner in respect of the death, and the Home Office pathologist Dr. Kenneth Scott confirmed that Paul Nixon had died from multiple injuries, including fractured ribs and pelvis, consistent with being run over by the coach. He also had a fractured skull consistent with being struck by a missile.

There had been some concerns that he had been stabbed but these injuries were described as being consistent with being struck by the underside of the coach. At that stage the body was not released to the family in case further suspects were arrested and another post mortem was required.

I came back from leave on the 15 April 1995, and the following week did my best to keep the 'day job' going whilst John Plimmer, and Detective Chief Inspector Williams, were tied up on the investigation. Most of my staff were engaged on this job but we still needed to deal with routine things and the steady flow of 'overnight prisoners' that were often lodged in the cells for the CID to deal with.

Satellite offices were set up in London and Manchester, to trace people, and support was provided by both local forces, as more than seven hundred statements were completed.

At the beginning of May 1995, thirty officers carried out a

series of raids, and arrested seven people in Irlam, in Manchester, and one in Carshalton in Surrey.

Further arrests followed, and I subsequently confirmed with the press that a total of thirteen had been made by the 9 May1995.

Ultimately a number of Manchester United fans were arrested, three of whom were initially charged with manslaughter, and violent disorder. Seven others faced charges relating to the actual disorder however charges were eventually dropped against the latter group seven months later for legal reasons.

Ten months later, at the end of a three day committal hearing at Walsall Magistrates Court, a Stipendiary Magistrate, Ian Gillespie, dismissed the charges against the three men charged with manslaughter, following further legal submissions at the close of the prosecution case.

John Plimmer indicated that as far as he was concerned the case was not closed, and that he was considering asking the Crown Prosecution Service to apply for a voluntary bill of indictment to get the matter back before the courts.

***

On Thursday 27 April 1995, I attended a briefing for *Operation Larkrise'* which was to take place the following day. We had already met twice in the previous week to put some detail into the operational planning. It was part of a borough-wide initiative to tackle the growing problem of drugs and was to be led by Superintendent Brian Wall.

In March 1995, highly addictive crack cocaine, valued at £12,000, was recovered from a house in Pleck, Walsall, and there was real concern within local communities.

At 5pm on Friday 28 April 1995, nearly one hundred officers sealed off Beddows Road in Ryecroft, in Walsall, and searched six addresses using search warrants. A large quantity of cannabis and cannabis plants were seized, with a street value of thousands of pounds, together with drug related equipment and an air rifle. Two women, and eight men, aged between twenty-years and fifty-years were arrested and taken to Walsall Police Station. It had been a good result in a location that had started to look like a police 'no go' area.

***

At 9.30pm, on Saturday 29 April 1995, an incident occurred at a Chinese Takeaway in Harden Road, Leamore which displayed the sheer madness of incidents of violence which occurred routinely in the area.

The victim, a twenty-nine-year old father of two, who was also an asthma sufferer, cycled to the restaurant to collect a meal for his family. As he entered he saw three men arguing with the shop owners.

One of the men told the victim, Paul Bryn, that he was going to steal his pedal cycle, and immediately punched him in the temple causing him to fall. As he did so his head struck a window causing the glass to smash. He was then repeatedly kicked on the ground, and as he was protecting himself he noticed that one of the three men was actually in the process of collecting a takeaway meal from the counter.

Carrying the meal this man calmly kicked Mr. Bryn in the right eye, as he lay on the floor, before all three made off with his pedal cycle. He was rushed to the Manor Hospital and treated for multiple bruising in an entirely unprovoked attack by a bunch of cowards.

On the 1 May 1995, *'Operation Hillcroft'* started, and I oversaw the commencement of another drugs operation in the borough, which was to last for three months.

***

Unfortunately May 1995 was to be remembered more for other things, as two personal tragedies struck members of staff on the Division. At lunchtime on Thursday 11 May 1995, two climbers discovered the body of PC Martin Chesters, aged forty-two-years, at the foot of Glyder Fach mountain in Snowdonia.

He had been on holiday, walking on his own in the Welsh mountains, when it appeared that he had taken a wrong turning, fallen one hundred and fifty feet down a rock face, and lain there for twenty-four-hours. Martin was an experienced crime-prevention officer based at Willenhall Police Station.

In the same month Clive Williams announced in the media a freak accident which resulted in Detective Inspector Stewart Grogan losing part of his left leg.

Stewart was alone on a Friday working in his daughter's garden, in Telford, when he got caught in the blades of a rotovator earth-moving machine, and was pinned against a wall.

A man mending a washing machine in the house heard his shouts and alerted the fire brigade who cut him free. He was taken to the Princess Royal Hospital in Telford where doctors amputated his left leg just below the knee. Clive said *"He is very positive, he is very brave. Maybe the full effects of it have not hit him yet. It is early days to say whether he will be coming back to work. He has a long way ahead of him for the leg to heal...."*

Stewart was forty-nine-years of age, with twenty-nine years' service, and worked for me in the Crime Bureau, and the Divisional Crime Unit.

You just never know what is going to happen to you in life and I reflected on the fact that prior to the incident I had wished him well for his annual leave, not knowing that the next time I would see him would be in a hospital bed. We had not been particularly close prior to the accident but after visiting him on a regular basis, during his recovery, I could only echo Clive's words and came to admire his tremendous fortitude and strength as he literally fought his way back to being able to lead an active life. He was already something of a fitness fanatic and it wasn't long before he was pushing himself to the very limits, and learning how to run with a prosthetic limb. He was without doubt a man of great courage who refused to complain about the nature of the accident.

On Tuesday 23 May 1995, more than one hundred police officers attended the funeral of PC Martin Chesters. He had been a police officer in Walsall for twenty- three-years, and only months before had been awarded his long service medal. Senior officers from the force attended, including Bob Packham, and pallbearers were provided by officers from the Crime Prevention, and Neighbourhood Watch staff.

It had just been announced that Bob Packham was to be promoted to Assistant Chief Constable, and would be leaving Walsall to go back to Headquarters. The move prompted a reaction from local MP Bruce George who said that he would be writing to the Chief Constable Ron Hadfield to say that the town needed a top officer who knew the area, and would be in post for a while, given that there had been seven police chiefs in the past ten years.

He said, *"Mr. Packham is a very good policeman. I congratulate him on his promotion and wish him well. Walsall is proving a great stepping-stone for high flying officers but it needs more consistency in its policing."*

I could only hope that some of his insight would 'rub off' on my career!

***

At 11.50pm, on Thursday 25 May 1995, violence reared its head again in Walsall town-centre. As a twenty-one-year old man was withdrawing cash from a dispenser outside the Safeway Supermarket, off Lower Rushall Street, two men grabbed him and pointed a pistol at his face. They demanded cash and stole his wallet before jumping into a red Ford Escort. He gave chase in his own vehicle, until one of his attackers leaned out of their vehicle and fired a shot at him, which fortunately missed.

At this point the victim thought better of it and pulled up

visibly shocked.

***

On the same date, MP Bruce George highlighted that crime had risen in Walsall since the 1970s by 150%, and yet since that time the establishment of police officers in the area had risen by only one hundred.

***

At 11pm, on Monday 29 May 1995, cars and homes were attacked in Wychbold Close, New Invention, Willenhall, as up to a dozen feuding neighbours armed with stones, sticks and catapults fought with each other. The windows of three houses were smashed, and three vehicles damaged in the incident, which resulted in several people receiving minor injuries. The local community closed ranks and refused to say why the incident had taken place, as six people were arrested and kept in custody for questioning.

***

At the end of May 1995 I was awarded my first medal, namely the Police Long Service and Good Conduct Medal, which is granted after twenty-two years' service, and is awarded under the provision of the Royal Warrant dated 14 June 1951 by the Secretary of State.

***

On the 2 June 1995 I spotted an advert in the Police Review from the Overseas Development Administration for a CID advisor in St Kitts and Nevis, a small independent state in the Eastern Caribbean. The

ODA, whose motto was *'Britain helping nations to help themselves'*, were looking to assist the Island's government to establish a force which would be devoid of inappropriate political influence, and the CID advisor needed skills in operational and intelligence policing, all of which I possessed.

The idea of two years working abroad appealed to me, even though it was to be classed as an 'unaccompanied' post, and I didn't want to disrupt my children's education. Within a week I applied with the full support of the force, but was unsuccessful. It was to be another eight years before my opportunity to work abroad was achieved.

***

On Friday 9 June 1995, at 6am, fifteen officers from the Divisional Crime Unit, and Regional Crime Squad, executed search warrants at five addresses, as part of *'Operation Hailes'*.

Five homes were searched in Johns Lane, Great Wyrley, Price Street Cannock, and three addresses in Pelsall – Trevor Road, Wilners View, and Forge Road. Two kilograms of cannabis, cannabis plants, a quantity of cocaine, and half a kilogram of ecstasy tablets were seized, with a street value of more than £30,000.

Cars, CS spray canisters, and rounds of ammunition were also found, as four men and four women aged between twenty-years and thirty-five years were arrested, and interviewed at three police stations.

At 9.30am on Friday 16 June 1995, a coordinated firearms

operation took place at a post office and newsagents, at The Square in New Invention, Willenhall. A dozen officers dressed as workmen kept watch outside and armed officers subsequently arrested one man, who it was believed was about to commit a robbery. Two other men in a stolen vehicle drove off, but after a short chase a police vehicle rammed it as they tried to reverse across a playing field. One man staggered out and levelled a pistol at police but he dropped it as armed officers surrounded him. A search of addresses in Wolverhampton later resulted in the recovery of forty-nine bullets.

On the evening of Tuesday 20 June 1995, two men, aged twenty-years, and twenty-three years, were standing in a small group outside the British Oak Licensed House in High Road, Willenhall, when a blue Ford Escort car pulled up containing five men, who were armed with wooden sticks, a hammer, and pool cues.

One of this group was also in possession of an acid spray and proceeded to spray both men in the face leaving them reeling in agony from burns. One of them ran four hundred yards to another pub, where he was hosed down with water, whilst the second man took refuge in a nearby house. Their attackers escaped and the victims were left with fifteen per cent burns to their heads and upper body, and needing specialist treatment in Trauma Hospital Units.

***

On Saturday 24 June 1995, the staff at Walsall Police Station highlighted their 'softer side' after twelve officers, led by Sergeant Colin Bill, completed a fifteen-mile trek through Derbyshire in aid of charity. Colin's four-year-old son attended Oakwood Special School, and after vandals wrecked a swing, just days after being installed, they decided to raise funds for a replacement.

Colin said, *"We were disheartened to find the swing had been damaged last week. We hope to raise £4,000 to repair it and continue to develop the playground."*

The officers were accompanied on their walk by Roz Ricketts, the station telephonist, who was wheelchair-bound. Roz was an inspiration to staff at the station, always smiling and cheerful, she was very determined to lead as full a life as possible, and was a great ambassador for the police.

***

At 2.20am on Sunday 25 June 1995, a seventeen-year-old youth who intervened in a fight involving fifteen other people, outside the Zone and Ethos Nightclubs in Bentley Mill Way, Darlaston, was stabbed in the back. He received a stab wound to his lower back which was three quarters of an inch deep, and ten inches long. Since opening in February the clubs had been plagued with public order problems, with frequent fights, and at least three CS gas attacks.

On the evening of Sunday 25 June 1995 an Asian family were at home in Bell Lane, Delves in Walsall, when a gang of up to twenty teenagers gathered outside and hurled bricks through the windows, as well as smashing the windows of a van parked outside. Damage running into several hundreds of pounds was caused, although fortunately no-one in the house was injured. A fifteen-year old youth was arrested and further arrests planned in what was felt to be an incident with racial overtones.

***

On Monday 26 June 1995, Alan Jones took over as the new chief superintendent at Walsall. One of his first acts was to launch an enquiry into why it had taken six hours for local police officers to attend to an incident, where an eighty-three year-old housebound pensioner had suffered a smashed living room window at the hands of mindless hooligans.

Whilst it was an incident that had not been classified as requiring an immediate response he nevertheless felt that as a vulnerable member of the community, who had been left traumatized and in tears, she should have been visited earlier. Alan was a very principled officer who clearly meant business and was determined to leave his mark on policing in the area. Whilst responding to genuine concerns he was also sending a very clear signal to the staff to be 'on their toes' at all times.

***

At 1pm on Tuesday 27 June 1995, a fight took place outside TP Riley School in Lichfield Road, Bloxwich, during a school break time, involving two fifteen-year old boys. As a result David Watson had an ear bitten off. He was taken to Wordsley Hospital for microsurgery, and underwent plastic surgery when surgeons were unable to sew the ear back on. The other fifteen-year-old boy was arrested and charged with an offence of wounding.

***

At 6am on Friday 7 July 1995, as part of the ongoing initiative to combat drug dealers, forty police officers raided ten houses in Walsall, Pelsall and Bentley. Ecstasy tablets and cannabis valued at

£10,000 were recovered, along with a number of cannabis plants, drugs paraphernalia, as well as dozens of stolen mobile telephones. It had been the seventh such raid in recent weeks, as part of *'Operation Hillcroft'*, and resulted in the arrest of seven men aged between eighteen-years to thirty-six-years.

On the same date the press reported on the results of *'Operation Belvedere'*, where five raids by the Divisional Crime Unit resulted in the recovery of power tools, a cement mixer, several complete central heating systems, three cars, and twenty car radios. Four men were arrested, two of whom were charged with dishonestly handling stolen property.

In a follow up operation, at 9pm later that same day, as part of *'Operation Hailes'*, fifty officers from the Divisional Crime Unit, and the Operations Support Unit, raided the 'Trees' Licensed House, in Queslett Road, Great Barr, armed with a search warrant issued under the Misuse of Drugs Act. The pub was packed with people at the time, and one man armed with a knife tried to attack the officers as they attempted to arrest him for dealing in drugs, but he was quickly overpowered and taken to Walsall Police Station, together with seven other men. Cannabis and amphetamine valued at £10,000 was recovered as customers scattered as police entered the premises.

On Monday 17 July 1995, eight people appeared at Aldridge Magistrates Court charged in connection with the recovery of cannabis worth £30,000 found in two homes in Pelsall. One of the accused was a pregnant mother of three children, charged with possession of controlled drugs with intent to supply.

***

On the evening of Monday 17 July 1995, I attended a formal ceremony, with my family, in the Lord Knights Suite at Tally Ho Police Training Centre, where together with thirteen other recipients, my medal was presented to me by the Chief Constable Ron Hadfield, amongst a degree of pomp and ceremony, with a police band playing on the stage, formal speeches, and official photographs.

The citation for the medal read,

'The Police Long Service and Good Conduct Medal was instituted under Royal Warrant by King George VI in 1951 and is awarded as a mark of the Sovereign's appreciation of long and meritorious service rendered by members of the Police Forces of the United Kingdom. For an officer to become eligible for this award the Chief Constable must make a recommendation to the Home Secretary and in so doing is required to certify that the officer has been a full time serving member of a Police Force, who has served efficiently for twenty two years and that during that period the officers, character and conduct has been very good.'

Sixty-six new-recruits were also officially sworn in as constables by a magistrate. They all stood up in the room and in unison, placed their hats on and repeated the words,

'I do solemnly and sincerely declare and affirm that I will well and truly serve our sovereign lady the Queen in the office of Constable, without favour or affection, malice or ill will: and that I will, to the best of my power, cause the peace to be kept and preserved and prevent all offences against the persons and properties of her Majesty's subjects: and that while I continue to hold the said office I will, to the best of my skill and knowledge,

discharge all the duties thereof faithfully according to law.'

It was a proud moment for them and their families and I suddenly started to feel very old!

***

On Wednesday 19 July 1995, further drugs warrants were executed.

On Thursday 20 July 1995, John Plimmer reported an 'explosion' in the crime figures, with a leap from just over 2,000 offences reported in Walsall in May, compared to 2,898 in June 1995.

Burglary offences, as well a vehicle related crime, had all risen sharply, and no doubt the huge quantities of drugs circulating in the borough were having some impact on acquisitive crime. Offences of wounding had also risen from sixty-eight to eighty-nine offences, and it was felt that the recent spell of hot weather had influenced the figures which were described as a 'freak month.'

On the same date I spoke to the Walsall Advertiser and highlighted the need for us to target drugs dealers, the fact that fifty people had been arrested for drugs offences in the previous two months alone, and that at least one more drug related death had occurred in that period.

It was also announced that a multi-agency 'Drugs Action Team' would be set up in the borough involving the Health Service, Police, Prison Service, Social Services, Education and Probation Services. Traditionally we had not always been good at communicating with each other and whilst it was a positive step forward it would take time to develop trust between the agencies.

***

On the same date some of the residents of Coalpool were out on the streets threatening each other with pick-axe handles and I started to pull together an operation. Experience told us that if we didn't nip criminal activity in 'the bud' quickly in this area we ran the risk of losing control.

***

On Thursday 27 July 1995, two further drugs warrants were executed in Bloxwich. At a flat in Croxdene Avenue, cannabis and amphetamine were recovered and four people arrested, two of whom were charged. At a house in Chapel Street, a small quantity of cannabis and a cannabis plant were recovered, and two persons detained, one of whom was subsequently cautioned.

***

On Friday 28 July 1995, thirty officers carried out early-morning homes raids in Coalpool, under an operation codenamed 'Beaconmoor', and arrested eight men aged between eighteen-years, to twenty-eight years, in relation to the disorder a week before. They were all known to each other and spent the day being interviewed about offences relating to possession of offensive weapons, possession of drugs, criminal damage to vehicles, and theft. We still had further targets to find.

***

On Tuesday 1 August 1995, the last drugs raid on *'Operation Hillcroft'* took place at a house in Ingram Road, Blakenall, Bloxwich, where cannabis valued at £100 was recovered, and a twenty-one-year-old man arrested.

Up to twenty-five officers had been engaged during the course of the operation, which had resulted overall in the arrest of forty-nine persons and controlled drugs with a street value of £40,000 being recovered. I appealed to the public for further information, and made it clear that we were determined to continue tackling the problem due its impact on crime in general in the area.

It was a well-known fact that an addict on so called 'hard drugs' such as heroin, needed hundreds of pounds a day to get enough 'fixes' to satisfy their habit. Given the social circumstances in which many of them found themselves the only way to find this sort of money was through crime.

***

On Wednesday 2 August 1995, just before 2am, a man was rushed to the Manor Hospital after being blasted with a shotgun. Shabir Khan, aged thirty-six-years, from Drayton Street in Pleck, Walsall received a wound to the groin and was detained in a stable condition in hospital. His wife and three children had been in the house at the time. He had been the victim of a firebomb attack in 1994.

This could so easily have been a murder enquiry, and I dealt with the initial press enquiries - before the case was taken on as an 'attempted murder' investigation by DI Martyn Thomas. The shotgun used in the attack was later found in the boot of a stolen car in Primley Avenue, together with a long black wig used as a disguise by the gunman. The car had been stolen twelve days earlier in Caldmore, Walsall, so the early indications were that there were some local connections.

***

On Saturday 5 August 1995, I oversaw the investigation into the wounding of a sixteen-year-old youth, on the Gillity Playing Fields, Walsall, the previous evening. He was 'messing about' with three friends when he was accused of bullying by his attacker, who told him to 'pick on someone his own size' before producing a knife with a seven inch blade, and stabbing him in the right leg.

His friends quickly raised the alarm and the victim was taken to the Manor Hospital bleeding heavily. He needed several blood transfusions and could have died due to the huge loss of blood. The mystery assailant, who had a tattoo on his right shoulder that showed a 'heart with a dagger through it', was with a female at the time, who took no part in the incident, and I appealed to her via the media to come forward.

***

On Thursday 31 August 1995, I was on the last day of a period of annual leave when, yet again, the division came under pressure with the discovery of the naked body of a man found in a fifteenth floor flat, at Darby House, in Caledon Street, Pleck, at 4.30am. The man, later named as Stephen Boulton, aged twenty-nine years, was found in bed with a dressing gown cord around his neck, and a post-mortem subsequently revealed the cause of death to be asphyxiation.

John Plimmer took charge of the investigation and an incident-room was set up at Walsall Police Station. The victim was later described as a 'practicing homosexual' in the media and a number of enquiries were commenced within the local gay community. A man was detained for questioning at a very early stage of the enquiry.

On Saturday 2 September 1995, Kevin Borthwick, aged twenty-six-years, was charged with the murder of Stephen Boulton. He was subsequently committed for trial in December 1995 but before that there was still a lot of work to be completed. Borthwick was convicted of murder in 1996 and sentenced to life imprisonment, but this was reduced to a manslaughter conviction on appeal.

***

At 3.30am on Thursday 14 September 1995, an argument took place outside a house in Leighs Road, Walsall, resulting in one man receiving superficial knife wounds, and another cuts and bruises. A third man, aged twenty-years, was shot in the chest with a pistol, and managed to stagger a hundred yards before collapsing. A bullet was found lodged in his heart by surgeons, and he was critically ill in hospital after losing more than five pints of blood.

The offence was classified as a case of attempt murder, and an incident-room set up at Walsall Police Station, as two men and a woman were arrested.

***

At this time I entered the promotion process again.

Forty-two of us got through the paper sift stage and I was nominated to attend yet another extended assessment process on Sunday the 17 September 1995, at Tally Ho! Police Training Centre, along with nineteen others. After the end of an exhausting day ten of us got through to the final interview stage, and another thirteen made it through on another date.

***

On Tuesday 19 September 1995, at 9.45pm, another senseless attack took place on the car park of the Barley Mow Pub in Goscote Lane, Bloxwich. A thirty- one-year-old man was sitting in his silver Mercedes car, when a gang of five white men, and one black man, pulled up in a Leyland Daf van and pulled him from his car. One of the group then proceeded to hit him with an iron bar, whilst others punched and kicked him in the head and back. As he was left reeling in agony on the ground they stole his vehicle and escaped.

***

On Saturday 23 September 1995, as the 'on call' duty CID officer, I oversaw the investigation into another suspected murder of a baby. As senior CID officers we took it in turns to be on 'on call' for incidents that took place out of normal office hours, however they might be defined, and in particular from Friday evenings through to Monday mornings. It meant that if you were not on call you got some degree of respite from the job, although that was not always guaranteed.

On this date an edition of the Walsall Express and Star carried the story with the headline,

'Police probe murder of two week baby', and read, 'A murder enquiry has been launched after the death of a two week old Walsall baby boy from a head injury. Two people are being questioned. Kieron Matthew Mcgee died before doctors could treat him. Police were today interviewing a man and a woman in connection with the death. The investigation was launched after a post mortem yesterday revealed that the baby had suffered one fatal head injury.*

Detective Chief Inspector Mike Layton, of Walsall CID said, "An ambulance was called to an address at Holdens Crescent in Coalpool on Wednesday. A two-week old child was taken to the Manor Hospital and was found to be dead on arrival. Subsequently, as a result of information received, a post-mortem was carried out by a Home Office pathologist and two people were arrested yesterday afternoon. A twenty-year-old female, and a twenty-year-old male, are in custody. It is fair to say we are treating it as a murder enquiry."

Officers from the Family Protection Unit, based at Darlaston Police Station, were today linking in with detectives from the divisional crime unit in the investigation. A neighbour this afternoon told how the boy's mother Tracey Wood ran round to a next door house to ask for help after thinking Kieron had died on Wednesday. Tracey lives at the semi-detached council house with her boyfriend Carl and two and a half year-old son Adam. "She said she thought the baby had stopped breathing. He was upstairs in the cot."....'

A follow up article on Monday 25 September 1995 read,

'Mum on murder charge - A twenty-year old Walsall woman

has been charged with murdering her two-week old baby boy.
Kieron Matthew McGee, who died at his home in Holdens Crescent
on Wednesday. His mother Tracey Wood was arrested on Friday
after a post mortem revealed Kieron had suffered a single fatal head
injury. After twenty- four hours questioning she was charged at
Green Lane Police Station with his murder. Detective Chief
Inspector Mike Layton said she was being bailed to appear before
Walsall Magistrates Court on October 2. Her twenty-five-year-old
boyfriend Carl McGee, who comes from Tamworth, was released
without charge after also being questioned.

An inquest is due to be opened on Kieron McGee on Friday
by Walsall Coroner Aidan Cotter. Today, Steve Pickersgill of the
Child Protection Unit said Tracey Wood's two and a half year old
son was being cared for by relatives. "The case is a tragedy for all
the people involved. The family have been very supportive and our
thoughts go out to them at this time" he said. "The police, in joint
consultation with social services, have arranged for her other little
boy to be looked after by other family members."....'

Steve Pickersgill was extremely committed to his work in the
Family Protection Unit and cared greatly about the victims he
encountered, both in terms of domestic violence, and child abuse.
Many victims of domestic violence are repeat victims, who suffer
scores of attacks before finding the inner strength to give evidence
against offenders. It takes a special kind of police officer to be
exposed, day in day out, to such human cruelty, and perhaps even
more so in cases involving children. Being a police officer the trick
is never to 'take on the grief of a victim' and whilst this sounds harsh
you have to remain detached, or risk being consumed by daily

outpourings of sadness. It was hard.

On Tuesday 26 September 1995 the success of a 'pilot' scheme in Walsall called, *'Tell a Friend. Be a Friend'*, was highlighted. A twenty-four hour telephone line commenced in March 1995 and officers visited primary schools, to give talks to teachers and pupils, about the 'tell-tale' signs of sexual, and emotional abuse. It was a timely intervention after a huge increase in child abuse cases, with more than eight hundred cases reported the previous year.

The inquest on Kieron McGee was opened and adjourned on the 29 September 1995.

***

My final promotion interview took place at 11.30am, on the 3 October 1995, and the interview panel consisted of ACC Clive Roche, who finished up as the Deputy Chief Constable, ACC Tim Brain, who finished up as the Chief Constable of Gloucestershire, and at that time was the youngest ACC in the Force, and Chief Superintendent Patricia Barnett who had a tough exterior, but actually had a 'heart of gold.'

Everything would rest on that sixty minutes and after fielding questions on grievance procedures, force re-organisation, finance, compulsory competitive tendering, the Audit Commission, deskilling, strategic aims, volume crime, secondary detections, objective setting and whether my CID experience gave me too narrow a perspective, I was done for the day. I left them with my prepared final response as to why I was suitable and went for a pint.

After the usual nervous wait I found out that I had been successful, along with nine other candidates.

***

On Friday 6 October 1995, as part of *'Operation Hillcroft II'*, we executed a drugs warrant at a house in Fairview Court, Western Avenue, Willenhall and recovered a quantity of cannabis resin, and amphetamines, valued at several hundred pounds. The operation was due to conclude, after twelve weeks, at the end of the month, and up to that point we had made twenty-four arrests. We added another two to the tally - two men, aged twenty-two-years, and twenty-five-years.

At 3pm on Thursday 12 October 1995, a flat was searched in Bayley House, Lindon Close, Brownhills, and cannabis valued at £200, which had been broken down into plastic dealer's bags, was recovered together with some stolen jewellery.

On Friday 13 October 1995, a search warrant was executed at a house in Queen Mary Street, Palfrey during an early morning raid. Three cannabis plants were recovered and a twenty-seven year old man arrested.

On Wednesday 18 October 1995, we executed warrants at two unconnected addresses in Tamworth Close, Brownhills. At one address a small amount of cannabis and a cannabis plant were recovered, whilst at the second officers found £200 worth of cannabis. Two arrests were made of men aged twenty-six-years, and twenty-eight years.

Later the same day I had a group photograph taken of myself with eighteen members of the Divisional Crime Team.

They worked extremely hard, and constantly needed to work long and flexible hours to meet the challenges of changing crime trends.

***

At that time we were particularly concerned about the spate of 'bogus official' burglaries being committed in the borough, with more than one hundred and fifty offences during the year, on victims whose ages ranged from seventy-one years to ninety-years.

On Thursday 19 October 1995, two men claiming to be from the Water Board stole £61 from the home of a seventy-five-year-old woman in Bloxwich Lane, Beechdale. These were notoriously difficult offences to detect, and due to the age of the victims it was often very difficult to get accurate descriptions and witness statements. It was a despicable crime which often left victims traumatised, and no longer able to feel safe in their own homes.

***

During one period of 'Acting' Detective Superintendent duties I oversaw two separate murder investigations on the division, which occurred over one weekend period, on consecutive evenings, and involved the combined arrests of twenty suspects in a three-day period.

The Walsall edition of the Express and Star dated Friday 20 October 1995, told the story of the first murder as follows,

> *'A teenager died today after a fight at a late-night burger van near a Walsall nightclub complex. Police are treating the*

death of seventeen-year-old Merrick Nightingale as murder.

Twelve people have been arrested. Merrick suffered serious head injuries in the fracas in Bentley Mill Way at 2.10am just yards from the Zone and Ethos nightclubs. He was certified dead at Walsall Manor Hospital shortly before 3am.

Detective Chief Inspector Mike Layton, leading the inquiry, said crowds of people walking home from Zone and Ethos at the time of the fight might have vital information. Detective Inspector Ian Dodd of Walsall CID added that it was clear that revelers from the nightclub were involved.

Merrick was walking home with friends when he stopped to buy food from a Mr. Sizzle van. Frank Smith, owner of Willenhall based Ringside Refreshments, said the attack happened just ten feet from the van. It was the first night at work for the twenty two year old man, who was serving in the van with his girlfriend. He went on "There was no problem at the van. The teenager who died had ordered a couple of hot dogs but never picked them up" said Mr. Smith "He was shouting and it appears that he fell out with his mates. Suddenly they were fighting and kicking."

Merrick's mother Lesley, who lives in Wavell Road, Bentley was being comforted today. His aunt Elaine Walker of Edinburgh Road, Bentley said "The family are all absolutely devastated. I just hope they catch whoever did this to Merrick"

A spokesman for the Rank Organisation, owners of Zone and Ethos, said they had expressed concerns to police and Walsall Council that the operation of food vans was encouraging people to hang around the area after the clubs had shut.

A post mortem was carried out this morning, by Dr. Kenneth Scott, who found the cause of death to be a depressed fracture to the skull. Police are investigating how the injury was caused.

Residents in nearby Bentley Mill Lane who slept through the commotion today called for the nightclub to be closed, claiming, "Enough is enough." Yvette Brown said "It was an accident waiting to happen – it was just a matter of time before someone was killed." Two sixteen year old girls, an eighteen year old woman, and six eighteen year old men are among a dozen people from Darlaston and Wednesbury who are helping police with their enquiries.'

In a follow up article the next day his family said, *"The fight which killed him lasted just twenty seconds."* An aunt said the whole family was still reeling from the news. She said her son Adam had seen the fight, which had occurred on Merrick's first trip to a nightclub, and tried to stop it. *"Adam said it was all over in about twenty seconds. He was trying to fight them off. He was lucky he wasn't hurt."*

By this time we had released the three females without charge, and three other men on police bail, whilst six other men remained in custody.

We opened the incident room at Walsall Police Station for this murder enquiry, under the name of *'Operation Packington'*, and in accordance with Home Office Guidelines we administered the enquiry by using the computerised system H.O.L.M.E.S. (Home Office Large Major Enquiry System).

The system took information from several sources, and then cross-referenced them in different indices. The sources included such things as actions allocated to staff, documents and exhibits recovered, house-to-house enquiry forms, messages, personal descriptive forms, questionnaires, reports, and witness statements whereas the indices related to the creation of nominals, vehicles, personal details, and sequence of events records. These elements of cross-referencing were designed to make sure that links were not missed.

In this way we were able to build up a comprehensive profile of individuals, and the events in which we believed that they had been involved, by piecing information together from these different sources. It was not a 'perfect science', and there was no magic formula to the process of identifying suspects, but the combination of technology, and human expertise, brought real structure to the process, and was designed to both prioritise work, as well as avoid important details becoming lost within the sheer volume of paper.

The system was also used as the 'core tool' for creating prosecution files, and as the Senior Investigating Officer for *'Operation Packington'*, I would in due course be required to indicate, to both prosecution and defence lawyers, the existence of all 'non-sensitive' or 'sensitive' material. To achieve this we used trained 'disclosure officers' to assess the nature of all material held within the incident room and to categorise it from the basic level, where we believed it could be disclosed 'in unedited form', right through processes relating to 'public interest immunity', such as information relating to national security, covert policing methods, or the protection of vulnerable witnesses and informants.

In one way arresting a suspect was the easy part. You had to consider all of the requirements of the law in the knowledge that one small failure to properly disclose evidence, or a failure to comply with the rules of evidence in relation to the detention and interview of suspects, could lead to the collapse of a case in court, and the potential for the guilty to escape justice.

With this in mind I had to keep a detailed *'Policy File'* in accordance with West Midlands Police Orders, which were amended in 1995, and a copy of which were maintained on the HOLMES system. Staffing levels, briefing times and welfare issues were referred to but key to the policy file was a requirement to list the major lines of enquiry. Dependent on the nature of the incident these would routinely feature any outcomes to be followed up in relation to the forensic post mortem examination of the deceased, the parameters of house-to-house enquiries, and forensic examination of the scene of the crime.

We would need to define the scale of any search of the area surrounding the scene, for instance if we were looking for a murder weapon, and possibly research into similar patterns of offences for instance in a rape enquiry. Crucially we would always need to 'TIE' – Trace, Interview and Eliminate, witnesses, and highlight those that were classed as 'significant' as well as establishing a motive for the crime. All of the major lines of enquiry had to be regularly reviewed and signed off by the Senior Investigating Officer when completed. It was a critical document which drove the direction of an enquiry and required a 'clear head' when completing.

***

The Express and Star subsequently contained details of the second murder,

'A man was killed today in a fight outside a takeaway restaurant in Walsall – sparking the town's second murder enquiry in 24 hours. Paul Adshead, aged 30, was attacked outside the Kentucky Fried Chicken in Bridge Street. Witnesses reported seeing his head being repeatedly struck against the window of the restaurant by a gang.

His death comes less than 24 hours after the murder of 17 year old Merrick Nightingale during a fight at a late night burger van in Bentley Mill Way. Detectives are not linking the two deaths. Mr Adshead, from Paterson Place, Shire Oak died from head injuries.

A full post mortem examination was being held today. Two other men aged 28 and 27, suffered head and eye injuries in the disturbances at 12.20am. Police officers and a passer-by qualified in first aid attempted to resuscitate Mr Adshead but he was pronounced dead on arrival at Walsall Manor Hospital. Taxi driver Mohammed Amin, chairman of Walsall Taxi Association, witnessed the resuscitation attempts and said "There was blood all over the men. The police and ambulance crew were there for a long time doing their best with mouth to mouth and heart massage.".

A police spokesman said "We believe the parties involved did not know one another." A spokeswoman for Kentucky Fried

Chicken said, "It was an incident outside the shop and did not involve anyone who had been inside. The manageress contacted the police as soon as she became aware there was a scuffle going on outside."....'

Three teenagers aged sixteen, seventeen and eighteen years, and four men aged twenty-one, twenty-two, twenty-seven and thirty-one years were arrested following this attack.

Enquiries revealed that the group of attackers had been sat outside the Kentucky Fried Chicken when they became involved in a verbal altercation with another group, who were looking for taxis, which included the deceased Paul Adshead. The confrontation turned violent, and in the fight that ensued, Mr. Adshead was punched, kicked and stamped on by Paul Tennant, and two others, even though he was already unconscious on the ground. After the attack they prevented Adshead's friends from coming to his assistance, and assaulted those who tried to do so.

A post-mortem examination revealed that Paul Adshead received fractures to his jaw, and nose, and received sixteen injuries in total to his head which were caused by heavy blows. He died from respiratory obstruction due to inhalation of gastric contents and blood, which basically meant that he had choked on his own vomit.

There was a great team spirit on the CID, and the two detective inspectors working with me, Ian Dodd and Adrian McAllister, did a fantastic job. By Monday morning both offences were cleared and a number of people charged with murder. All this was done without asking for support from other divisions, or force headquarters, and we stayed within the contingency funding made available.

On Monday 23 October 1995 eighteen-year olds Robert Norton, Darren Kimberley, Jason Bates, and Callum McCall, and seventeen-year old David Greatrex appeared at Walsall Magistrates charged with the murder of Merrick Nightingale. Before a packed court, defence solicitors made no application on behalf of the five, who were all from Darlaston, and they were remanded in custody for one week.

On the same date Peter Tolley aged thirty-one years, Paul Tennant aged twenty-one years, Craig Perry aged eighteen-years, and seventeen-year-old James Bridges, appeared before the same courts, charged with the murder of Paul Adshead. One of the four, Peter Tolley, a married man with three children, repeatedly shook his head as the case was outlined by Miss Alison Hickman-Smith prosecuting and shouted, *"Not guilty. No not at all. I was nowhere near him."* from the dock. All four were refused bail and remanded in custody for a week.

Footnote: On the 10 July 1997 Paul Tennant, Craig Perry and James Bridges were convicted of murder.

In dismissing a subsequent appeal by Tennant against his life sentence, with a minimum tariff of sixteen-years, Mr. Justice Longstaff said that he had 'displayed considerable brutality.' Tennant had admitted to drinking eight bottles of Budweiser prior to the offence and claimed to have an underlying epileptic condition.

***

As if to serve as a reminder as to where I had come from, and the journey I had taken in my twenty-seven years police service to date, I received an unexpected letter dated the 22 October 1995 from a retired clerk in the British Transport Police, who lived locally. The letter read,

'Dear Mike, I know you must be a very busy fella with all that has been going on in the Walsall area. But after having heard you speaking on Ed Doolan's show last week I thought I would drop you a line to wish you well in your career. It seems not so very long ago when you first joined the B.T. Police at Rail House in Broad Street Birmingham. My wife and I wish you well in all you do. Regards Denis (EMMS) Ex Divisional Office B.T. Police (Clerk) PS I've been retired for eleven years now how time flies. All the very best.'

I had first met Denis when I joined the British Transport Police as a police cadet in 1968 and felt very humbled that he had taken the time to write to me after hearing me talking on Ed Doolan's Local Radio show about crime in the Walsall area. Years later I attended the funeral of Fred Taylor, a BTP Sergeant referred to in the letter. It was one of many I have attended over the years and, as was the norm, was attended by many serving and retired officers, with a police flag draped over the coffin together with a police helmet on top. The police service has always been one for tradition, and he received the customary salute on entering the church.

***

At 6.30am on Tuesday 24 October 1995, twenty-four officers were involved in raiding three flats at Newcomen Court, in Ivatt Close, in

Rushall. Twenty-two cannabis plants were being cultivated in one flat, whilst another was found being grown in a second flat in the same block. Both of the premises were vacant at the time, but with the evidence secured it would only be a matter of time before we found those responsible. In a third flat, cannabis resin valued at £100 was found and a nineteen-year-old female arrested.

We were now nearly up to thirty arrests for *'Operation Hillcroft II',* and after doing yet another press appeal I made my way down to the police college to attend a course. My head was still spinning with the sheer scale of the activity over the last four days but with a three-hour drive ahead of me I had plenty of time to put my thoughts in order.

***

Between the 24 October 1995, and the 3 November 1995, I attended a *'Management of Serious and Series Crimes'* course, at the Police College in Bramshill, which was regarded as a key element of training for Senior Investigating Officers.

The course was run by the reasonably new National Crime Faculty, within the college, and the students consisted mainly of detective chief inspectors, but with a smattering of detective superintendents. There were twenty-two of us on the course from forces across the UK.

***

On the 19 January 1982, the Home Secretary made a statement to the House of Commons in relation to a review of the so called *'Yorkshire Ripper'* case, which was carried out by Lawrence Byford, one of Her Majesties Inspectors of Constabulary, supported by an external advisory team which was set up in November 1980. The review also took account of the views of relatives of the victims. It proved to be a turning point in the way in which such major enquiries were to be investigated by police in the UK:

'The report highlighted major errors of judgement by the police and some inefficiencies in the conduct of the operation at various levels. In particular excessive credence was given to the letters and tape from a man claiming responsibility for the series of murders and signing himself 'Jack the Ripper.'

Another serious handicap to the investigation was the ineffectiveness of the major incident room which became overloaded with unprocessed information. With hindsight, it is now clear that if these errors and inefficiencies had not occurred Sutcliffe would have been identified as a prime suspect sooner than he was......I would remind the House that the Ripper case gave rise to the largest criminal investigation ever conducted in this country imposing a great strain on all concerned.....

I now turn therefore to the lessons for the future.....these deal comprehensively with the management requirements of the investigation of a series of major crimes; the training of senior detectives and personnel working in major incident rooms; the command of investigations involving a number of crimes which cross force boundaries; the harnessing for such investigations of the best detective and forensic science skills in the country; and the use of computer technology.'

In December 1982 Home Officer circular number 114/1982

was issued which articulated the various strands of training which those involved in investigating major crimes would be required to undertake, as well as highlighting the nature of the key relationship between the police and the media in terms of solving crimes.

All of this would take time to implement, indeed it was not until the 1 January 1984 that *'Standardised Incident Room Procedures'* were introduced and the murder of Susan Maxwell, aged eleven-years, highlighted the fact that at the time of her murder in July 1982 there was no nationally approved computer package available to police. By 1986 some progress had been made and West Yorkshire used a 'HOLMES' computer system to manage their investigation into the death of Sarah Jayne Harper aged ten-years. These were the foundations that my generation of senior police investigators would build on.

***

The course I was about to complete was designed to enhance skills in these key areas as well as putting students under a degree of pressure during the course of a practical exercise. It was certainly not designed to be a 'rest and recuperation' course.

It was a highly practical course which included presentations from senior colleagues based on actual murder investigations and major enquiries that they had dealt with. Many had hit national media headlines and were presented 'warts and all' so that we could learn the lessons of others.

There was nothing 'glamorous' about these presentations. Each of these experienced investigators had found themselves in the 'public eye' with ever-constant scrutiny from a media that could turn from positive to negative at will. They were under close scrutiny from the families of victims who wanted justice for their loved ones, and they were under constant scrutiny from their senior officers who wanted results that would stand the test of integrity and legality.

The Senior Investigating Officers (SIO's) showed themselves to be determined, but fallible, and above all human. Police officers need to eat and sleep, and cope with their own personal situations, the same as any normal person. They also make mistakes but in the public eye they are rarely forgiven.

***

With a 9am start, the first presentation I sat through, on Wednesday 25 October 1995, related to the murder of a female child, and Detective Superintendent Doug Smith from Cleveland Constabulary went through the case study.

Rosie Palmer was murdered in Hartlepool on the 30 June 1994. The three year-old was abducted, raped, and murdered after buying an ice cream from a van just twenty meters from home. Her partially clothed body was found in a house fifty meters from her home on the 3 July 1994. It was the third visit to the premises by police and the second time it had been searched.

The occupant Shaun Anthony Armstrong was widely disliked in the area, and known as *'Tony the Pervert'*. In 1993 a social worker had said that he was likely to be a risk to any child he came into contact. There was an outcry from the local community when the child's body was found and questions were raised with politicians as to why it had taken so long to find it. Armstrong was sentenced to life imprisonment on the 27 July 1995.

Statistically, we were told that if a child was missing for more than six hours there was a distinct likelihood that they were dead. We learnt about the value of ensuring that properly trained *'POLSA'* search officers were deployed, using defined search parameters, and discussed the 'golden hours' where actions taken, or indeed not taken, could determine the success or otherwise of an enquiry.

We learnt not to exclude any possibility, however unlikely it might seem, and not to take anyone on 'face value.' In this case relationships between various agencies were examined, and in particular the role of Social Services, the Local Authority, and Health Services, as well as the Police. Playing the 'blame game' when things went wrong achieved nothing.

***

At 4pm, also on Wednesday 25 October 1995, another case study was presented by Detective Superintendent Albert Patrick from the Metropolitan Police, and in this case involved murders within the 'gay community.' Known as the *'Gay Slayer',* Colin Ireland was sentenced to five life sentences on the 20 December 1993, at the Old Bailey, for the murder of five people, four of whom he strangled within a seventeen-day period. The thirty-nine year old was 6'2" tall and a survival expert, from Southend, in Essex.

His five victims were: Peter Walker, aged forty-five-years, found bound and naked at his home in Battersea, London,

Christopher Dunn, aged thirty-seven years, found strangled at his North London home, Andrew Collier, aged thirty-three years, found murdered in his home in North East London, Perry Bradley, aged thirty-five years, found strangled at his home in West London, and Emanuel Spiteri, aged forty- one years, found naked and murdered in his home in South East London.

All of them were homosexual men, who were said to engage in sado- masochistic sex, and all of them visited the Colherne Pub in Brompton Road. This meant that Ireland was able to tie up his victims, or handcuff them with their consent, before killing them.

This case provided a valuable insight into the mind of a serial killer who planned his attacks meticulously and was extremely forensic aware, spending hours at the scenes of his crimes to remove all potential traces of his presence. He destroyed his own clothing each time he committed a murder, and even waited at premises until the streets were busy so that he could easily blend into the background when leaving. He chose a very common type of cord to make it difficult for the police to trace its origins.

Colin Ireland was captured on a CCTV camera, with his victim Emanuel Spiteri, and CCTV evidence proved to be a key element of the subsequent prosecution. We also heard how detailed technical analysis in relation to a suspect's height assisted the investigation team. We were given valuable advice as to how to engage with potentially vulnerable sections of the community, and how to manage the media. We learnt that there was no such thing as doing an, 'off the record' interview, and if the information was not to be released it should not be said.

***

This was not an 'eight hour day' course and in order to consolidate the information we had consumed, the day concluded with a presentation from the Forensic Science Service.

***

On Thursday 26 October 1995, a presentation by DCI John Marshall from Northumbria Police focused on a serial murderer, and the importance of detailed forensic post-mortems of victims. We were encouraged to get second opinions, where appropriate, and to consider personality and offender profiling when dealing with such individuals. In this case the offender, Steven Grieveson, aged forty-two-years, displayed specific character traits which would have assisted the investigators if known.

Grieveson was arrested for the murder of eighteen-year old Thomas Kelly in 1993, and the murders of two fifteen-year olds, David Hanson and David Grieff, in 1994. All of the murders took place in Sunderland, Tyne and Wear and at his subsequent trial it was disclosed that he had committed them to conceal his sexuality. The victims were strangled and efforts made to burn the bodies.

In 2012 whilst serving a life sentence he was further convicted of the murder of a fourteen-year-old boy in 1990 and as recently as February 2014 interviewed in respect of yet another murder committed in 1992.

***

At 2pm on Thursday 26 October 1995 another case study was presented by Detective Chief Inspector Keith Bell from Nottinghamshire Constabulary, which focused on the abduction of a child from a hospital, and emphasized the sheer scale of activity within the incident room with over three thousand messages being raised, nearly a thousand statements taken, and more than fifteen hundred actions allocated.

Advice was given in relation to working with health authorities, social services, as well as media management. In this case it had been decided to delay the publication of video pictures and an, 'identikit' of the suspect to the media for seven days, and timing was an important consideration, and the subject of much debate.

The facts he recounted were that at 3.20pm on Friday 1 July 1994, Abbie Humphries, just three-hours-old, was in the arms of her father, in a private bedroom at the Queens Medical Centre in Nottingham, when a woman purporting to be a nurse entered the room and removed the child from the father on the pretext of taking it for a routine hearing test.

It was quickly established that the baby had in fact been abducted and a huge investigation commenced. The enquiry was beset by problems with hoax calls and at one stage even a 'physic' got in touch to say that she had information, whilst the press reported on the availability of a £50,000 reward. Abbie was eventually recovered at a house in Brendon Drive, Woolaton sixteen days later.

During the course of the enquiry the house had already been visited twice by police. Julie Kelly aged twenty-two years, was charged the following day with unlawfully taking Abbie from her parents and when she appeared in Court on Monday 18 July 1994 via her solicitor she expressed her 'deep regrets' for her actions.

***

David Phillips, the Chief Constable of Kent Constabulary, came to give a talk on 'Crime and the Criminal', immediately after the last case study, in which he stressed the need for investigations to be intelligence-led. He was a very accomplished speaker who I had listened to before and he strode up and down the auditorium, using his hands for effect, and without using notes. His key words in his introduction were *'Time-Vision-Energy'* and at that time many saw him as the architect of the concept.

***

On Monday 30 October 1995, at the beginning of week two of the course, Detective Chief Superintendent Phil Pyke presented a case study in relation to the murder of Sandra Parkinson in July 1994. She had been raped and strangled before being dumped down a forty-five-foot cliff in Salcombe, South Devon.

Alan Conner, aged thirty-two years, was subsequently found hanging from a tree in Brampton, Cambridgeshire, on the 6 August 1994. He left a suicide note confessing to the killing. As a result of genetic tests this was subsequently confirmed forensically. This case highlighted the pressing need for a national DNA database to be created after it was revealed that the National Criminal Intelligence Service were exploring links between the offender and six other murders, twenty two rapes, and five other sex attacks.

***

At 4pm on Monday 30 October 1995, one of the most emotive of the presentations was delivered by Detective Superintendent Albert Kirby, from Merseyside Police, who was the Senior Investigating Officer on the James Bulger murder case. Everyone in the packed room listened intently to the details of the case, which had previously captured the headlines in national newspapers for days.

At 3.30pm on the 12 February 1993, Jamie, who was just short of his third birthday, was led away from a Liverpool shopping-centre, by two ten-year-old boys Jon Venables, and Robert Thompson, whilst his mother was distracted. One of them held his hand as they led the crying toddler on a two and a half mile walk to a rarely used piece of railway line in Walton.

There they beat the boy with sticks and bricks, and finally killed him by dropping a twenty-two-pound piece of steel railway track onto his head. They then placed his body across the line and, by the time it was found two days later, it had been cut in half by a freight train. The police quickly established that he was already dead prior to this happening and a murder hunt followed.

You could have heard a 'pin drop' as video from shopping-centre cameras showed Jamie walking away with the killers. The CCTV was to prove their undoing and they were soon arrested, tried, and convicted of murder. Because of their age it was necessary to provide evidence of 'guilty knowledge' on their part and the services of two consultant forensic psychiatrists were obtained.

During the course of their trial in November 1993, the jury of nine men, and three women, heard evidence from the interview of one of the accused who described how they had *'stoned him with bricks but that he would not lie down'*. After being knocked out James showed signs of life as they piled bricks on his face. The jury was visibly shocked as they were shown fifty photographs of his injuries. When his body was found the lower half of his body was stripped.

Although the killers were sentenced to life imprisonment, the Judge, Mr. Justice Morland, set a minimum of just eight years, even though he had said in his closing comments, *"The killing of James Bulger was an act of unparalleled evil and barbarity. In my judgement your conduct was both cunning and very wicked."*

The case has continued to hit the press in more recent years as Venables and Thompson served their sentences, and were received back into society under assumed names, and with one of them subsequently being accused of further offences.

***

Immediately after this case study we were briefed on the evening of Monday 30 October 1995 and then commenced three very long days on a practical exercise, where, working in four syndicates, we attempted to conduct an effective 'investigation' into a simulated murder case, which drew together many of the components of the real cases we had learnt from.

The briefing was given by an Assistant Chief Constable from Avon and Somerset Police, and afterwards we were provided with a large document to assess. I undertook, within my syndicate, to analyse twenty-seven pages of it overnight and identified some of the key 'nominals' and events in the case. This was a team-effort, and whilst it was an exercise, we were being scrutinised by the staff, and there were three 'observers' from other Forces, so none of us were looking to be found wanting. By the time I had read everything, and listed sixteen significant features, it was well after midnight but it had to be done and I had to be ready for a 9am sharp start.

This was after all how it was in reality.

After going through a number of scenarios we were required to present our thoughts on what the significant features of the case were, what motives might exist, and what our views were on whether the culprit lived locally. The instructors were running to a script based on real life issues and we were being tested to see if we had picked up on potential lines of investigation. We were shown video clips, as the tasking process continued, at regular intervals, and were given specific times within tightly prescribed timeframes to present our findings.

Just to complicate matters the discovery of two other bodies was added to the mix, and we had to decide whether to link them to the investigation or not.

Based on that decision we had to prepare a press release, and deliver its contents, using an appeal to the public to highlight key issues, and the description of suspects.

On day three we developed an arrest strategy for suspects and then did an operational debrief for three hours. It was very focused stuff designed to be as realistic as possible.

To make sure that we understood the sheer scale of our personal responsibilities, the course concluded with a presentation and case study, relating to Robert Black, which was presented by Detective Chief Inspector Roger Orr from Lothian and Borders Police.

On Thursday 19 May 1994, Robert Black, a forty-seven-year-old van driver, from Stamford Hill in London, received ten life sentences in relation to ten counts of murder in connection with the deaths of Susan Maxwell, Caroline Hogg, and Sarah Harper, all children, whose bodies were dumped in the Midlands. The bodies of Susan Maxwell aged eleven years, and Caroline Hogg aged five years, were both found in Uttoxeter, within twenty-six miles of each other, whilst Sarah Harper, aged ten years, was found in the River Trent near Nottingham.

Black was already serving a life sentence in Scotland for abduction and sex offences, and although Mr. Justice MacPherson of Cluny indicated a minimum of thirty-five-years in prison, he said that in reality he expected him to be detained for the rest of his life.

He was found guilty of three charges of murder, two of kidnap, and one of false imprisonment, and three charges of preventing the proper burials of the three girls. He was also found guilty of kidnapping fifteen-year-old Theresa Thornhill, in Nottingham, in 1988. It took the jury thirteen hours of deliberation, after a five-week trial at Newcastle Upon Tyne Crown Court, to reach their verdicts.

As the mothers of the three girls looked on in court, Black

showed no emotion as the Judge ordered him to be 'taken down' to the cells after the verdict.

This had proved to be an absolutely massive police investigation which in many ways created the 'bedrock' as to how 'linked major investigations' were to be conducted by the police service in the United Kingdom for years to come.

***

During the two weeks of the course we also received presentations on a variety of databases and forensic techniques, such as the 'CATCHEM' database, which was a distillation of facts from a comprehensive study of child sexually motivated murders, and the persons who committed them over a period of thirty-two years.

We had lectures on DNA and Mass Blood Screening, Offender Profiling, Locating the Stranger Rapist, Forensic Pathology, and were updated on the work of the National Project Team for Investigative Interviewing.

I discovered the difference between 'organised' and 'disorganised' crime scenes, and the development of 'PAGIT' which was designed to link HOLMES incident rooms so as to create a central research facility for cross-border crimes. The list of information to be crammed in seemed endless, but all of it was critical.

We also did a session on stress awareness, and completed a sixty-four question test, which we scored individually. To some extent we were still in denial as a service about the effects of stress on police officers and 'going for a pint' was still the preferred remedy of many.

I left the course with a better understanding that *'the helmet of knowledge'* was as much a myth as the *'cloak of experience'* which assumed wrongly that seniority in service and rank always equaled knowledge and competence.

It was also abundantly clear that delegation of responsibility did not absolve responsibility, and that delegation to someone without the necessary knowledge and experience was in essence abdication. I resolved to do my best not to fall victim to these shortcomings as I pondered during the long drive home to Birmingham.

***

Then it was back to work and reality. At 1.40pm on Thursday 9 November 1995, two masked men in balaclavas burst into the Kings Hill Post Office in Darlaston Road, and threatened to shoot the male member of staff. Despite the alarm being activated they managed to smash a hole in the security screen and made off with cash in a car that had been stolen from Birmingham. In the run up to Christmas such offences were more prevalent as criminals anticipated that post offices, and building societies in particular, would be handling greater levels of cash.

***

On Wednesday 15 November 1995, the funeral of Paul Adshead took place at St James Church. The Vicar of Brownhills, the

Reverend Colin Thomas, described him as a *'victim who had been in the wrong place at the wrong time'*. *'Amazing Grace'* and *'The Day They Gavest Lord Is Ended'* were sung at the service.

***

On Thursday 16 November 1995, the Walsall edition of the Express and Star recounted,

'Police found more than £600 worth of cannabis during a drugs raid at a house in Walsall during which a thirty seven year-old man was arrested. The house in Anson Road, Bentley was raided by officers from the Divisional Crime Unit at 5pm yesterday. The arrested person was charged with possession of drugs with intent to supply and bailed to Walsall Magistrates Court. DCI Mike Layton said "This was part of the ongoing divisional strategy to combat drugs in the Borough. We formally concluded Operation Hillcroft on October 30 but drugs offences remain one of our priorities" Mr Layton made an appeal for further information.'

We followed this up on Thursday 23 November 1995 with further early morning raids, at addresses in Bloxwich, and Walsall, involving sixteen uniform and plain clothes officers. Hundreds of pounds worth of drugs were recovered. A further ten officers raided a home in Shelfield at 5pm. As a result of the search warrants we recovered cannabis resin, and cannabis plants, as well as a CS gas canister. Five people aged eighteen-years to twenty-six years were arrested.

At 6.30pm on Friday 24 November 1995, eight officers executed a warrant at a house on the Pheasey Estate and recovered cannabis resin, and amphetamine, with a street value of £1,000. Two men, aged twenty-seven years, were charged with possession of drugs with intent to supply.

On Thursday 30 November 1995, the Divisional Crime Unit were again deployed to execute a search warrant, but this time it was to recover £10,000 worth of stolen motor parts from a house in Goscote. The parts had been stolen from a van in Walsall, three days previously, which had then been burnt out. A thirty-five year old man was arrested and charged with receiving stolen property.

At 1pm on Friday 1 December 1995, officers from Bloxwich and Willenhall CID executed a search warrant at a house in Hadley Road, Beechdale. A cannabis factory containing heating, lighting, and irrigation equipment, together with more than one hundred plants with a street value of £15,000 were recovered. The raid was as a result of a tip-off from the public, and a twenty-nine year old man was arrested and charged with cultivating cannabis, and possession with intent to supply.

***

On Monday 4 December 1995, the Chief Constable held a meeting with all of the divisional management teams and instructed them to come up with a plan for dealing with service delivery calls during that month, and in the run up to Christmas.

We were already heavily committed with various operations but I was required to submit an urgent report within twenty-four hours to the chief superintendent outlining proposals for CID deployments.

Traditionally the CID did not always carry police radios but my proposals reversed this and created the principle of 'crime cars', which would respond quickly to all burglary dwelling houses, and in particular those defined as 'distraction burglaries.' These tended to be offences committed on elderly and vulnerable persons and often entailed a 'bogus official' gaining entry to a house and keeping the victim talking whilst an accomplice stole property. Sometimes they pretended to be gas officials pretending to be investigating a leak. On other occasions if youngsters were involved they would pretend to have lost a ball in the back garden. We were already running an operation on this type of offence called *'Nightstar'* and this approach would supplement that.

I also suggested creating interview teams in the cell-block at Walsall Police Station, where we averaged forty prisoners processed each day. We needed to free up uniform officers as quickly as possible, to get back out on the streets, and I put four CID officers into the block to assist.

During the course of the month we also conducted *'Operation Sidewinder'* in relation to robbery and burglary offences at commercial premises, as well as *'Operation Five Towns',* which focused on vehicle crime.

On Tuesday 5 December 1995, the Walsall edition of the Express and Star carried the following story,

'Dozens of suspected burglars were targeted today when police carried out a series of dawn swoops on addresses throughout Walsall. More than sixty officers raided homes as part of Operation Christmas Cracker. They seized stolen property including

televisions, hi-fis, video recorders, jewellery, and car parts worth more than £5,500. Detective Chief Inspector Mike Layton of Walsall CID said eleven people had been arrested by noon and they expected to make further arrests this afternoon. "We are delighted with the operation which is still ongoing" he said. The raids were part of Britain's biggest nationwide police crackdown on burglars.

Throughout the country police arrested 569 people in thousands of dawn raids. Twelve thousand officers took part in 4,000 raids in forty different police force areas'

In the West Midlands more than one hundred addresses as a whole were visited with eighty-one arrests and stolen property valued at £36,000 recovered. Given the size of the force I was satisfied that we had played our part.

***

On Friday 8 December 1995, four more drugs raids followed. In the morning officers recovered amphetamine and cash from a house in Aldridge, and later in the day recovered cannabis resin and amphetamine, plus thousands of pounds, at a Shelfield address. A third raid recovered crack cocaine, valued at £100, from a flat in Walsall, and as yet another warrant was executed, twelve cannabis plants were found in a house in Roebuck Road, Leamore. Five people were arrested in total.

***

On the evening of Wednesday 13 December 1995, a fight occurred in Webster Road, Coalpool, involving five persons. One man, aged twenty-five-years, was hit in the face by airgun pellets when shots were fired, and after being treated at Walsall Manor Hospital for minor injuries he was arrested together with a twenty-two-year-old man. Part of the road was cordoned off as a search was made for the other three men, and scenes of crime staff examined a vehicle, and the windows of a house, also damaged by shots being fired. I oversaw the investigation, whilst the detective superintendent was away, and it was soon apparent that this was as a result of an ongoing dispute between families from Webster Road, and nearby Beddows Road.

Once again I found myself appealing for information in the press but I knew that given the nature of the area people would be reluctant to come forward. It simply was not done to 'grass' on your neighbours and this had all the hallmarks of a local power struggle.

***

On a lighter note, on the same date, I received a 'mock' WC200 West Midlands Police crime report through the post from 1198 Eileen Bennett, one of my detective constables. She had heard that I had cancelled the traditional Divisional Crime Unit CID Christmas party at the Social Club attached to Aldridge Police Station, and whilst I had done it for good operational reasons, the decision had nevertheless gone down like a 'lead balloon'.

The offence on the report was listed as, *'Theft (of Christmas Function).The Modus Operandi section in the report read 'Known offender believing work was what detectives were paid to do decided without consultation to cancel social event causing extreme distress and fear of dehydration by all hard working detectives (It matters not that heaps of money will be saved and no hangovers). The property stolen was listed as 'Hangover' recovered 'Money saved' and damaged 'Not the liver'. The report of police action read 'Sir, This matter was reported through the grapevine and as a person not effected by the theft I felt it my duty to bring this matter to your attention. Personally I don't care cos I'm off to Australia but we must stick together!'*

I took it in good stead and the decision stood – the reality was that with everyone working flat out we simply could not afford the time to socialise. Who said that 'Scrooge' was dead!

On Wednesday 20 December 1995, John Plimmer made the headlines with the results of *'Operation Hailes'* when he claimed that the operation had effectively ended the link between eighty per cent of Walsall's drugs suppliers, and drugs importers based in Amsterdam.

At 5am on this date, with the support of Dutch police, the Operations Support Unit, Force Drugs Squad, and the National Criminal Intelligence Service, search warrants were executed at twenty-one homes in Walsall and Cannock, resulting in the recovery of cannabis valued of £350,000. Over one hundred and twenty officers were involved in the raids. A total of twenty one arrests were made in Pelsall, Rushall, Willenhall, Bloxwich, and Norton Canes and at one house, described as a cannabis factory, enough plants were recovered to fill a skip. All of those arrested were local to Walsall, apart from one man who came from the West Country. At the same time warrants were also executed in Avon and Somerset and Merseyside.

***

We managed to get through the Christmas holiday relatively unscathed but on Friday 29 December 1995 I was busy again, overseeing the investigation into an arson attack at 4am that day on a house in Chaucer Road, Harden. Someone set fire to a wooden veranda attached to the house, and a suspect was seen running away from the scene, with footprints in the snow leaving clear evidence of the route the attacker had taken.

Five people in the house, including a twelve-week old baby, and two other young children, were lucky to escape as the heat from the blaze shattered windows, and triggered a smoke alarm. The inside of the house was badly smoke-damaged with upstairs walls blackened by thick smoke. This could so easily have been a murder enquiry.

***

On Tuesday 2 January 1996, robbers saw the New Year in when, at 9.14am, two men, wearing balaclavas, burst into Little Bloxwich Post Office, in Stoney Lane, armed with a crowbar which they used to smash a security screen. As two female employees dived to the floor for cover the attackers grabbed cash bags, containing £2,000, before making off in a car parked at the rear of the nearby Nags Head pub. The raid was over in less than a minute.

***

On the afternoon of Thursday 11 January 1996, fourteen officers from the Divisional Crime Unit, and Area CID officers, executed warrants at two addresses in Morris Avenue, Bentley and Wolverhampton Road, Walsall. Amphetamine Sulphate, otherwise known as 'speed', to the value of £100,000, was recovered, together with a 'sawn-off' shotgun.

Two men aged forty-eight years, and thirty-years, were arrested. The drugs weighed ten pounds and it was a significant seizure. My team was building up expertise on drugs matters on a daily basis and the intelligence structure we had put in place on the division was really paying dividends.

***

At 6.30pm on Thursday 11 January 1996, the problems in Webster Road emerged again when a gang wielding baseball bats forced their way into a house. They attacked Darren Wain, aged twenty-seven-years, in front of his family, which included nine children, and left him with a broken nose before running off. Elaine Wain, aged thirty-five years, told the press that up to five men, some with guns, chased Darren into the garden before beating him, as the children looked on terrified. She claimed that, in a six month hate-campaign, eleven cars and a van belonging to them had been petrol-bombed, and that she had already been driven out of one property as three families tried to control the Coalpool Estate.

Her sister Debbie said at the time, *"It has become like the Bronx. People are selling drugs to children and wrecking the estate. But they are not going to drive me out. The only way I will be leaving is in a box."*

Two days previous we had already made three arrests for aggravated burglary, when another incident had happened at the same house. The offenders had been charged and bailed.

Between 8pm and 8.30pm, on the same day, a group of up to fifteen masked men, were seen in Webster Road and Beddows Road in Coalpool, firing shotguns in the air. Shortly before 8.30pm this group opened fire on another group in Beddows Road, before making off. Kevin Hickinbottom, aged twenty-five-years, of Beddows Road was hit in the face, and taken to Manor Hospital, along with a twenty-three- year-old who suffered shotgun pellet wounds in his arm and leg. They were both released after treatment.

At about 1am on the morning of Friday 12 January 1996, the Wain's Ford Sierra motor car was set alight outside their house, at 39 Webster Road.

In a follow-up operation, in the immediate aftermath, we made six arrests of local men, all from the Coalpool area, aged 20,24,28,29,and 31 years, as well as the twenty-three year old who had been injured. I suspected that we had not been informed about all of the incidents that had taken place and whilst all of the answers were going to be 'close to home' it was not going to be easy finding any independent witnesses.

***

At 11.20am on Friday 12 January 1996, a lone armed robber raided a Walsall Bank and a finance company in the space of a few minutes. The attacker first of all entered the Provident Assurance in Bridge Street, Walsall Town Centre, threatened staff with a firearm and stole cash and jewellery. Minutes later he entered the Yorkshire Bank, in nearby Digbeth, and again stole money. Customers in both premises, including in one case a child, were left terrified by the experience.

I attended the location, together with other CID officers, to secure the scenes for forensic examination, and to take witness statements. The town-centre was sealed off by uniform officers wearing bulletproof vests, as an extensive, but fruitless, search was carried out for the offender who was described as a white male in his fifties wearing a blue bobble hat. I spoke to the press at the scene and, given that witnesses described him as smelling of alcohol, made an appeal to licensees in the area who might have served him.

***

On Saturday 13 January 1996, three brothers, John, Kevin, and Lee Hickinbottom from Beddows Road, and Holdens Crescent, appeared at Walsall Magistrates Court charged with violent disorder in relation to the Coalpool incidents, and were remanded in custody. They were then followed into the dock by Brian Wain, Chad Wain, and John Sharp from Webster Road, Dartmouth Avenue, and Goscote Lane who were also charged with violent disorder. They were likewise remanded in custody for a week although eventually all six were granted bail, together with a seventh defendant, on condition that they lived at addresses outside Walsall, and did not interfere with witnesses.

On Wednesday 17 January 1996 the Walsall edition of the Express and Star carried a follow up story,

'Police have arrested eight people in a series of dawn raids – codenamed Operation Mollybrook – by 40 officers on homes in the troubled Coalpool area of Walsall today. The raids follow an

alleged Wild West – style gun rampage through the streets of Coalpool on Thursday night in which two people were shot. Detective Chief Inspector Mike Layton of Walsall CID said the police were determined to stamp out violence and drug dealing in the area. There were no reports of trouble during the raids. Mr. Layton said they were pleased with the success of the operation, but were still looking to make more arrests. "We are not going to tolerate public-order incidents in this area or anywhere else in Walsall." Three men in their 20's are being questioned about violent disorder. A twenty-five year old man was arrested on suspicion of conspiracy to supply drugs, and two others for possessing cannabis. Another twenty-five year old man was arrested on suspicion of theft, and a thirty-one year old man was arrested on an outstanding warrant........'

***

Elsewhere on the division robberies continued unabated, with a violent attack, the previous day, on a fifty-six year old Willenhall newsagent from New Invention, who required three stitches after being punched in the face and threatened with a knife by two raiders wearing masks. He didn't realise the extent of his injury until noticing bloody footprints on the shop floor. They also threatened his sixteen-year old female assistant before making off with just £30 from the till. It was typical of the senseless violence inflicted on innocent people in such situations, as adrenalin, drug, or alcohol fueled offenders 'pumped themselves up' prior to committing offences.

***

On Tuesday 23 January 1996, the five young men charged with the murder of Merrick Nightingale appeared at Walsall Magistrates Court and were committed to the Crown Court to be dealt with.

***

On Wednesday 24 January 1996, we continued with the burglary operation under the code name *'Sidewinder',* which resulted in the arrest of seventeen people, who were charged with burglary and robbery offences.

The operation was partly in response to a 10% rise in crime figures, over the previous year, with particular concerns over burglaries at commercial premises which numbered more than 3,500, and street robberies, with sixty alone during the month of December. The good news was that as a division we had an overall detection rate of 28% against a Force average of 24%, and good progress had been made in relation to detecting the 'bogus official' type burglaries which made life miserable for the elderly in particular.

***

On Wednesday 7 February 1996, a further operation was conducted in Coalpool as we sought to keep the pressure up.

***

On Friday 9 February 1996, the Health Service in Walsall released figures showing that the number of people being referred to 'Lantern House', Drug and Alcohol Centre in Lower Hall Lane had risen by nearly a third, to five hundred and twenty eight cases on the previous year. At the same time there had been a significant decrease in the age profile, with the youngest being aged just eleven-years.

There was an increasing use of amphetamines, crack cocaine, ecstasy and anabolic steroids in the area, as well as cannabis, LSD, heroin, and tranquilizers. By now we had started to work in partnership with education, probation and health services as part of the newly formed Walsall Drug Action Team. Working together was new territory for all of us and it took a while for trust to develop. Our primary aim was to take the dealers out of circulation but logic told us that education, prevention and rehabilitation were also central to a borough wide strategic approach, and the evidence showed that we needed to reach the young at the earliest possible moment.

***

On Tuesday 13 February 1996 we again put a large police presence into Coalpool.

***

On Saturday 17 February 1996 another weekend was disrupted with the discovery of the body of a partially-clothed man, found by Police Sergeant Graham Parrish, lying in a pool of blood between Heath Road and Simmonds Place in Darlaston. The victim, who was in his twenties, had his shirt ripped, and his trousers were torn and around his ankles. He was found by the officer as he checked the rear of premises. The deceased was later identified as Stephen Worthington, aged twenty-six-years, from Barlow Road in Wednesbury.

The area was cordoned off at 2.50am and John Plimmer, who was in charge of the investigation, and myself, attended the scene. In John's own words to the press the victim had taken *"One hell of a*

Beating" and was thought to have been hit with a concrete post. It was a dark and bleak place to die, in the cold and the mud.

Somewhat unusually a direct public appeal was soon made for Jason Michael Doughty, aged twenty-three-years, from the Wednesbury area to come forward. The reason for this was a phone call received by Ken Tudor, Sandwell Chief Reporter with the Express and Star, who picked up the phone in his office at 7.20am. The person on the line started by saying, *"There's a body behind Simmonds in Darlaston. It's on a dirt track at the side of the road."* He went on to explain exactly why he had killed the man and said, *"He went through a window and I followed him. I caught up with him on a dirt track and clobbered him.....it's a gory mess, a pretty gory mess."*

In this case we had a confession before we had a prisoner.

The man gave himself up later that day and when arrested was found to have a leg injury where he had severed an Achilles tendon. He was treated at Walsall Manor Hospital and discharged back into police custody.

A post-mortem on the victim by the Home Office Pathologist, Dr. Peter Acland, confirmed the cause of death as severe head injuries.

***

On Monday 19 February 1996 I went to Stafford Crown Court and sat through the 'plea and directions' hearing for the five men charged with the murder of Merrick Nightingale.

Callum McCall aged eighteen-years of Glyn Avenue, Robert Norton aged nineteen-years of Dangerfield Lane, Darren Kimbley aged eighteen-years of Herberts Park Road, David Greatrex aged seventeen-years of Rough Hay Road, and Jason Bates aged eighteen-years, of Victory Avenue, all pleaded not guilty. McCall, Norton, Kimbley, and Bates also denied committing an affray, whilst Greatrex admitted that offence. The case was adjourned for trial with Bates being remanded in custody, and the others on bail.

***

On the morning of Tuesday 20 February 1996, Jason Doughty, aged twenty-three years, appeared at Walsall Magistrates Court charged with the murder of his cousin Stephen John Worthington. He hobbled into Court with the aid of crutches, and one hand bandaged. With two police officers either side of him, he was allowed to sit whilst the charge was read out. There was no application for bail and he was remanded in custody for one week.

Paul, a former detective inspector, remembers the case, *"I was called out to the murder in Darlaston in the early hours, and at the scene saw John Plimmer and Mike Layton. I was put in charge of the outside crews. It all started following a dispute over a girlfriend, and finished with Worthington running from a house, and being chased by the offender, who caught him on waste ground behind a flat, after he fell over. The offender in pursuit suffered a leg injury.*

The victim had sustained significant head injuries from a concrete post being dropped onto him, whilst he was on the ground. One line of enquiry was that the suspect had contacted police and wanted to speak to some officers that he knew. I went to the

offender's relative's house in Wednesbury, at about 6am, but the
offender had already left to go to another unknown address,
although we found blood at the scene from his injuries.

I called out the two officers who knew the offender and at
about midday we went to an address, in Wednesbury town-centre,
where we found our suspect. He was arrested and taken back to
Walsall Police Station for interview and charge. I did the file for the
Crown Prosecution Service – it was my first murder file. He was
convicted at crown court and sentenced to life imprisonment."

***

Also on Tuesday 20 February 1996, in a follow-up operation to the
Coalpool disturbances, we searched a house in Ogley Road,
Brownhills, and recovered a 'sawn- off' shotgun, and more than one
hundred cartridges. We would need to see if we could get a forensic
match on the gun discharged in Webster Road but taking a firearm
'off the streets' was always welcome. We also recovered a vehicle,
which we believed to be stolen, and arrested six men and one
woman, who were held overnight.

***

During the same week, Walsall fire service announced that it had
stepped up its security arrangements as a result of the end of the IRA
ceasefire. Two bombings in London had increased speculation that a
bombing campaign might spread to the rest of the mainland.
Motorists were also warned by the police to be more careful after a
car, which appeared to have been abandoned, was discovered by
traffic wardens parked outside the Town Hall. This led to a full

evacuation of staff at the Town Hall, and the area being cordoned off by police, until the owner was found. The emergency services were nervous and with good cause.

For those who would say, 'it would never happen here', on Thursday 3 April 1997 two explosive devices were planted by the IRA as part of their 'pre-election campaign', on stanchions at Junction 9 of the M6 motorway in Walsall.

During the same period in March 1996, another case relating to the use of explosives in Walsall, a century before, was uncovered by the Local History Centre and recounted as follows,

'Six anarchists stood trial for threatening the foundations of British society with Walsall-made bombs. Four of them were convicted on the evidence of a small amount of hair, and clay, some colourful anarchist literature, and a very convenient confession.

Walsall anarchist Joe Deakin was the founder member of the Walsall Socialist Club and joined forces with a group, which included a fugitive from France, wanted for incitement to murder. Their plan was to produce thirty-six egg-shaped bombs with which to carry out attacks.

By October 1891 they were still in the planning stages, when they received written instructions as to how to make the bombs. On the 12 and 13 January 1892 they were arrested but the case looked 'dire' until Chief Constable Taylor managed to work Deakin into a frenzy and convince him that two others had confessed. He told the police that the hand-grenade bombs were to be aimed at Czarist Russia. Deakin got five years penal servitude, and on his release campaigned for the local Labour Party. The Chief Constable got a diamond tie pin from the Czar.'

***

On Thursday 7 March 1996, the inquest on Stephen Worthington was opened and adjourned.

***

On Monday 11 March 1996, an armed robber described as 'having a face like a bulldog', held a revolver to the heads of two women at Annie's Jewellers in George Street, Walsall, and stole £2,000 in cash, and a large quantity of jewellery. Their attacker threatened to 'blow them away' and tied them up in a back room, before calmly walking away from the premises.

On Tuesday 12 March 1996, the CID at Walsall took the unusual step of publishing the name, and photograph, of Stephen Hendy, aged forty years, who was wanted in connection with six violent robberies at banks, where a pistol was brandished. He was described as a violent individual who used disguises, and had even been known to dress as a woman. The British Bankers Association put up a £15,000 reward for his arrest. Hendy was arrested ten days later, when he was found asleep in the back of a lorry, on a lorry park in Pleck. He was subsequently charged with five robberies where thousands of pounds had been stolen and possession of an imitation firearm.

***

At 2pm on Wednesday 13 March 1996, during the course of the

ongoing drugs initiative, a flat was searched in Jones House, Penkridge Street, just five hundred yards from Walsall Police Station. Four barrels containing seventy-five litres of acid used for manufacturing amphetamine sulphate was recovered and a thirty-one year old arrested.

On Thursday 14 March 1996, during the course of *'Operation Banff'*, fifteen officers raided ten homes in Walsall and arrested ten people. At one house shoes valued at £3,000 were recovered, stolen from a van found burnt-out.

***

At the end of March 1996 a crackdown was announced on car crime in the borough, with five thousand offences relating to vehicles in just ten months, of which just seven hundred had been detected. Crime in general had risen 10% over the previous year but the division's 28% detection rate was still more than 4% higher than the Force average. This was set against the backcloth of the police in Walsall revealing that they had received some 81,000 calls for assistance in the previous twelve months.

***

On Tuesday 26 March 1996, three armed robbers burst into a post-office in St Anne's Road, at 11.40am armed with a pistol. As two terrified female customers fled, the robbers forced open a security door and sprayed the postmaster, and his wife, with CS spray. As he fought back they ran off empty-handed, and made good their escape in a stolen car, but not before he was threatened with a hammer. The attackers were described as two white men, and one black man, wearing balaclavas and masks.

***

On the 27 March 1996, two of those charged with the murder of Clarence Cooper were convicted, and a third convicted of manslaughter, in an investigation that had seen nearly six hundred statements taken. A fourth defendant had previously been acquitted. Life sentences followed.

***

The story in one of Walsall's local newspapers read, *'Four senior police officers have won promotion in Walsall where the detection rate is currently the highest in the West Midlands. Figures for April to September showed almost a third of crimes in H Division at Walsall were solved, the best results in the Force. Detective Chief Inspector Mike Layton of H Division CID has been promoted to Detective Superintendent, Detective Inspector Adrian McCallister of Willenhall Sub Division, and Detective Inspectors Martyn Thomas and Ian Dodd from Walsall all became Detective Chief Inspectors. Detective Superintendent John Plimmer Head of H Division CID said, "In my 26 years' service I have never known so many of a Division's top officers win promotion at the same time.*

Figure 34: The Fulbrook licensed House - 2016

Figure 35: Waste ground, rear of Simmonds Place, Darlaston, murder scene

Chapter Ten

The Rubber Heel Squad

(Stephen Burrows):

The departmental nickname apparently arose, because apocryphally, officers from the department charged with investigating the conduct of their colleagues wore rubber heels so that they could creep up unheard. The official name was, *'Complaints and Discipline Department'*, and later *'Professional Standards'*.

The ways in which police officers get into trouble have not altered much over the years, apart from the misuse of technology, which can amplify and publicise to the point of no return, stupidity and bad behaviour that might have in the past escaped public condemnation.

On my induction course, a grizzled old superintendent wagged a finger at our class of fresh young officers about to embark upon thirty-year's service, and imparted a few nuggets of advice that have stuck with me ever since. In fact, it strikes me that they are a good guide for life in general, never mind for police officers. The first thing he said was:

"You have to be better than everyone else because you have the power to take away their liberty. You have to be the example and beyond reproach. You have to live above the standards you expect of the public."

He then outlined his personal philosophy when judging his

own conduct:

"Before I do or say anything I always consider how it would look on the front page of the Daily Mail and what my mum would think if she saw it."

He concluded by telling us the areas where most policing pitfalls arose, which he entitled *'the four 'P's'*. I reproduce these below but have updated them to illustrate that they are still current today:

- **Paperwork** - The bane of the police officer's life. Many a good 'thief-taker' has failed because he, or she, could not put together a court-file, or simply could not manage the demands of completing all the necessary documentation on time and to standard. Falling behind on paperwork leads to the 'dark-holing' of items, cases failing, and enquiries into the causes. Having an irate Judge terminating a case due to the paperwork not being submitted, and sending his observations to a Chief Constable, is likely to indicate an early exit from the police service.

- **Pocketbooks** - Prior to the Police and Criminal Evidence Act coming into force in 1985, much evidence, including 'contemporaneously recorded' interviews, was contained in an officer's pocket notebook. There was a set of evidential rules called 'Judge's Rules', that governed how evidence was obtained and presented. These rules had emanated from stated-cases over many decades. They did however, place infinite trust in an individual police officer's honesty and integrity. Unfortunately, a number of cases, some of which were high-profile, involving perjury and willfully filling in evidential gaps, resulted in wrongful convictions, and undermined the credibility of 'Judge's Rules'. The situation prompted a review of the law, resulting in the introduction of the Police and Criminal Evidence Act, more commonly known as PACE, which is still in force today.

The PACE Act governs all aspects of arrest, search, detention, interviewing and identification, and has been built upon by case-law and detailed Codes of Practice. Thus the term 'pocketbooks', is broadened to become 'evidence' and the pitfall for officers acting under PACE in this respect is either the falsifying of evidence or 'adding a bit in', to fill any gaps that might cause a case to fail at court through a lack of continuity.

This rare practice strikes at the heart of an officer's honesty and integrity, any breach of which will usually prove fatal to a police career. It also spawned the phrase, *'noble cause corruption'*, whereby misguided officers added in a vital piece of evidence to ensure that a criminal they knew to be a 'bad-un', got their 'comeuppance'. This was 'noble', so the reasoning went, because it removed a bad person from the streets, usually a drug-dealer or member of an organised crime syndicate, who was proving difficult to convict conventionally due to witness fears and the like. The problem is of course, that the officer is not only lying and falsifying evidence, but is actually subverting the hundreds of years-old criminal justice process of this country.

A police officer's job is to arrest, investigate fairly and impartially to ascertain the truth, and to present the facts to a court, where a jury determine innocence or guilt with the burden upon the prosecution to prove guilt *'beyond reasonable doubt'*.

• **Prostitutes** - For this, read improper sexual conduct of any kind and add in anything likely to bring the police service into disrepute. The newspapers like nothing better than the heady mixture of sex and cops.

• **'Pop'** - This involves doing really stupid things whilst under the influence of alcohol. Drug abuse can be added in these days, as well as another 'addiction' – gambling.

To these older 'banana skins' can now be added:

• **The Internet and Social Media** - Making stupid comments, breaching security, posting embarrassing photographs and other transgressions online that result in enquiries regarding conduct, bringing the service into disrepute or letting criminals know exactly what is going on as regards warrants, procedures and police techniques.

• **'Digging a Deeper Hole'** - An officer makes a mistake or does something wrong. It may be trivial; it may be serious. There is a choice to make, often at a moment of stress, panic and unclear thinking – Do they:

a) Make a clean breast of it and take the medicine but retain integrity?

or,

b) Try to cover it up by lying or falsifying documents? I have lost count of the number of discipline enquires I have conducted, or sat in judgment upon, where the original offence would have resulted in a warning but the attempted 'cover up' warranted dismissal.

***

In 1993 I commenced working in the Complaints and Discipline Department, based in Lloyd House Headquarters, as a detective inspector. I had been in the CID as an, 'attached man,' and on the plain clothes department as described earlier, but this was my first permanent 'detective' post. I am sure that 'career detectives' would not have seen it as such but it was actually a role in which one handled investigations from start to finish, decided lines of enquiry, conducted the interviews, obtained all the evidence and completed all the necessary files.

Discipline investigations could be incredibly complex and difficult, dealing with, on the one-hand, hardened criminal complainants, and on the other hand that very small minority of officers who knew exactly how to thwart and impede an enquiry should they so wish.

There was also the constant challenge of maintaining the ethics of the investigation, and not being in any way tempted to jump to the defence of officers. It had to be a search for the truth and nothing more. In fact, keeping a focus on establishing the truth was *the* key to being successful.

By way of an example, I once received a complaint from someone who had been given a parking ticket for parking on double yellow lines. This may sound trivial, but they were actually alleging that the officer in question had falsified the evidence because they were racially prejudiced, and in fact they had not been parked on double-yellows. To make it worse they also alleged that the officer had been verbally abusive. This was serious, as racism, if proven, could easily have resulted in dismissal. Some photographs were provided that showed the complainants vehicle clearly parked legally just before the double yellows began.

I visited the complainant who was very polite and plausible and recounted a 'horror story' of oppressive behaviour and racist abuse by the officer.

I then interviewed the officer who denied every word of the allegations and maintained that the vehicle had been illegally parked and that the Asian driver had been the abusive one.

There were no witnesses and it was one word against another - who to believe?

I was scratching my head when I looked once more at the photographs taken by the complainant and noticed another car parked directly behind the offending vehicle. The registration number was visible, so I was able to trace the registered keeper and telephone them, with little hope they would be able to assist.

On the contrary, they remembered the incident very well. Their attention had been drawn to an Asian man who had been illegally parked, yelling and shouting at a policeman. They clearly recalled that after the officer had left, the man had moved his car to a legal space that had appeared directly in front of where the witness was parked. The man then disappeared for a few minutes and re-appeared with a camera. A witness statement was duly provided to that effect.

I later had the pleasure of watching the complainant read the witness statement. The complaint was withdrawn and the man was left in no doubt that he had come close to a charge for wasting police time and potentially attempting to pervert the course of justice, if it had ever become a criminal case.

***

Most of the demand, probably 90%, in the department, came from complaints, usually following arrest, or contact with an officer in a confrontational circumstance. If there was a court-case pending as a result of the initial contact, we had to make a decision as to whether the complaint was 'part-and-parcel' of the criminal case and could have evidential implications. This was true in the overwhelming majority of complaints and resulted in the matter being deemed *'sub-judice'*.

This meant that the complaint investigation had to wait until after completion of the criminal case. Complaint investigators would attend the trial or magistrate court hearing and listen to the evidence presented.

After a verdict had been delivered, unless there was an appeal, we could then make an appointment to see the complainant, with or without their legal representative – their choice. Sometimes this involved visiting prisons if the complainant had been found guilty and given a custodial sentence.

This meeting would invariably result in the complaint being withdrawn. It is no exaggeration to state that probably three-quarters of complaints stemming from an incident involving criminal proceedings were made to try and 'muddy the waters', cast doubt upon the officer's conduct and secure a 'not-guilty' verdict.

On average, less than five percent of complaints annually were 'substantiated' – resulting in some sort of proceeding, either discipline, or criminal, against the officer.

Officers are subject to a Discipline Code and can be dealt with on a criminal or discipline basis, or both, a rare illustration of 'double jeopardy' in the British criminal justice system.

This low percentage rate of 'conviction' for officers inevitably led to, and still does, calls for a totally independent investigative body, resulting in the establishment of the Police Complaints Authority, and latterly the Independent Police Complaints Commission.

The problem that these organisations had, and in my opinion still have, is that in my view the most effective investigators of police officers are police officers. As such they have never been able to train non-police investigators to fully understand the culture and also possess inside knowledge of the police service.

I worked in the complaints arena for several years, and of course can only speak for what I witnessed and experienced during those years. The reality, as I found it, was that the overwhelming majority of allegations were false, malicious, or spurious and were not supported by the evidence.

My other observation is that the complainants often could not resist 'gilding the lily', piling colourful allegations onto a fairly simple issue until their statement of events was so far divorced from reality as to be mainly fantasy, a fact that the investigation usually revealed. An allegation proved to contain lies was fatally flawed and could not hope to proceed, even if there was a nugget of truth somewhere within.

I was not naïve, however. There were, and are a minority of officers who are either stupid, bad at their jobs or, more worryingly corrupt, and they need to be identified and either dismissed, reformed or put before the courts, dependent upon the severity of the conduct.

I will conclude the chapter with two examples of wrongdoing where officers were imprisoned.

**

The other regular clientele of the complaints department were those who were frankly mad. We used to operate an 'on call' system whereby we took turns to answer direct telephone calls, or see members of the public who presented themselves at Lloyd House, Police Headquarters reception.

We had a set of 'regulars' who must have made thousands of complaints between them over the years. The procedures for discipline investigations allowed forces to present a case to the Police Complaints Authority to have such persons deemed to be 'malicious complainants', and many of them were. Some were rather sad people, often with clear mental health issues, but their complaints had to all be registered and dealt with in some way.

The particular one that springs to mind, who I met several

times in Lloyd House reception, was in fact an ex female police inspector in her seventies. She spoke clearly, rationally and with impeccable grammar as she recounted during her visits how undercover officers broke into her room at night and implanted devices in her head enabling them to control her and use her to keep observations!

***

My first example of serious misconduct on behalf of an officer also covers a number of the 'not to dos' detailed at the start of the chapter.It was a small plain-clothes unit, a sergeant, and three or four officers, tasked with investigating vehicle crime. They kept observations, made arrests, recruited informants, the usual methods of addressing the problem, and were successful.

Occasionally they would have a 'probationer' attached to the unit for a few weeks to gain experience.

One evening the sergeant, one officer, and the probationer, completed their tour of duty and decided to go for a drink. Instead of returning the unmarked police vehicle and using their own, they went to the pub in the police car.

Having imbibed, they set off to return the vehicle to the police station in order to book off duty. The PC, who was over the alcohol limit, drove, whilst the sergeant was in the passenger seat, and the probationer in the back seat.

They were in a police vehicle, technically still on duty. They had an impressionable young officer with them and should not have taken him to the pub. The driver drank enough to be over the limit.

The sergeant, being the 'ranking' officer was 'in charge' and 'responsible', had a duty to maintain discipline, adhere to the law and to act with common sense.

The driver lost control and collided with a lamppost. Thankfully they were all unhurt. At this moment, there was a crucial decision point.

They could have confessed. It is entirely possible that the driver and the sergeant would have lost their jobs, but there was a chance that honesty could have been put in mitigation and the position of the hapless probationer could have been protected.

They decided otherwise. They left the scene of the accident. The sergeant then phoned the control room and reported the police vehicle stolen and later filled in a crime report to that effect. Immediately they were in the territory of 'attempting to pervert the course of justice', an extremely serious offence, especially for a police officer.

The probationer was then browbeaten into silence and they all booked off duty. Early the next morning the sergeant and constable went to the probationer's home and took him somewhere in order to concoct and rehearse their 'story'.

Initially they got away with it, but the pressure on the probationer must have been enormous and rumours began to circulate as to what had taken place. Eventually the issue was reported to the complaints and discipline department. The fake story began to unravel.

A coordinated arrest and premises search operation was set

up in respect of the sergeant, and the constable driver. The probationer by now was being treated as a witness.

Together with a colleague from the department, I had the unpleasant task of arresting the sergeant and searching the address. We found evidence in diaries and later a confession was made, followed by a guilty plea.

Prison sentences of two years followed for a variety of criminal offences, including attempting to pervert the course of justice and technically 'stealing' the police vehicle by using it to go to the pub. Both offices were subsequently dismissed from the service. One initial mistake, compounded by a failed attempt to cover it up, led to this disastrous consequence.

***

My second example involves one of the deadliest addictions, that of gambling.

Most police stations used to have a social club. These were provided in order that officers had their own 'safe place' to socialise after a shift and the clubs often hosted Christmas parties, retirement 'do's' and other social events. They were of course licensed to sell alcohol, always seemed to have a couple of 'one armed bandits', and were usually run by a committee of volunteer officers, one of whom would be 'treasurer'.

The overwhelming majority of clubs ran perfectly and provided a fantastic service for police officers; indeed this author has many happy memories of 'a quick pint' with the shift after 2pm till

10pm shift.

A number of factors sounded the death knell for the clubs, most, if not all of which have now closed. Shift patterns changed, and it became less and less normal for a whole shift to book on and off together - in other words, the time slot for socialising together gradually evaporated.

The culture of 'drinking and driving' became unacceptable in society and in the police. It became the norm for dismissal to follow a drink-drive conviction and fewer officers would drink even a single pint and drive.

Finally, questions began to be asked about the cost in terms of premises, space and officer time, coupled with a view from senior management that the police should not be in the business of hosting licensed premises.

The closure of police clubs has thus proved to be a source of unresolved controversy and disagreement between officers, but the closure of a club was actually the catalyst that wrecked the career of the officer in this example.

He was the long-standing treasurer of a police social-club, a volunteer with many years of service, popular and viewed as a man of integrity who had been handling the club finances for as long as could be remembered. The type of person without whom police clubs could not have existed.

He was an 'ever-present' in the club, helping out behind the bar, ordering stock, cashing up at the end of an evening, and compiling the books for the independent accountant's verification.

As elsewhere, this particular club was run as a limited company, independent of West Midlands Police, with the officer 'volunteers' comprising 'The Board'.

Everyone expected to see the treasurer if they attended the club in the evening, often playing the 'jackpot' machines for an hour or more at a time. Perhaps this behaviour should have aroused a question, but it was commonplace in all the clubs that certain officers 'fed' the machines compulsively. In those days nothing was thought of it other than the odd comment about them funding the club on their own, or 'pissing it up the wall'. It was their choice how they spent their money, and if they wasted it on drink and gambling, they were not the first, and certainly would not be the last.

Into the routine of the social club in question fell the bombshell that it was to be closed and the space used for police purposes, along with a number of others at the time. A rear-guard action by the committee and regulars was fought to no avail and the closure occurred, celebrated, as elsewhere, with a final drink and a sale of fixtures and fittings owned by the club.

The point had come at which the club accounts had to be finalised and decisions made as to the destination of any surplus monies, often donated to charity in practice. After some prevarication and delay, it became apparent that there was a significant 'hole' in the accounts, and that around thirteen thousand pounds were missing.

I ended up investigating the mystery. It was a puzzle to begin with as every previous year's accounts had balanced, and been signed off by the accountant.

The Treasurer wrung his hands, could not understand it, had there been a theft? Unfortunately for him, the missing amount was too large to have been stolen in a single theft, so suspicion inevitably turned to those who had access to the takings on a regular basis. This included bar-staff, committee members and the treasurer himself.

There is nothing worse as a police officer than being involved on the wrong side of a corruption enquiry, as the taint of suspicion persists whilst the investigation proceeds – often at a slow pace, relationships deteriorate, and a gradual realisation dawns that someone, a friend and colleague, is dishonest and has successfully hidden the fact.

The spotlight turned towards the cashing up and banking process and it became obvious that the treasurer was usually trusted to do this alone – after all he had been doing it for years. He would empty the gaming machines and tills, reconcile the money to the till rolls, place it in a safe overnight and bank it the next day.

Inspection of the records indicated that there were missing till rolls and discrepancies, including stock held.

During lengthy interviews the treasurer steadfastly denied any wrongdoing and could not explain what had happened - the mystery continued.

I began to look at motive, and the 'fruit machine' behaviour came to notice. The treasurer, it seemed, spent a lot more time gambling than had initially appeared. I pursued the gambling line of enquiry and eventually located a local 'bookmakers' frequented by him. It did not take long before a history of daily betting on the horses was revealed.

Eventually the sorry tale emerged, although it was never admitted in interview. An addiction to gambling was the root of the issue. The treasurer's increasing habit had gradually become financed by his own money and short-term unofficial 'loans' from the bar takings.

At first it was small amounts, and any losses could be covered by his own funds, or lax book-keeping. A fictitious amount was carried as a float in the safe, which was never physically checked by the accountant or anyone else, there was lax reconciliation between takings and till rolls; the machines were even easier to 'cream' some cash from. Hence he had managed to balance the books in time for each annual audit.

I never did find out how long the 'fiddling' had been going on for, but he was charged with theft over a period of four year's accounts. I personally believe that the gambling had spiralled out of control during the final eighteen months of the club. He began losing more and placing higher stakes in an attempt to win the money back. It was all under control so long as the police club 'bank' was in operation and the 'balancing' float was never checked, but the club closure spelt curtains for this enterprise.

The treasurer later pleaded guilty, lost his job and went to prison. It was hard not to feel sorry for him as gambling addiction is an illness, but he had betrayed his office of constable, his friends and colleagues, so incarceration was inevitable. I never enjoyed seeing police officers go to prison but I also never had any doubts about the need to confront unacceptable conduct of this type.

My experiences and knowledge of discipline investigation were to lead directly to the point at which my career path met my co-author's in *'Operation Elmtree'*, an investigation that forms the core of the epilogue to this book.

Epilogue

(This chapter was written jointly and each individual segment of recollection is preceded by the author's name in italics).

(Michael Layton):

At 11.45am on Thursday 18 April 1996 I had an appointment with the chief constable at Lloyd House, Force Headquarters, where I was formally informed of my new posting. Once again it was to be a promotion within the CID.

Once it had been published in Force Orders I received a nice note from an officer who had been a fellow detective sergeant at Steelhouse Lane Police Station in the 80s. It read *'Det. Supt Layton – Mike, I guess this will be the last time that I can get away with first name terms but I wanted to pass on my congratulations and wish you all the best. Keep the blue touch-paper burning. With regards....'* He must have had a crystal ball!

Amongst best wishes on yet another 'leaving' card was a double edged comment from one anonymous member of staff with a sense of humour who said simply, *'Like a wart you grew on me. Best wishes at Lloyd House.'*

On the 29 April 1996 I was promoted to the rank of detective superintendent, (CID Support), and found myself back in force headquarters at Lloyd House in Birmingham. My responsibilities included the management of twenty-one coroner's officers, the Firearms and Explosives Department, Headquarters Major Incident Room staff, and the coordination of major incident resources across the whole of the West Midlands. I also had oversight of the Headquarters Family Protection Unit so, all in all, a mixed bag of disciplines. Whilst the promotion was welcome, the job itself was nothing short of a 'poison chalice', and a thankless task, as I was soon to find out.

I met the previous post-holder at Lloyd House, at 10am on Wednesday 24 April 1996, for a bit of a handover. He had already cleared his desk and left me with a few files and papers and that was it – he was gone and looking rather relieved!

On top of my 'day job', one of the first things I was given to do by the head of CID was to conduct a review on the force policy relating to post-sentence prison visits, and the practice of 'writing off' crimes in accordance with Home Office guidelines. Whilst it was quite appropriate at the time to conduct these interviews they sometimes attracted controversy with allegations that convicted criminals were just 'clearing the books' for the police, when visited in prison.

Two months earlier, two West Midlands police officers had been suspended over allegations that they had induced offenders to sign blank police statements, which were later filled in with unsolved crimes in order to boost the clear-up figures.

A criminal investigation was launched by the Complaints and Discipline Department, and as the force defended its policy and procedures as being ethical, the chair of the Police Authority was obliged to pass comment. A local Labour MP Dr. Lynne Jones weighed in saying, *"If the allegations prove to be true then the officers should be dealt with appropriately. Justice has got to be seen to be done and bad apples must be rooted out."*

On Friday 3 May 1996 at 6.30pm, I had a 'leaving function' in the social club at Walsall Police Station. I was very proud of what we had been collectively able to achieve and I wanted to wish my colleagues the very best in the future. I deliberately wanted it to be a 'low-key' affair, although more than a hundred people were present. As is the norm I was presented with some gifts, and a few kind words were expressed by Alan Jones, the Chief Superintendent, along with the usual ritual jokes at my expense.

In responding I paid tribute to the spirit of the H Division. In talking about success I reminded the audience that Indira Gandhi had once said that there were two kinds of people, namely, *'those who do the work, and those who take the credit'* and urged them to be in the first group as they would find less competition! I reflected on the sadder moments on the division and remarked on Stewart Grogan who twelve months to the day had experienced his accident. I paid tribute to Alan Jones for his support and commented, *"One of the quickest ways to meet new people is to pick up someone else's ball on the golf course and to start playing with it. Mr. Jones has a propensity for squeezing other people's balls so it must be good advice."* At the end I joked that Arnold Schwarzenegger had said, *"I'll be back,"* and that whilst I wouldn't make prophecies you could never tell.

Little did I know that in less than a year I would be reintroducing myself to many of them again, but this time I would be 'the boss' and that the prophecy would come true.

***

As I was leaving the division, there was a new arrival in May 1996 in the shape of Dave Faulkner who, as a detective constable, had just spent nine years on the Force Drugs Squad, and was something of an expert in drugs and covert policing tactics. He describes his early experiences at Walsall:

"Being on the CID we often used to pick up prisoners who had been left in the cells overnight for us to deal with. When there weren't any we often went out first thing in the morning to try to pick up people wanted for various offences.

Being a 'Brummie' I quickly realised that the culture was totally different. In Birmingham if you knocked on someone's door you normally got loads of 'verbal grief' but that was as good as it got and then they would come in quietly but invariably tell you nothing when interviewed.

In Walsall when you knocked the door they always wanted to fight. I couldn't believe the number of times that I finished up rolling around the floor in someone's hallway. The difference was that once we got them to the police station and had given them a 'fag' to calm down, they would talk to you all day and we often cultivated informants.

In the first few weeks, because of my drugs squad background, a couple of younger officers came to me for advice. They were looking to execute a drugs warrant at an upstairs maisonette on the Beechdale Estate but the problem was that the drugs dealer had a good view all round from his upstairs windows.

430

They had already tried once to execute a warrant once but he had got rid of the 'gear' before they could get the door open.

I had a bag of 'props' that I had used on the drugs squad, and I solved the problem by dressing up as a postman in a blue jacket and blue hat. I presented myself at the door of the premises with a big parcel in my hand and knocked it. The dealer started talking to me from the other side of the door and initially said that he wasn't expecting anything. I told him that I would take the parcel back to the depot and that he would have to pick it up from there. At this point he changed his mind and opened the door and we all piled in. He was well 'pissed off' when we recovered the cocaine and didn't think that we had played 'fair' at all – it was not in the rules!!

A couple of weeks later Mick Swinnerton approached me with a similar problem at another address in Bloxwich. Once again I got dressed up in the postman's outfit and went through the same scenario. The dealer was a bit of a 'Hippy' and had a reinforced door. Again at first he was reluctant to open the door until I said that he would have to collect it from the depot. Curiosity got the better of him and he opened it at which point officers standing out of sight at the side rushed in. We recovered a stack of drugs and once again he was thoroughly upset with the police tactics.

There was a slight twist to the end of the story – a week later I was in the CID office when a uniform officer came in to advise someone about a case of assault. He said that he had a postman at the counter with a parcel which he had tried to deliver to the address of another cannabis dealer on the Beechdale Estate. After knocking on the door the person came out and hit him with a baseball bat!!

Things did not always go to plan. I was out with the Divisional Observations Team one day and we were trying to do mobile surveillance of sorts on a heroin addict and drugs dealer, who was also a disqualified driver. He used to pick his drugs up in Walsall and then take them back to his house in Bloxwich where he would hide his 'stash', sometimes in the front garden.

I had the 'eyeball' on the target who stopped at some traffic lights and indicated to go left. I was behind him in the outside lane and I radioed the team to say that in order not to 'show out' I would drive straight on, and someone would need to go with the target. When the lights changed I duly drove straight on but when I looked in my rear view mirror I noticed that the whole of the team were following me. I called up and queried what was going on and the answer was that they were trying to avoid showing out as well so followed me. I used a few choice words to explain that we had now lost the target! Fortunately we had got static observations in place at his address and picked him up again when he arrived. They saw him hide some drugs in the garden hedge so he still had his day in court."

***

On Tuesday 7 May 1996, at 8.30am, I met the staff from the HOLMES Unit. Whilst they were only a small team, they were experts in their field of work and were invaluable in terms of being able to set up the computer systems for major incident rooms at short notice.

They could be quite protective about their roles but I had come across this type of behaviour often and it didn't bother me. They had previously operated on the basis of being left to their own devices but this wasn't my style and they would need to embrace change!

As the coordinator for major incident resource staffing across the force, I was expected to play 'honest-broker' with my fellow detective superintendents on divisions, none of whom wanted to give up their scarce CID resources for other people's major enquiries. Hence I spent most of my time trying to apply diplomacy, and to manage expectations to the point where 'no meant no' to unreasonable requests.

Sometimes my phone calls would go deliberately unanswered, and I even got cut off once during one irate exchange, but as I adopted the same tactic people started to realise that they needed me more than I needed them. In truth it was a thankless task where everyone thought that they 'were hard done by', and I was stuck in the middle.

I also introduced a system of financial reviews on each major incident to make sure that there was due diligence in respect of the contingency funding allocated from headquarters CID to divisions. At the same time I created a system for monitoring abstractions of staff across the force, and published the figures to each divisional crime manager and HR Manager, so that they could all see each other's figures. Armed with these extra tools I worked with Senior Investigating Officers to look at *Operations Asia, Laura, Manyana, and Bahamas*, which were all murder enquiries. As a result of this I was able to engage positively in decisions about returning a number of staff to their own divisions.

'Operation Manyana' related to a shooting incident in an

isolated lane in Handsworth Wood on Christmas Eve 1995, where the injured man required protection from the force Tactical Firearms Unit whilst he was hospitalised. This case was eventually linked to *'Operation Oaktree'*, three days later, following a fatal shooting in a residential area of Handsworth Wood.

Concerns had already been raised by senior officers in the force about an increase in gun-related crime, particularly in the Birmingham Inner-City areas, and these incidents just added to the debate. It was clear that some of this activity was being fuelled by 'organised' gangs and that the force would need to sharpen its approach to intelligence, and to consider whether to dedicate more resources to this particular area of criminality.

***

At 10am on Tuesday 14 May 1996, I met the coordinator for all of the coroners' officers, who, in the main, were very experienced retired police officers who had returned to the Force in a civilian role.

The coordinator's post had only recently been created, and he was a former inspector from the force, also with relevant experience. Whilst the officers were employed by the West Midlands Police Authority and, 'on paper', they came under the overall line management of the Head of CID, and formed part of Headquarters CID Support, the reality was that, on a day-to-day basis, they reported directly to one of the seven HM Coroners who covered the West Midlands area. I later met with each of the Coroners on an individual basis.

On Wednesday 5 June 1996, I conducted an interview for the Chief Inspectors post in the HQ Family Protection Unit, which was one of my less controversial tasks, and resulted in Steve Burrows taking up the post – our first meeting.

***

(Stephen Burrows):

I went for the job because I was on *'Operation Gunter'*, a corruption enquiry, at the time, had recently passed a promotion board, and became aware of a vacant DCI role that it seemed no-one wanted. For some strange reason it was seen as a woman's job, probably because it had 'family' in the title. I had a feeling, which proved to be correct, that the new Chief Constable, Edward Crew, would shake the Force up. In my experience, this usually meant that all promotion opportunities to senior rank stopped whilst a 'new broom' approach was implemented, so I decided to go for the role that no-one wanted, and got it.

My interview was the first time Mike and I had crossed paths despite working many of the same locations for many years – and living within a couple of miles of each other, as we found out subsequently. To my relief it was a really interesting and challenging job, another one of those 'lifting of the stone' scenarios similar to domestic abuse, with demand rising, new skills required, and specialist resources scarce. This was because the new chief constable's philosophy was to strip out specialist units, return staff to local command units and attempt to develop 'omni- competent' police officers who could perform a wide variety of tasks. This approach was never going to satisfy the requirements for skilled investigators into child abuse and I was prepared for a battle. I started by visiting all of the divisional Family Protection Units to review them.

They were totally under-resourced and a lot of the staff were stressed, and completely overwhelmed by their workloads. A lot of the officers in the units were women, and at that point the force had not really introduced the same level of flexible working arrangements that they have today so the long hours and distressing subject material were adding to the pressure.

My office at Lloyd House was on the same floor as all of the senior CID management, and next door to Mike's. I was a late entry into the CID and I regarded myself as a something of a 'CID moderniser'. I was not afraid to say what I thought, and wore my 'heart on my sleeve', especially when I engaged with people who I believed were out of touch and not willing to change.

This honest approach did not suit everyone, and I often found myself being politely ignored, and occasionally not so politely. I was beholden to none of them so it didn't bother me.

***

(Michael Layton):

Being part of such a large force meant that suspicious deaths and murder enquiries came with relentless frequency. Jon Lighton retired as an Inspector in West Midlands Police and recalls one such murder investigation that he played a very small role in, but remembers it well due to the stoic behaviour of a 'street girl' that he was asked to interview.

On the 15 August 1996, sixteen-year-old Lucy Burchell went missing from the Walsall area. The teenager had turned to prostitution after watching an ITV series called *'Band of Gold'* which portrayed a 'vice-girl' in Bradford. Described as a bright and happy teenager, she was studying for her GCSE examinations, during the daytime, and in the evenings could be found leading a secret life outside the 'Dog and Partridge' pub in the Caldmore area of Walsall.

The area was plagued with street prostitution, and residents were used to seeing strangers in the area. Sometimes they were 'punters' looking for girls, and sometimes they were plain-clothes police officers looking to make arrests.

Lucy's body was found in some undergrowth five days later next to the Locarno Ballroom in Edgbaston Reservoir, Ladywood. She had died from a heroin overdose and two men subsequently stood trial for offences relating to the death.

Jon was working as a PC on the Divisional Crime Unit at Ladywood at the time and recalls:

"I was asked to go with a CID officer to Walsall to get some background information from a prostitute who was familiar with the Caldmore area. From my recollection she was a local girl, attractive, and was I think wearing a dirty blonde wig. She was in her early twenties and had worked the area for a while. She was a

confident girl who didn't work for a pimp. She came forward after the suspects for the murder were arrested. She knew them, as they used to visit a local Indian restaurant, and they had paid for her services.

She knew a lot about the 'punters' who used the area and said that some of them showed no respect towards the girls at all and tried to mess them about. She was a strong character and described one incident where a client had asked her to provide a list of her 'services' and how much each would cost. He then decided that he wanted a 'blow-job' but half way through changed his mind and said that he wanted sex.

The girl described in no uncertain terms challenging him with words to the effect, 'You don't go to McDonald's, order a cheeseburger, take a bite, and then take it back and ask for a 'big mac' instead do you?' It was a very sad case but for many of the girls working the area they felt that they had no choice but to carry on."

***

As one of the Headquarters CID management it was not unusual for us to be the first port of call when members of the Chief Officer team had a crime related issue to be sorted.

On Thursday 12 September 1996 the Chief Constable of the West Midlands Police agreed to a request, from South Wales Police, to establish an enquiry team to investigate previous management decisions made in 1989 with regard to alleged criminal activities involving child abuse at a Children's Home. At the same time the

South Wales Police referred the matter on a voluntary basis to the then Police Complaints Authority (PCA).

Bob Packham, the Assistant Chief Constable (Crime), was nominated to head the enquiry, which was classified as a Category D, in accordance with West Midlands Police policy on major crime – (a sort of 'catch all' category at the other end of the spectrum to a murder enquiry where the offenders' identity was not immediately known.)

Shortly after this decision had been made my phone rang and I answered it promptly in my office at headquarters. I recognised the voice of the ACC, who had his office on the floor immediately above me, *"Mike are you busy for the next couple of days.....?"* This was not a question, it was a request, and the only answer to give was to confirm that I was both willing and available to assist him. It just didn't do to try to say 'no' and thus I became the Senior Investigating Officer, (SIO), for *'Operation Elmtree'*, and a couple of days turned into six months.

We quickly decided to make use of the HOLMES computer system and we identified a room at Cowbridge Police Station, in South Wales, in which to base the enquiry team. It was a non-operational station which housed some of the South Wales headquarters CID, but was ideal for our purposes as we 'kept ourselves to ourselves.' The locks were changed on the doors and security was tight.

Cowbridge Police Station was described by one historian in the following terms, *'In April 1859 Mr. Nicholl-Carne put forward the question of providing a Police Station with two cells and*

accommodation for two constables at Cowbridge. The Chief
Constable reported that the constables had been permitted to use the
cells under the Town Hall which are 'very damp, badly ventilated
and without the usual convenience. After heavy falls of rain there is
half inch or more of water on the floor and of course the cells there
are quite unavailable. I consider them quite unfit for prisoners'. The
contract for the building of the Police Station was given to Mr. M.
Moore at a price of one thousand five hundred and sixteen pounds.
The new building, a graceful one, was completed in 1862.'

A sketch of the stone-clad building with large arched windows, and a prominent chimney stack was subsequently drawn by a constable with the initials ESR and collar number 1186.

Clearly we were the temporary occupants of a piece of history.

I was fortunate enough to be able to nominate my own deputy SIO, and chose Steve Burrows, who had the required experience of complaints and discipline procedure and investigation. We gathered a small team of investigators and incident room staff around us and at its height seventeen police officers and police staff, were engaged on the enquiry, including Detective Sergeant Steve Trenbirth who had worked with me on *'Operation Red Card'.*

We briefed the team fully, on the 16 September 1996, before starting to work Monday to Friday's in Wales, and going home at weekends. Not good for family life but then nothing had changed for me over the years.

(Stephen Burrows):

We used to drive home on a Friday afternoon from Wales. During this period I actually moved house to Worcester and my wife had to deal with everything, including the discovery of an outbreak of 'dry rot' at our old house that held up the sale. Mike insisted that all the police vehicles were kept at police stations over the weekend periods, and we routinely drove past my new house whilst on the motorway. I could nearly see it from the M5.

Mike would ironically invite me to wave to my wife as we drove all the way back to Halesowen to drop the car off, before I drove all the way back down the motorway to Worcester again. Mike asked for total commitment and would accept nothing less. A couple of the investigators did not last very long and were returned to their divisions. They hadn't done anything wrong but were simply not on the same page and were having difficulty with investigating police officers.

We stayed in a hotel called *'The Bear'*, on Cowbridge High Street, which was very pleasant, with friendly staff, if not a little reminiscent of *'Fawlty Towers'*. Welcoming literature quoted *'The Bear Hotel offers you all the modern day comforts whilst still retaining the charm and character of a hotel whose history can be traced back to the 12th Century'*.

Evening meals tended to be very extended affairs, as the service operated at one speed which could not be classed as fast. You could start eating at 7pm, and still be finishing your meal at 11pm, with no time to get to the bar! My most interesting experience was one particular breakfast, when the only member of staff on duty in the restaurant was a French waitress, who spoke little English. It took us a while to realise that the chef had not turned up and that it was either toast, or toast, on the menu. We eventually gave up and headed to the supermarket for sandwiches!

Some of the team were into fitness. One of them in particular was fanatical about running, and would think nothing of running ten miles. I used to go to the small gym at the Bear because I knew it was the only place that Mike wouldn't find me. Exercise was not then on his list of priorities!

(Michael Layton):

Cowbridge is a beautiful market town in the Vale of Glamorgan, once occupied by the Romans, and just ten miles from Cardiff. It has a long High Street, and contains at least fifty-five listed buildings, and small shops full of 'knick-knacks' with places where you could enjoy a drink, and pass the day away. It was a place where everyone knew everyone, and nothing really happened.

***

A more complicated sequence of events would be difficult to create for *'Operation Elmtree'* but with persistence we slowly managed to put some of the pieces of the jigsaw puzzle together, as follows.

At the beginning of 1989, an allegation of indecent assault was received by Merseyside Police, from a nine-year-old boy following an incident at a swimming baths in the Wirral. The suspect left the scene before the arrival of police but was seen at the same location a month later, and the registration number of his vehicle taken. Enquiries revealed that he was a social worker at a Children's

Home.

A few weeks later, officers from South Wales Police visited the Children's Home in an effort to speak to the suspect but he was not there, and a message was left for him to make contact with the police. Later that evening the suspect spoke to his mother and that was to be the last time she would hear his voice.

The following day, the body of the suspect was found in a car in a remote quarry in the Gwent Police area. A hosepipe was attached to the exhaust of the vehicle and he had apparently died by breathing in carbon monoxide fumes. A Coroner's Inquest subsequently confirmed a verdict of suicide.

Three months after his death, two suitcases were recovered by officers from the British Transport Police from the 'Left Luggage' lockers at Cardiff Railway Station. The suitcases contained material which could be classed as having paedophilic content, and it transpired that they belonged to the dead suspect.

Initial enquiries were overseen by a detective inspector from the British Transport Police, who went on to have a distinguished police career. He was a man of great principles who, in essence, felt deeply hurt that he had been 'dragged into' an investigation where his personal ethics and integrity were called into question. Apart from the fact that the suitcases had been recovered on railway property, there were no offences disclosed within their jurisdiction, and subsequent efforts at trying to point towards this being a BTP led enquiry, simply did not hold water.

Ultimately he passed the suitcases, and the contents, to a

detective inspector from South Wales Police. The suitcases, and the contents, were photographed and some of the contents were passed over to two officers from the Metropolitan Police, who were investigating the activities of yet another suspected paedophile based in London who was suspected of corresponding with the dead social worker. This man later served a prison sentence for indecency offences.

(Stephen Burrows):

One of our lines of enquiry was to try to recover the case-file for the particular London prosecution. We went to the relevant London police station, with no real hope of finding anything, and were quickly told that all of the case-papers had been destroyed. I asked if there was anyone at the station who had been working there for some time, and they produced an old guy who had been there for years.

He told us about an archive, that clearly no-one else knew about, and took us to a tiny door in one of the walls of the building. We contorted ourselves through what was more a hatch than a door, and like Howard Carter with Tutankhamen, found treasure. There were racks and racks of files, all of which were in chronological order. We found our documents.

(Michael Layton):

Despite the fact that an operational name was allocated to the initial 1989 enquiries by South Wales Police, the end result was that all further enquiries were ultimately ceased, on the basis that the suspect was dead, and therefore there were no prospects of a prosecution. The suitcases and their contents were made the subject of a destruction order and duly disposed of.

It transpired that another social worker at the same Children's Home had previously been confronted by senior staff about his behaviour with children, whilst on an organised holiday. He had been working with children for years, and was subsequently given an informal warning and continued working at the home until it closed in 1991. Five years later, further complaints were made against him relating to indecent assaults on children, and in due course he went to prison for five years.

In 1995, another social-worker from the home was also sent to prison for sexual abuse, and yet another worker charged with similar offences, he was later found not guilty at court.

It was by now clear that there were serious concerns for the safety of children at this children's home and in 1996 South Wales Police set up a specific investigation to look at cases of alleged child abuse. As part of the search for information they set up a confidential hotline, and an officer who had been involved in the limited enquiries relating to the suitcases in 1989 made contact, and voiced his reservations about the way in which the earlier case had been handled.

It was at this point that South Wales Police decided that an outside-force should conduct an enquiry into the police actions in respect of the 1989 events and voluntarily referred the matter to the PCA. West Midlands Police were asked to do the investigation, which was to be supervised by the PCA.

Lines of enquiry were established and agreed by both Forces, and the PCA, and the West Midlands Police team set about trying to make sense of events from seven years previously, whilst at the same time trying to establish appropriate working relationships with officers from South Wales with whom we came into contact.

(Stephen Burrows):

In the early days we received a warm welcome in some quarters, but a lot of initial bluster and false 'bonhomie' dissipated very quickly when people realised that we would not be leaving after a couple of days and that a superficial report was not an option.

We had great support from our nominated contact in the Police Complaints Authority, who had an office in London. He always wore a waistcoat and had a bit of an 'aristocratic air' about him. I stood in his office in St. Georges Street, London one day and had a full view of Westminster Abbey. He was likeable and business-like, but absolutely resolute and determined. He was not, nor had ever been a police officer, and at heart I think he secretly loved the concept of being involved in investigations, but I couldn't fault his approach.

One of the lines of enquiry that was added, at a later stage, was to research professional and social links between those involved in the case. This particular line of enquiry also referred specifically to the issue of Freemasonry within the police service and social services, and became an issue when a senior social-worker declared his membership at an early stage to one of the investigation team on first contact. Whilst deemed to be sensitive, freemasonry was also very topical at the time, as the Association of Chief Police Officers had taken the view that being a police officer and a Freemason were not compatible.

(Michael Layton):

Neither Steve nor I are Freemasons nor have we ever been. Having arrested a leading Freemason who was a scrap-metal dealer, some years before, my views on the subject were fairly well-known, as a number of police colleagues made subtle enquiries about the case. I was prepared to keep an open mind but all-male gatherings and things like playing golf did not interest me, and I always studiously ignored strange handshakes. I have worked with officers over the years that have made no secret of their membership, and far more who never revealed it. I had no interest either way what they occupied themselves with in their spare time as long as it did not affect their work.

As a result of this line of enquiry I visited Freemasons' Hall in Great Queen Street, London with Steve, to ask for assistance, and received a lot of positive support, and a tour of the very impressive building which was funded by 1,321 Lodges. They all contributed to the building costs, which well exceeded one million pounds, and the building was formally dedicated on the 19 July 1933. I was also given two books on Freemasonry, one entitled *'United Grand Lodge- Constitutions, Supreme Grand Chapter Regulations, and Grand Charity –Constitution and Regulations – 1995'* and the other *'Masonic Year Book 1996-1997.'*

I subsequently kept them on a shelf in my office, for some years, and watched people's reactions with interest if they noticed them. In those days it was said that some 14,000 men were joining

English Freemasonry every year which was said to operate on 'a system of morality.' It therefore followed that some of them must have been in my office, at some time or another, on a balance of probabilities.

The reality was that whilst we did indeed identify a number of people who were Freemasons we never uncovered any evidence of wrongdoing as a result of them being a member.

(Stephen Burrows):

I had a set party-piece when Mike and I were seeing people together. We were a well- rehearsed double act and talked openly about everything. I would recount the story from memory, and quite often when I mentioned Tredegar, where the suicide took place, I was told by local officers that my pronunciation was not right.

By the end of the enquiry I could recite the whole story without notes, like a parrot. Before Mike asked the question about Freemasons we would sometimes have a bet with each other, as to whether they were, or not. It was just a bit of light-heartedness, but we often got deflections to the questions, and strangely sometimes got the most reaction from those who were not members. At every interaction between forces surrounding the 'suitcase enquiry' in 1989, we found people who were Freemasons.

We had nothing against Freemasons, indeed one of our team was open about his involvement, and I had previously worked with a colleague on a very sensitive enquiry, who was very open about his membership. When we went down to the Freemasons Hall in

London I was struck by the lack of accurate record keeping, in some cases, with the membership computer being a tired-looking stand-alone machine. Before this investigation I had been approached on three separate occasions by different police officers to become a Freemason, but as Inspector Morse once said to Lewis *'I don't join things'* and politely declined.

(Michael Layton):

Given that we had confirmed that the suitcases and their contents had been photographed by South Wales Police, we decided to see if we could find copies of them, albeit we knew it was going to be a 'long shot'.

On the 26 September 1996, together with three members of the team, I visited the Photographic Department at the police headquarters in Bridgend. The staff on duty were very helpful and invited us into a room which was full of box, after box, of photograph negatives. We looked at each other and realised that this was going to be like looking 'for a needle in a haystack', but spread ourselves around the room and started sifting through the boxes. After more than an hour we found the negatives, which in fact were about to be destroyed in accordance with force policy. Luck had been with us.

When we got the negatives developed they showed two blue suitcases containing numerous items which included books, photographs and newspaper cuttings about indecency cases, as well as a horrible looking device for self- masturbation with some jelly. There was clearly a mass of items and material which with hindsight could have been researched further. Whilst it was frustrating that the contents had not been properly laid out and photographed in full it was nevertheless a crucial recovery. We had already been told that potentially there were three cases, and that one of them was brown, but the photographs confirmed otherwise.

In an effort to get to the truth we raised hundreds of actions for the enquiry team to complete, took scores of witness statements, and recovered numerous items of paperwork, all of which were logged and cross-checked on the HOLMES computer system.

We spent time trying to help officers with their recollections by trying to find official pocket books which should have been filed in an archive when completed.

Sometimes we were successful, and sometimes they were found to be missing. In one case of particular interest they were all missing. Steve often says that the phrase, *'I have no recollection',* became a familiar mantra, and even when we found a pocketbook, to assist with people's memory, officers would simply assert that, *'if it is in my pocketbook it must have happened, but I have no recollection'.*

Clearly it was not unreasonable, with the passage of time, for some people to have difficulty in remembering detail but it certainly happened with regularity. In one case we even had to work hard to get someone to even recall a colleague whom he had worked closely with - what hope was there!

We also employed the services of the force senior intelligence analyst, who was tasked with producing a detailed sequence of events chart, covering several specific aspects and the actions of the four police forces who had been involved in some way or another. In addition she prepared a number of structural organisation charts, and association charts, and more than proved the value of having trained staff with analytical skills.

On Monday 14 October 1996 we went to London for an exploratory meeting at the Director of Public Prosecutions office.

At the end of October 1996 we completed the majority of the local enquiries in Wales and I moved most of the team back to an Incident Room at Halesowen Police Station in the West Midlands on the 28 October 1996. Eventually I reduced the team down to just seven staff, which included myself, and Steve, two detective constables, Detective Sergeant Steve Trenbirth, and a typist and indexer.

After consultation with the PCA in London, and the office of the Director of Public Prosecutions, we determined that we would interview a number of serving, and retired, police officers, and social workers, under caution in relation to allegations of *'Misconduct in Public Office'*.

This is an offence at common law triable only on indictment at the crown court, and carries a maximum sentence of life imprisonment. It is confined to those who are public-office holders and is committed when the office holder acts, or fails to act, in a way that constitutes a breach of the duties of that office. The prosecution has to prove that the person willfully neglected to perform his duties and/or willfully misconducts themselves without reasonable excuse or justification, and the nature of the misconduct calls for 'public condemnation'.

Steve Burrows developed detailed interview plans, and in due course the interviews took place and were recorded contemporaneously. Throughout I was required to complete and maintain a detailed policy log detailing the rationale behind each of my decisions.

(Stephen Burrows):

We had endless agonising over when people were witnesses, and when they needed to be treated as suspects. Some of the younger officers found difficulties in treating police officers in this way and we had to explain the rationale in detail. I recall going to see one retired police officer who clearly regarded me as a 'young whippersnapper.'

I was treating him as a witness but then he crossed the line. He was clearly being evasive, and I terminated the interview, and told him that I would see him again in different circumstances. His face was a picture and he clearly wasn't used to being spoken to in this manner.

When seen subsequently, the same individual presented himself with a clipboard, and a number of prepared statements. It was a very clear effort at taking control of the situation but he lasted five minutes before starting to answer our questions.

(Michael Layton):

A file of evidence was subsequently submitted to the Director of Public Prosecutions and ultimately the decision was reached to charge a retired senior member of social services with misconduct in public office, based on those original decision-making processes. It was determined that there was insufficient evidence to bring charges against anyone else but it had to be borne in mind that the DPP had to be satisfied that there was both a public interest, as well as a reasonable prospect of obtaining a conviction.

In brief, the case put forward was that as a result of the decision not to investigate more fully the recovery of the suitcases, and the death of the social worker, other members of local-authority employed staff went on to commit further abuse on children at the Home, whereas robust enquiries might well have revealed the extent of abuse at the home, thus preventing three years of further suffering for the children, between 1989 and 1992, when the home closed.

The individual duly appeared at a crown court in Wales and the prosecution case was presented, which included a witness who was abused at the Children's Home after the recovery of the suitcases. She was a compelling and powerful witness.

(Stephen Burrows):

It was a logistical nightmare getting all the witnesses to court. Many of them lived in different parts of the country and were 'reluctant witnesses'. In the end we got them all there and presented what we believed to be a good case.

At the conclusion of the prosecution case the Judge directed the jury to find the defendant formally 'Not Guilty' on the basis that the prosecution had not reached the evidential threshold in relation to intent. Whilst it was a frustrating and disappointing result, given the bravery shown by our key witness, I had long since stopped trying to understand the workings of the judiciary and accepted the situation as it was.

We will never know what the outcome would have been had the case been left for the jury to decide. We had done our job and I couldn't fault the efforts of the team, who had shown great commitment, whatever their role had been.

It is a case Mike and I have never forgotten not just for its complexity, but also for the fact that there was no real justice for the victims. History has shown that they were not the only group of vulnerable people to be failed by the system then, and who continue to be failed by the system now. It was a sad indictment on society as a whole and whilst the officer who acted as a 'whistle-blower' in bringing these events to light showed great courage, the police service did not come out of it in a positive light.

I believed that the 'whistle-blower' was credible right from the start. I'd been involved in investigating complaints against the police for a while, and with him I felt instantly that he was telling the truth and that he had lived with this for years.

(Both):

Looking back across the years we were applying the norms of 1996 to the events of 1989 and people questioned us as to why we were pushing this line of approach given that policies were different then, or indeed non-existent.

If we now applied procedures in place in 2016, with events in 1996, and consider what the reaction today would be, to even a 'whiff' of a paedophile ring at a children's home, we suspect that the outcome of the enquiry might have been different. It was hard work. We were in a search for the truth but some just thought that we had exceeded our original terms of reference.

***

The conclusion of the initial phase of *'Operation Elmtree'*, (the court proceedings took place some three years later), coincided with the restructuring of the West Midlands Police into semi-independent *'Operational Command Units'*, more commonly known as OCU's, by the new Chief Constable, Edward Crew.

Michael Layton was subsequently promoted in uniform to Chief Superintendent, and chosen to command 'H2' OCU, a 'black country' command area covering Willenhall, Darlaston, Bloxwich and Brownhills.

His request that Stephen Burrows be posted to H2 OCU, as his Detective Chief Inspector, was approved and they commenced working together on the fledgling OCU on the 1 April 1997 - but that is another story, recounted in 'Walsall's Front Line' (2017)

Michael Layton & Stephen Burrows 2016, revised for paperback April 2017.

Figure 36: Michael Layton's Medals: Queen's Police Medal (2003), Queen's Golden Jubilee Medal (2002), Police Long Service and Good Conduct Medal (1995)

Figure 37: Stephen Burrow's Medals Queen's Diamond Jubilee Medal (2012), Queen's Golden Jubilee Medal (2002), Police Long Service and Good Conduct Medal (2006)

Figure 38: The Authors, Michael Layton & Stephen Burrows

Acknowledgements:

Walsall Edition of the Express and Star Newspaper

Walsall Local History Centre

'Danny' – Retired Detective Inspector (West Midlands Police)

'Roger' – Former Chief Inspector (Royal Ulster Constabulary)

'Paul' – Former Detective Inspector (West Midlands Police)

Ivan Kelsey – Former Enquiry Office Assistant (West Midlands Police)

David Faulkner – Retired Detective Constable MIU (West Midlands Police)

Richard Shakespeare – Retired Police Constable (West Mercia Police)

Steve Barnbrook – Retired Police Sergeant (British Transport Police)

Jon Lighton – Retired Police Inspector (West Midlands Police)

Andy Gould (Cartoonist)

Debbie Menzel – Former West Midlands Police, (West Midlands Police Museum)

Frances Tebbutt – Critical Reader and photographs

Bob Davies – Critical Reader

Megan Davies – Critical Reader

Victoria Burrows – Proofreading

List of Visual Material

Key: Stephen Burrows – SB, Frances Tebbutt - FT, Barry Crowley – BC, Andy Gould - AG

1 Citation, Carnegie Award, Thomas Wright FT

2 Certificate, Carnegie Award, Thomas Wright FT

3 Public Order Training – petrol bombs

4 Bramshill Police College 1986 SB

5 Special Course 1987 - Caving SB

6 Special Course 1987 - Abseiling SB

7 Special Course 1987 - Rafting SB

8 Special Course 1987 - Sailing SB

9 Corporation Street, Birmingham circa 1970's FT

10 Bull Ring Market, Birmingham circa 1970's FT

11 Manzoni Gardens, Birmingham circa 1970's FT

12 High Street, looking towards Oasis Market, Birmingham circa 1970's FT

13 Bull Ring, Birmingham circa 1970's FT

14 Rotunda building, Birmingham circa 1970's FT

15 Detective Inspector Mike Layton, 1990 BC

16 Main office of Force Intelligence, 1990 BC

17 Walsall Football Club, Bescot, 2016 BC

18 NCIS caricature, 1993 AG

19 Willenhall Police Station, 2016 BC

20 Darlaston Police Station, 2016 BC

21 Walsall Police Station, 2016 BC

22 Humorous Crime Report–'Stolen CID Xmas Party'
31.12.1995 BC

23 Inspector Steve Burrows, 1992 SB

24 Steelhouse Lane Police Station, Birmingham 2016 BC

25 St Phillips Cathedral, Birmingham circa 1970's FT

26 Rear of Rackhams store, Bull Street, Birmingham circa
1970's FT

27 Corporation Street at Cherry Street, Birmingham circa
1970's FT

28 Union Street, Birmingham circa 1970's FT

29 Victoria Square, Birmingham circa 1970's FT

30 Ramp to Birmingham Shopping Centre FT

31 New Street, Birmingham circa 1970's FT

32 Chief Constable's Commendation 1987 SB

33 Leaflet circulated by covert officers during Operation Portdale July 1994 BC

34 The Fullbrook Licenced House, Weston Street, Walsall 2016 BC

35 Waste ground, rear of Simmonds Place, Darlaston, 2016 BC

36 Medals presented to Michael Layton - Queen's Police Medal (2003), BC Queen's Golden Jubilee Medal (2002), Police Long Service and Good Conduct Medal (1995)

37 Medals presented to Stephen Burrows - Queen's Diamond Jubilee Medal SB (2012), Queen's Golden Jubilee Medal (2002), Police Long Service andGood Conduct Medal (2006)

38 The Authors, Michael Layton and Stephen Burrows, (2006)

PLEA FROM THE AUTHORS

Hello dear reader. Thank you for reading to the end of the book, we hope that means that you enjoyed it. Whether or not you did, we would just like to thank you for buying it, and giving us your valuable time to try and entertain you.

If you would like to find out more about our other fiction and non-fiction books then please search on our names on Amazon. We also have Facebook, Linkedin and Twitter accounts.

If you enjoyed this book we would be extremely grateful if you would consider leaving a review on Amazon.co uk, (or the Amazon site for your country). To do this, find the book page online, scroll down, and use the 'review button'.

The most important part of a book's success is how many positive reviews it has, so if you leave one then you are directly helping and encouraging us to continue on our journey as authors. Thank you in advance to anyone who does.

Michael Layton & Stephen Burrows

Printed in Great Britain
by Amazon